COMPLETE JERRY HAHN METHOD FOR JAZZ GUITAR

To Access the Online Audio Go To:
www.melbay.com/99116BCDEB

2 3 4 5 6 7 8 9 0

© 2003 BY MEL BAY PUBLICATIONS, INC., PACIFIC, MO 63069.
ALL RIGHTS RESERVED. INTERNATIONAL COPYRIGHT SECURED. B.M.I. MADE AND PRINTED IN U.S.A.
No part of this publication may be reproduced in whole or in part, or stored in a retrieval system, or transmitted in any form
or by any means, electronic, mechanical, photocopy, recording, or otherwise, without written permission of the publisher.

Visit us on the Web at www.melbay.com — E-mail us at email@melbay.com

CD Contents

1. Tune up
2. Picking Technique
3. Basic Warm-ups - No.1
4. Basic Warm-ups - No.2
5. Basic Warm-ups - No.3
6. Blues Scales and Patterns - No.1
7. Blues Scales and Patterns - No.2
8. Blues Scales and Patterns - No.3
9. Blues Scales and Patterns - No.4
10. Chord Positions for Cross-Picking Exercise
11. Alternating Picking - No.1 - 4
12. Alternating Picking - No.5 - 8
13. V7-I Patterns - No.1 - 4
14. V7-I Patterns - No.5 - 9
15. V7-I Patterns - No.10 - 12
16. II7-V7 Patterns - No. 1 - 4
17. II7-V7 Patterns - No. 5 - 8
18. II7-V7 Patterns - No. 9 - 12
19. Bm7b5-E7 Patterns - No. 1 - 4
20. Bm7b5-E7 Patterns - No. 5 - 8
21. Bm7b5-E7 Patterns - No. 9 - 12
22. G Minor Patterns for Improvisation - No. 1 - 4
23. G Minor Patterns for Improvisation - No. 5 - 8
24. G Minor Patterns for Improvisation - No. 9 - 12
25. Polytonal Improvisation Scales and Arpeggios
26. Polytonal Improvisation - No. 1 - 4
27. Polytonal Improvisation - No. 5 - 8
28. Polytonal Improvisation - No. 9 - 12
29. Polytonal Patterns - No. 1
30. Polytonal Patterns - No. 2 and Pentatonics No. 1 - 5
31. Pentatonics - No. 6 - 9
32. Pentatonics - No. 10 - 14
33. Pentatonics - No. 15
34. D Dorian
35. Eb Dorian
36. Jazz Language
37. Changing Positions
38. Complete Fingerboard Knowledge - Malachi
39. Jazz Blues Solo
40. II-V7-I Cycle
41. Giant Steps Ahead
42. Giant Steps Ahead first six measures and 1st and 2nd measures Patterns No. 1 - 4
43. Giant Steps Ahead 1st and 2nd measure Patterns No. 5 - 7
44. Giant Steps Ahead 5th and 6th measure Patterns No. 1 - 5
45. All the Things You're Not - Slow Version
46. All the Things You're Not - Fast Version
47. Joy Springtime - Slow Version
48. Joy Springtime - Fast Version
49. Joy Springtime - Original Version
50. Comping Rhythm Changes - Study # 1
51. Comping Rhythm Changes - Study # 2
52. Titus
53. Rhythm Changes Solo - Slow Version
54. Rhythm Changes Solo - Fast Version
55. Rhythm Changes 1st and 2nd measure Lines 1 - 6
56. Rhythm Changes 1st and 2nd measure Lines 7 - 12
57. Comping - No. 1 - 2
58. Comping - No. 3 - 5
59. Modal Comping - No. 1 - 3
60. Modal Comping - No. 4 - 6
61. Twelve Bar Blues - a and b
62. Twelve Bar Blues - c and d
63. Twelve Bar Blues - e, f and g
64. Twelve Bar Progressive Blues
65. Twelve Bar Progressive Blues Solo
66. Study # 1 in G (Twelve Bar Blues)
67. Study # 2 in C (Twelve Bar Blues)
68. Study # 3 in Bb (Twelve Bar Blues)
69. Study # 4 in Ab (Donna Lee or Indiana)
70. Chelsea Rose
71. What a Friend We Have in Jesus
72. Improvisation Course Lesson I Solo Example
73. Improvisation Course Lesson II Solo Example
74. Improvisation Course Lesson III Solo Example
75. Improvisation Course Lesson IV Solo Example - In the Breeze
76. Transfiguration

Table of Contents

Practicing - Ideas and Suggestions 4
Fingerboard Chart 5
Key to Notational Symbols 6
Picking Technique 7
Parent Scales and Modes 8

Exercises - Basic Warm-ups 10
Blues Scales and Patterns 13
G Major Scales and Arpeggios -
   in Five Different Positions 15
G Major Scale - 2nd Position 16
G Major Scale - 5th Position 17
G Major Scale - 7th Position 18
G Major Scale - 9th (10th) Position 19
G Major Scale - 12th Position 20
D♭ Major - 1st Position 21
D♭ Major - 3rd (4th) Position 22
D♭ Major - 6th Position 23
D♭ Major - 8th Position 24
D♭ Major - 11th Position 25
G7 Scales and Arpeggios 26
G Minor Scales, Arpeggios and Chords 29
G Melodic Minor 33
G Lydian 35
G Lydian Dominant 37
G Locrian 39
G Altered Dominant 43
G Major Extended 46
C Major Extended 47
Diminished Scales and Arpeggios 48
Patterns for Diminished Scales 50
Whole-Tone Scales and Patterns 52
Cross-Picking Exercises 57
Chord Positions for Cross-Picking Exercises 58
Alternating Picking 59
Cross Picking Part II 63
Seventh Position 66
Alternative Picking Patterns 68
V7-I Patterns 72
II7 V7 Patterns 75
Bmi7♭5-E7 Patterns 78
G Minor Patterns for Improvisation 82
Polytonal Improvisation 85

Polytonal Patterns 88
Pentatonics 91
Modal Improvisation 95
D Dorian 95
E♭ Dorian 99
The Language of Jazz 101
Jazz Language 102
Changing Positions 103
Complete Fingerboard Knowledge - Malachi 104
Jazz Blues Solo 105
II-V7-I Cycle 108
Giant Steps Ahead 111
All the Things You're Not 116
Joy Springtime 119
Rhythm Changes 125
Comping Rhythm Changes 126
Titus 131
Rhythm Changes Solo 132
Chord Forms 136
Major 137
Minor 138
Dominant Seventh 139
Chords with Open Strings 141
Comping 142
Modal Comping 144
Twelve Bar Blues 146
Twelve Bar Progressive Blues 147
Harmonized Bass Lines 149
Study #1 in G 150
Study #2 in C 151
Study #3 in B♭ 152
Study #4 153
Chelsea Rose 156
What a Friend We Have in Jesus 157

Improvisation - Lesson I 158
Improvisation - Lesson II 161
Improvisation - Lesson III 163
Improvisation - Lesson IV 166
Solo to "In the Breeze" 168
Transfiguration 170
Listening 175
Jerry Hahn 176

Practicing
Ideas and Suggestions

Maintain a record book of all of your concentrated practice time, down to the minute. Assign yourself a minimum amount of daily practice. Make a list of the different aspects of your musicianship which need the most practice and assign a certain amount of practice time to each aspect.

Whenever possible, use a metronome. Set the metronome with a tempo that is slow enough for you to play a particular piece of music without mistakes. Repeat at a slow tempo several times before moving to a slightly faster tempo. Experiment with a metronome. It will make your practice time effective and will produce positive results. Invest in quartz or electric metronome. They are the most accurate and easiest to work with.

Fingerboard Chart

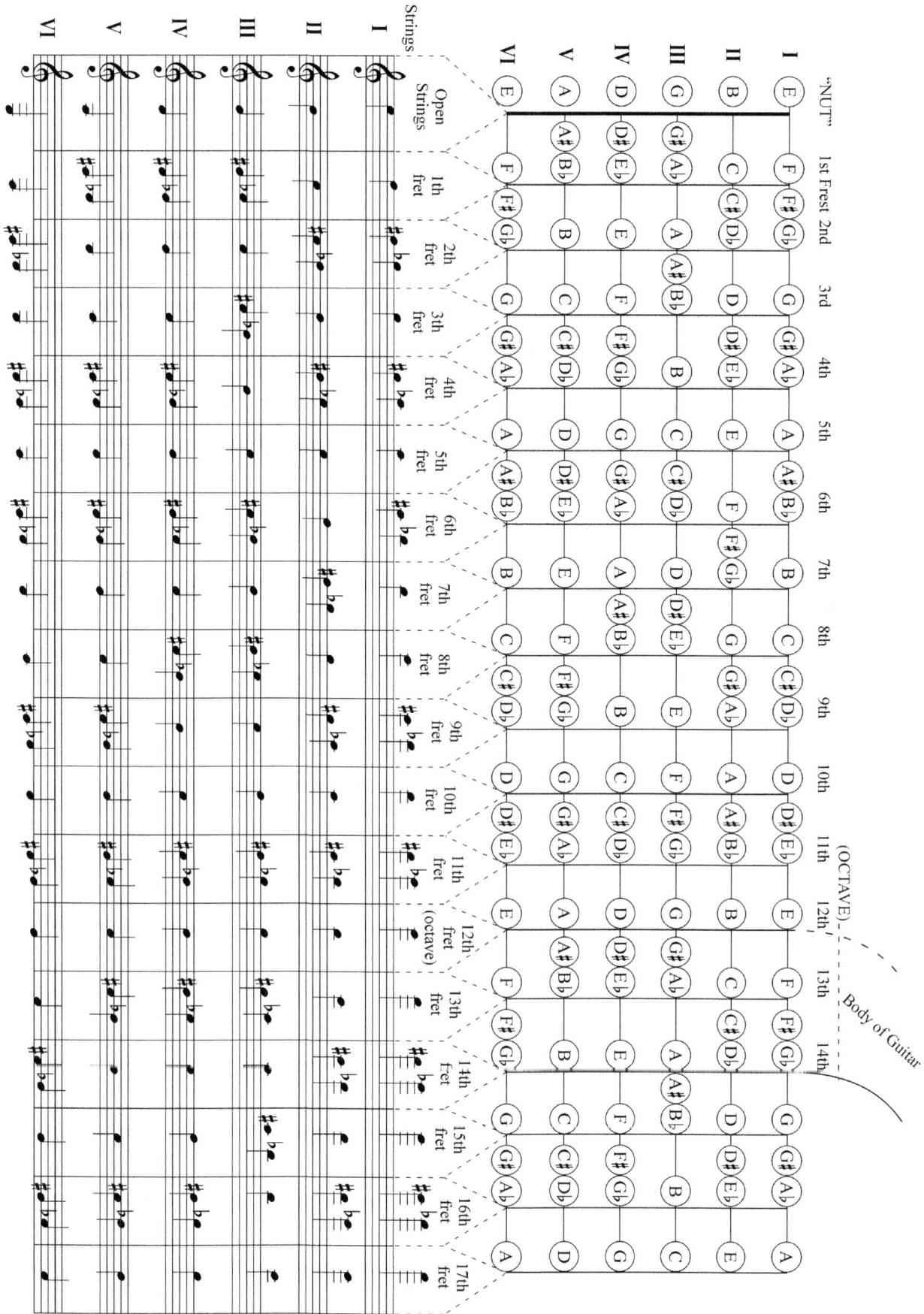

Key to Notational Symbols

Keep in mind that certain symbols are found in either the tab or the standard notation only, not both. For additional clarity, consult both systems.

4 ⊷ : Left-hand fingering is designated by small Arabic numerals near note heads (1 = 1st finger, 2 = 2nd finger, 3 = 3rd finger, 4 = pinky, T = thumb).

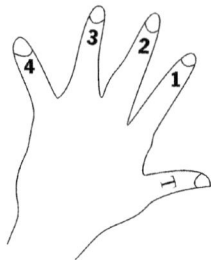

② ⊷ : A circled number (1-6) indicates the string on which a particular note is to be played.

⊓ : Pick downstroke.

V : Pick upstroke.

B
7 (9) : Bend; play the first note and bend to the required pitch (bend note is in parentheses).

B
(9) 7 : A reverse bend; strike an already bent note, then allow it to return to its unbent pitch (bent note is in parentheses).

Picking Technique

There doesn't seem to be a standard technique for playing the guitar as a person might find with other instruments. I have observed the various picking techniques of many of the best jazz guitarists in the country. Most of them have their own personal approach to the pick. What I have tried to do is to incorporate what I considered the best of all of their approaches into my own. Howard Roberts and Johnny Smith have been my main influences. Johnny Smith emphasizes the picking motion originating at the elbow, while Howard Roberts incorporates quite a bit of thumb and index finger movement in his picking motion. For me the best picking technique is an even distribution of forearm, wrist, and finger movement. Personally I like a heavy pick, I feel a guitarist can pick softly with a heavy pick, but he can't pick hard with a light pick.

The closer you play towards the bridge you will probably use more wrist and finger movement. The left side of the pick is usually turned slightly downward, especially when picking the lower bass strings.

To incorporate finger movement into your picking technique you should move the pick back and forth by bending your thumb and index finger. *

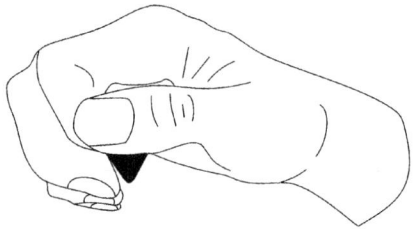

Figure 3 - The pick is held with my index finger and thumb only. The pick should not be touched by any other finger. It is in the exact center of the last joint of the thumb and is perpendicular to the thumb.

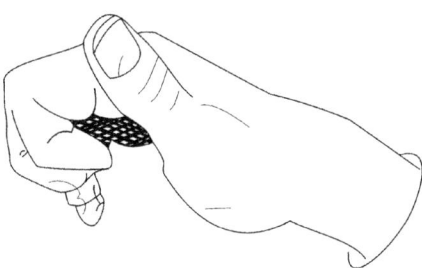

Figure 1 - I bend my index finger quite a bit

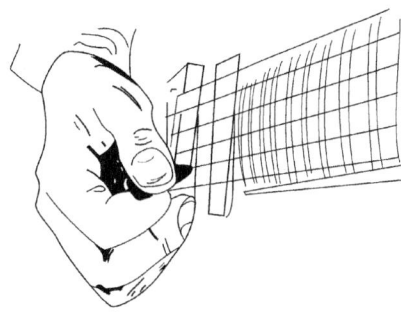

Figure 4 - The right hand should be relaxed with the little fingernail and may be the ring fingernail gliding on the pick guard which is adjusted to be 3/16 of an inch below the strings. The fingertips should not be anchored in an immoveable position anywhere on the pickguard.

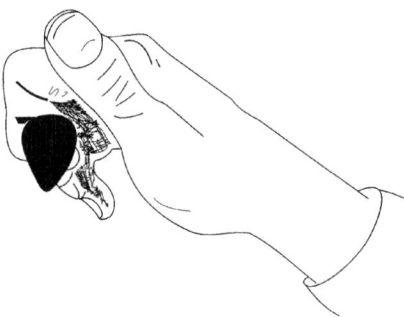

Figure 2 - The pick is placed on the side of my index finger.

* Practice these exercises moving only your thumb and index finger.

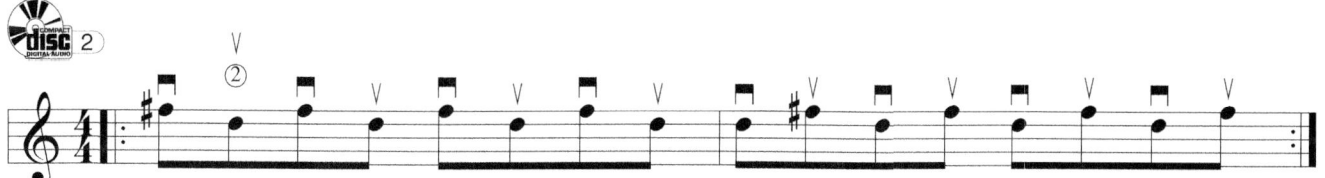

Parent Scales and Modes

This section concerns the use of scales and how they relate to chords. These scales are absolutely necessary in jazz improvisation. Harmonic knowledge is essential to determine the chord tones of these scales. The first seven scales are modes derived from various major scales. All of the scales have a tonic of C. They should be transposed to all keys and different positions.

Scale #1 (Ionian) is related to the C major chord family (C maj., C maj.7, C6, C6/9, etc.).

Scale #2 (Dorian) is applicable to most minor chords (Cm7, Cm6, Cm9, Cm11, etc.). This scale is utilized more than any other minor scale in jazz.

Scale #3 (Phrygian) for the most part is related to Latin harmonic structures and progressions.

Scale #4 (Lydian) is related to the C major chord family (C maj., C maj.7, C6, C6/9, C maj.♭5, etc.).

Scale #5 (Mixolydian) is of the dominant 7th family of chords (C7, C9, C11, C7 sus 4, and C13).

Scale #6 (Aeolian) is also referred to as the "pure" or relative minor. It applies to minor chords (particularly in the tonic key). The sixth tone is to be considered when selecting the appropriate minor scale (depending on the scale of the preceding or following chord).

Scale #7 (Locrian) and #8 (Locrian #2) sound best with a Cø (Cm7♭5) chord. Scale #7 has the same notes as the major scale starting on the tonic one-half step above (D♭ major).

Scale #9 (Lydian Dominant) works with any dominant C7 type chord, especially one with a ♭5 or ♯11.

Scale #10 (Whole-Tone) can be played with augmented or C7♭5 chords.

Scale #11 (Whole-Step/Half-Step Diminished) is played over a diminished chord. The C, E♭, G♭ and A are all tonics and chord tones since a diminished scale is symmetrical.

Scale #12 (Half-Step/Whole-Step Diminished) fits into the altered dominant 7th category (7♭9, 7♯9, 7♭5, etc.)

Scale #13 (Altered Dominant) is also referred to as a diminished whole-tone scale. This scale is played over a chord which usually has an altered 5th and altered 9th present. It has the same scale as the Lydian Dominant scale located a tri-tone from the tonic C (G♭).

Scale #14 (Blues) is a horizontal minor-modal type of scale which can be played over any chord in a traditional twelve-bar blues. It is the basic scale of rock.

Scale #15 (Pentatonic) is a major scale without the fourth and seventh. It can be used as a substitute scale when it is constructed on notes other than the root.

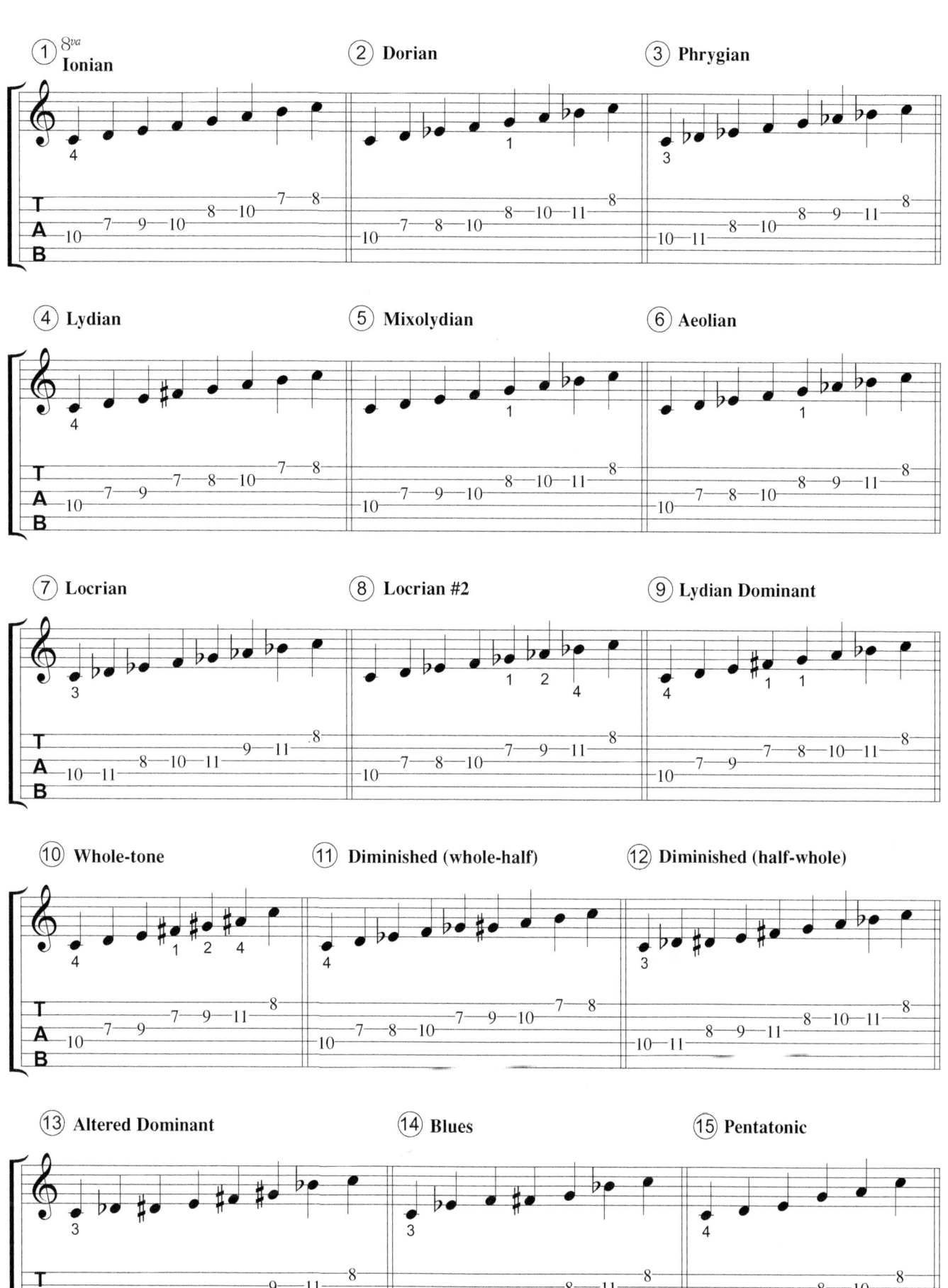

Exercises
Basic Warm-ups

    This entire section is to be played with alternating picking. Exercise #1 is a helpful exercise to teach a beginner in order to establish good left-hand position. When practicing exercise #1, the fingers should not be lifted until there is a change of string. Scale #15 (Pentatonic) is a major scale without the fourth and seventh. It can be used as a substitute scale when it is constructed on notes other than the root.

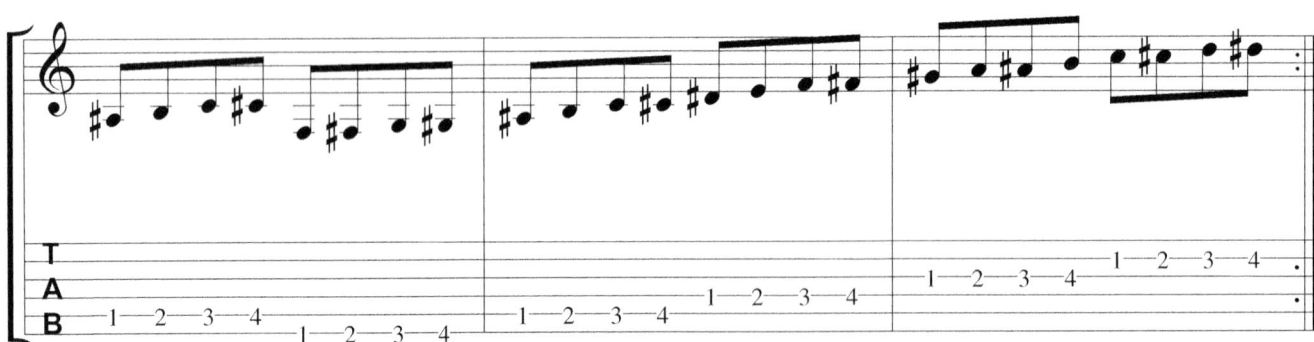

10

Exercises #2 and #3 should played two times per string. These exercises are primarily concerned with the development of the little finger. Exercise #2 is the favorite.

Exercises #4, and 5 and 6 are left-handed exercises which should be extended to cover the entire fingerboard. #6 can start on a higher fret if you wish.

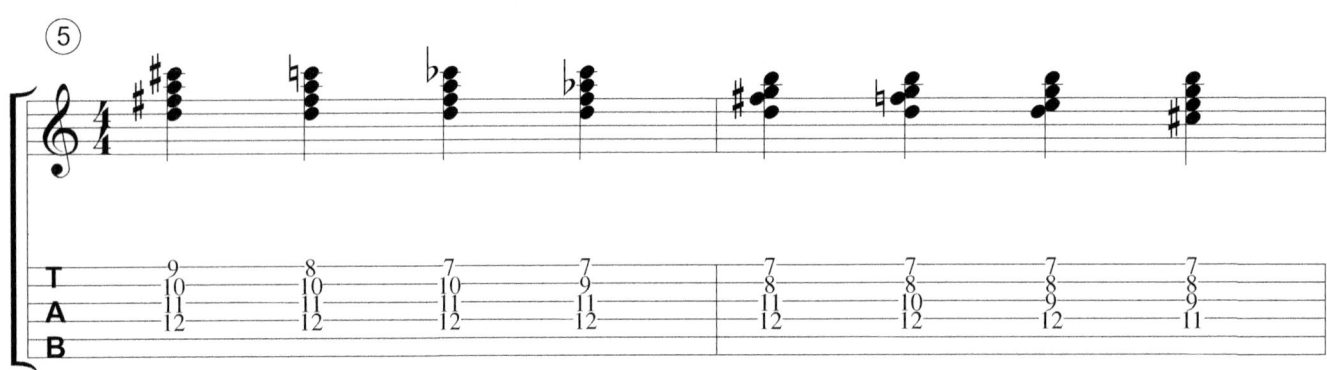

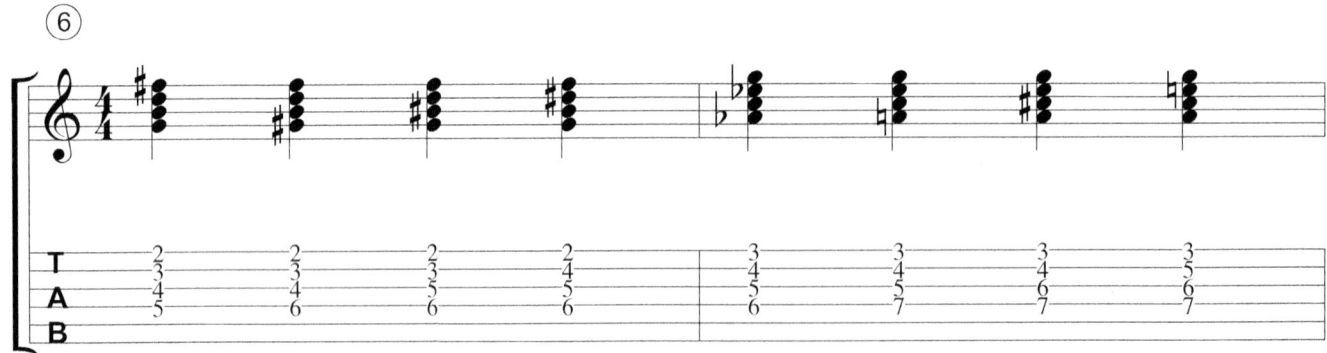

Blues Scales and Patterns

The majority of blues and rock guitarists derive most of their improvisation from basic blues scales and patterns. Here are some basic positions for blues scales and patterns in the key of A. These should be transposed and practiced in all of the other keys, especially E, C, G, B♭ and F. Refer to page 6 to understand the bend string notation symbol.

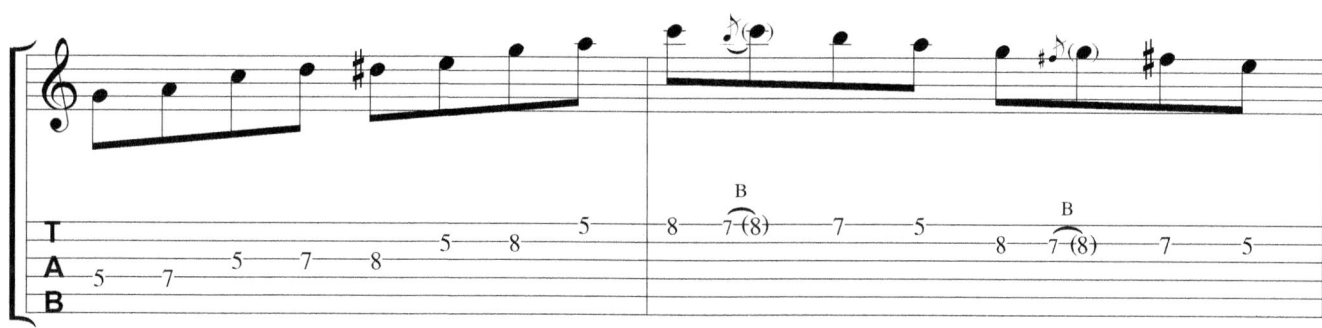

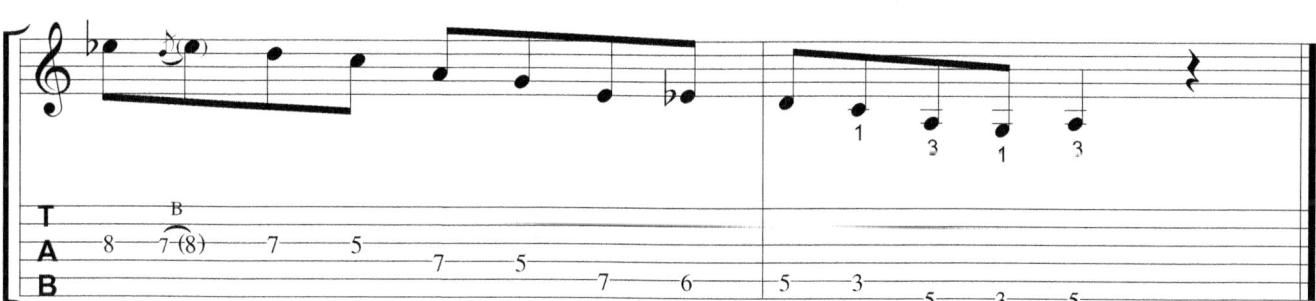

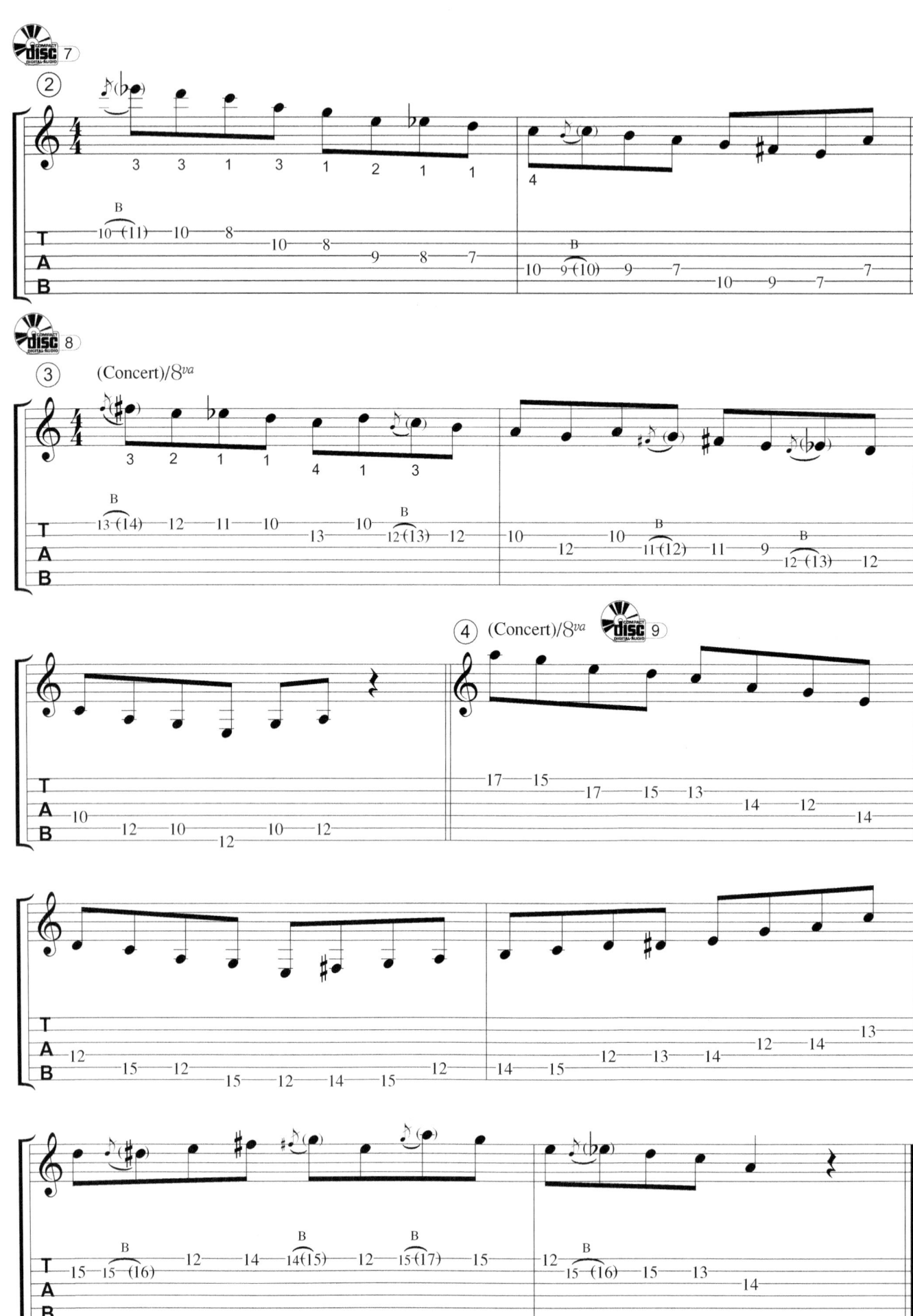

G Major Scales and Arpeggios
in Five Different Positions

    Scales, arpeggios and corresponding chords are very important to fingerboard knowledge and association. You should incorporate them into your daily practice schedule with a metronome (preferably an electronic or a quartz). Alternating picking is a must when practicing scales and arpeggios. This entire book should be memorized, especially the scales, arpeggios and exercises.

    Notice that all of the scales and arpeggios begin and end on the root. You should memorize the finger, string and fret that begins each scale so that you can transpose them into other keys. The first note of the first G major scale is played on the sixth string, third fret with the second finger. So, if you wanted to play that same scale in the key C, you would find the note C on the sixth string, with the second finger (which would be on the 8th fret). Then you would be in the correct position to play that particular scale in the key of C.

G Major Scale - 2nd Position

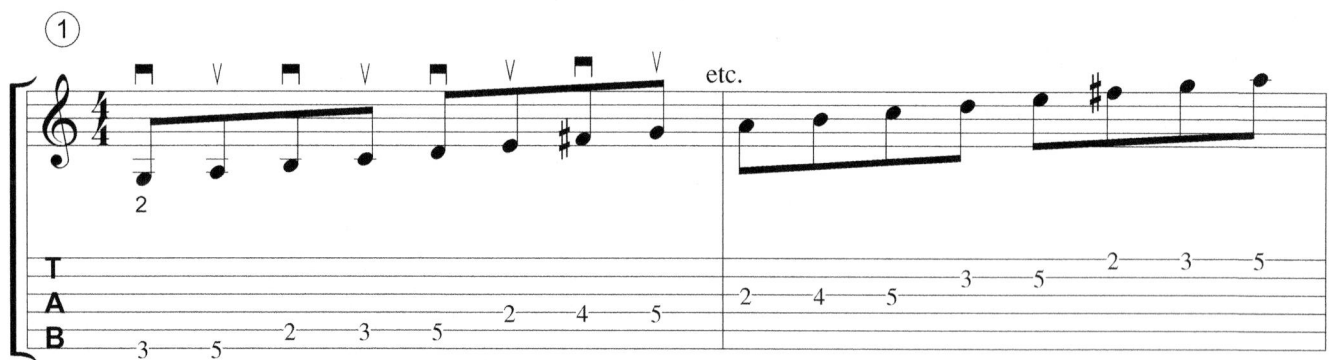

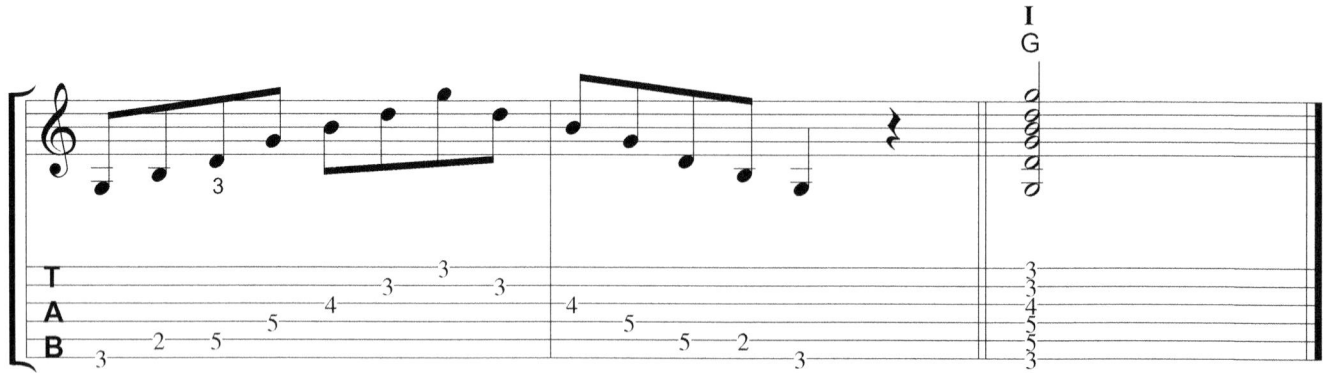

G Major Scale - 5th Position

Even though the first note is on the third fret, most of this scale is in 5th position.

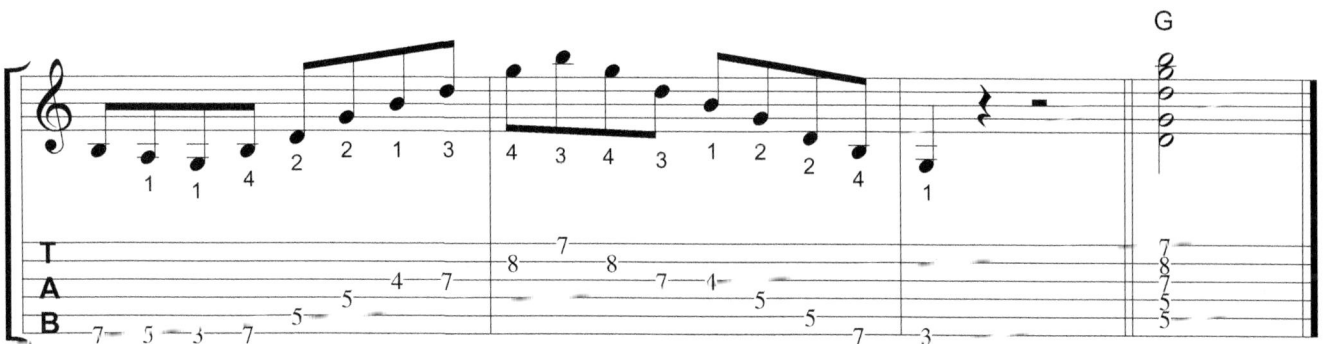

G Major Scale - 7th Position

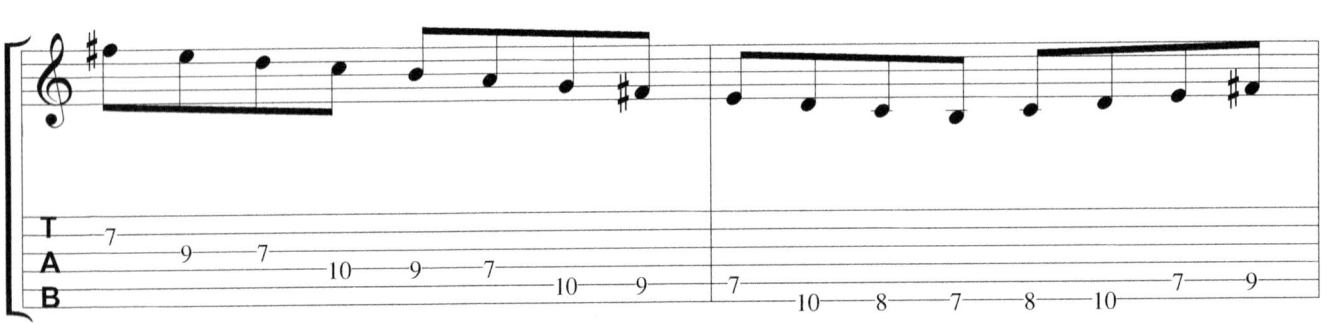
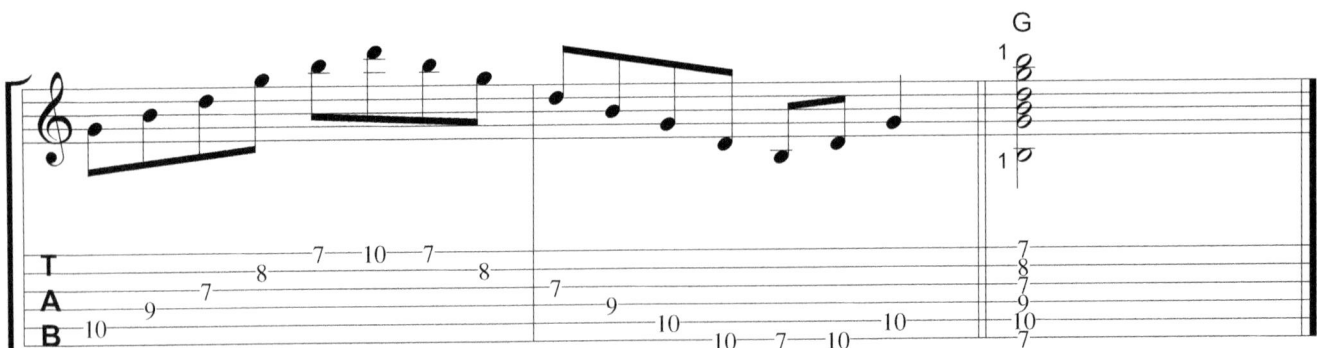

G Major Scale - 9th (10th) Position

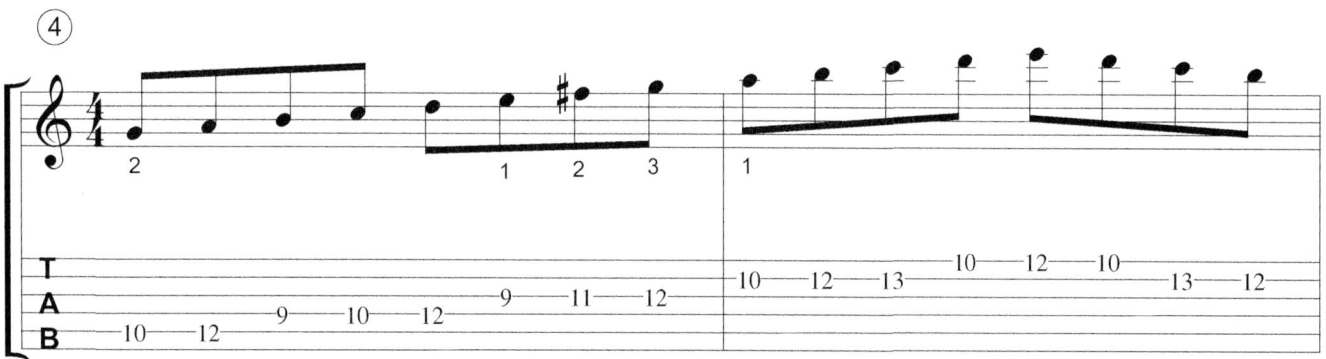
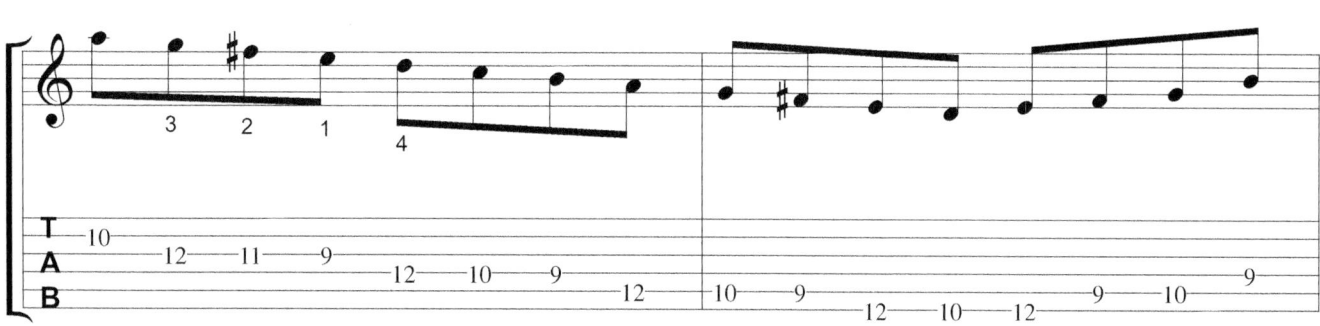
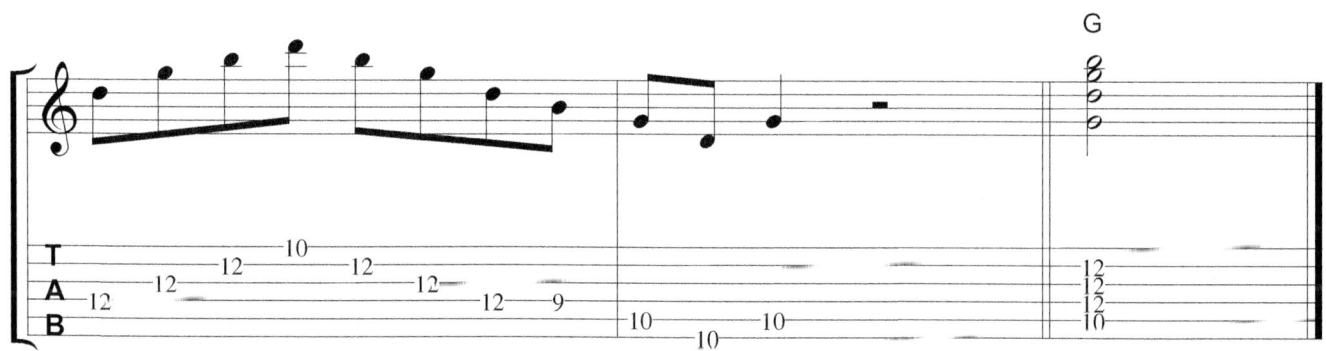

G Major Scale - 12th Position

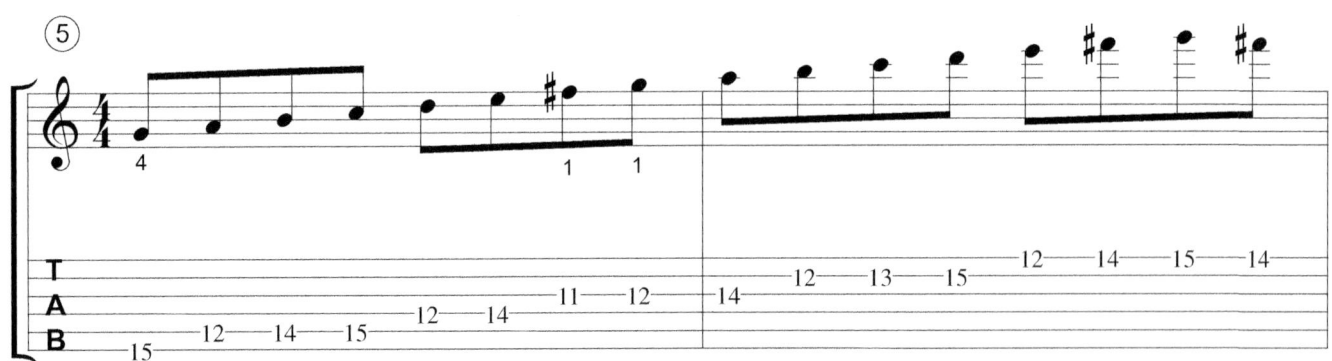
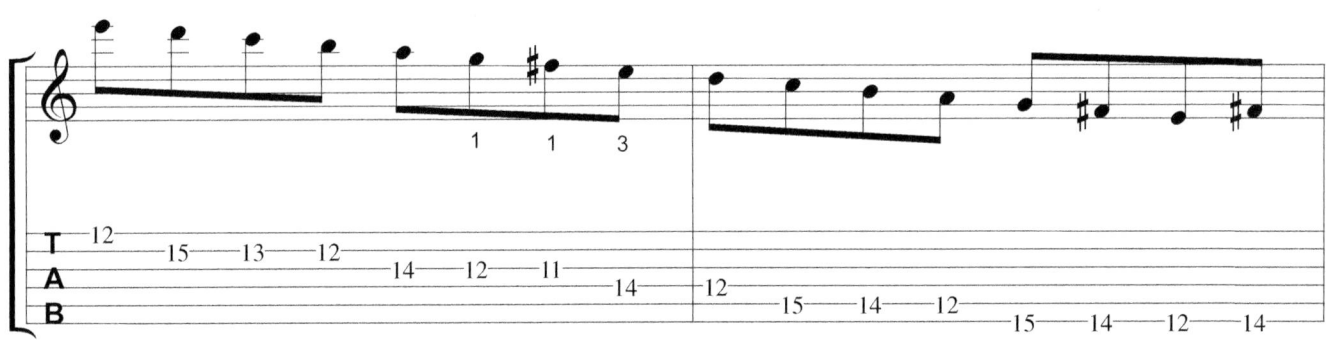
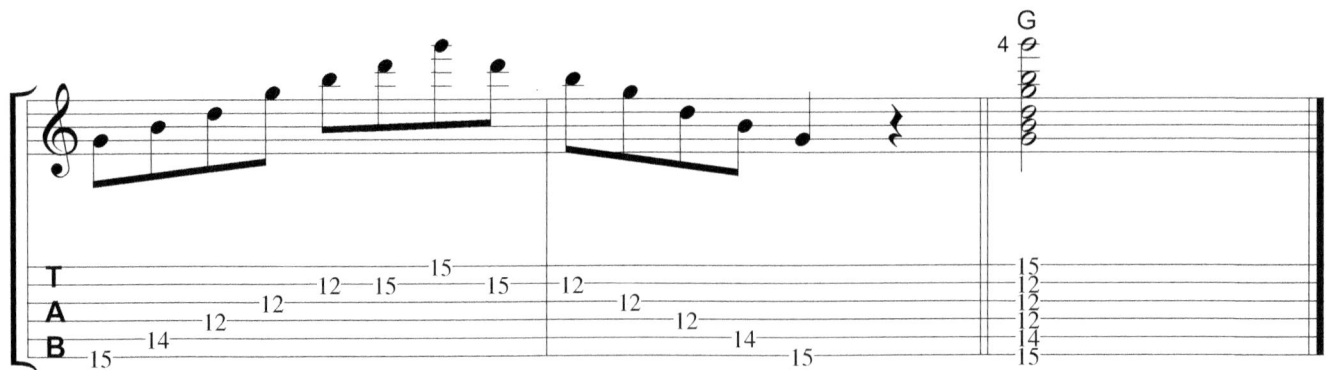

D♭ Major - 1st Position

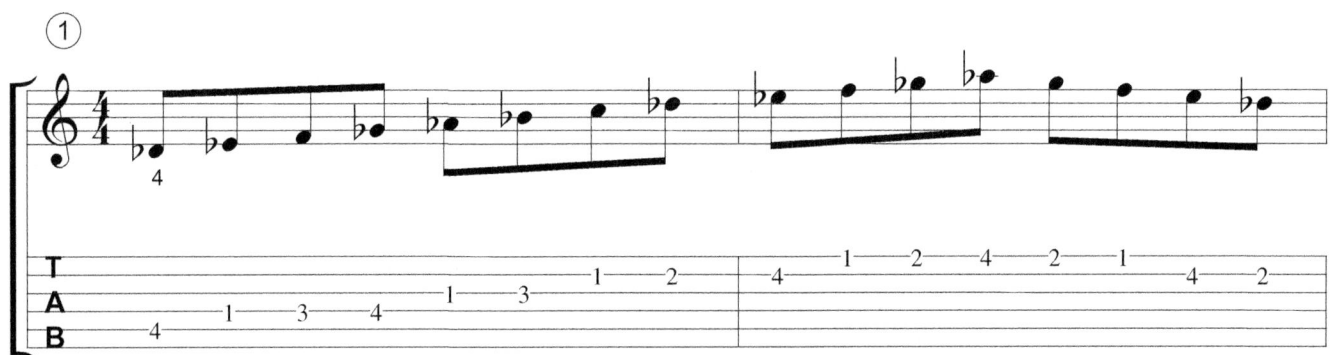

D♭ Major - 3rd(4th) Position

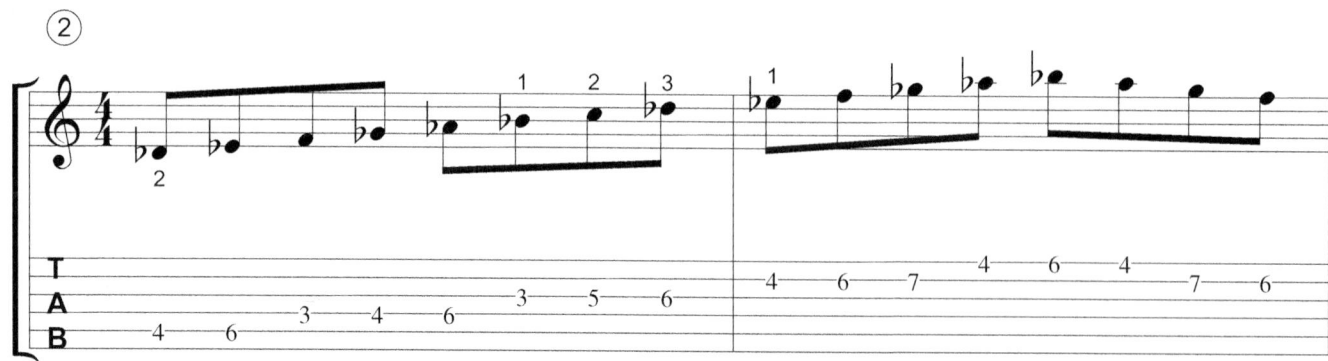

D♭ Major - 6th Position

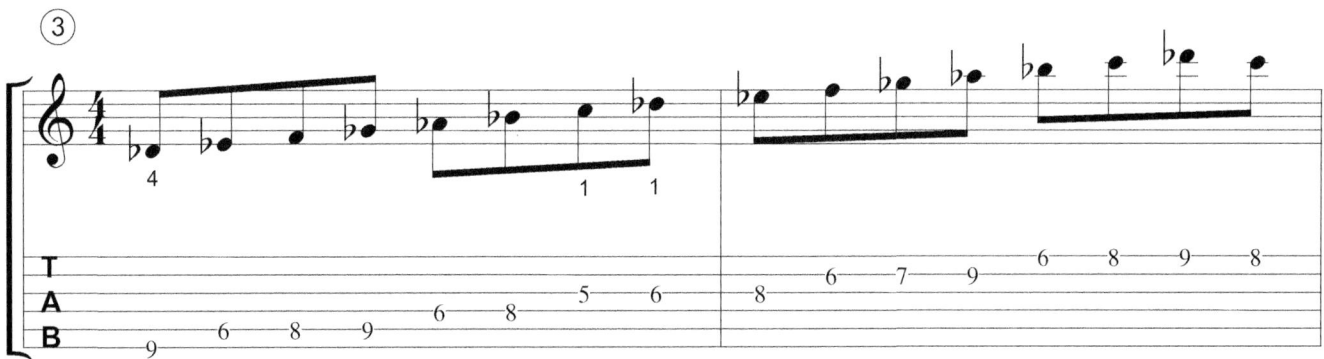
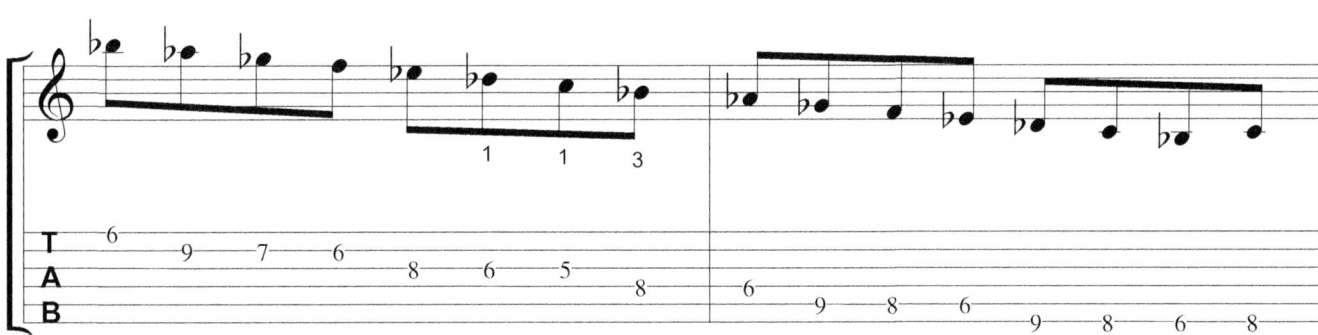
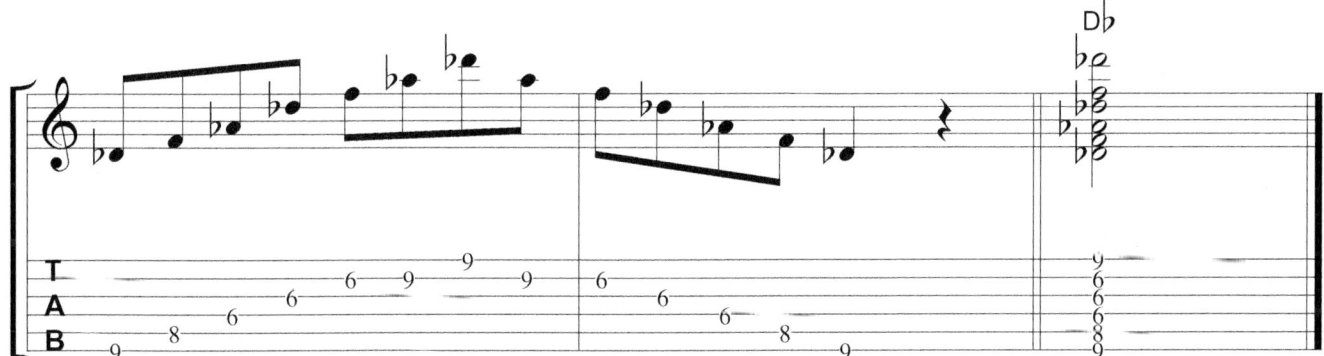

D♭ Major - 8th Position

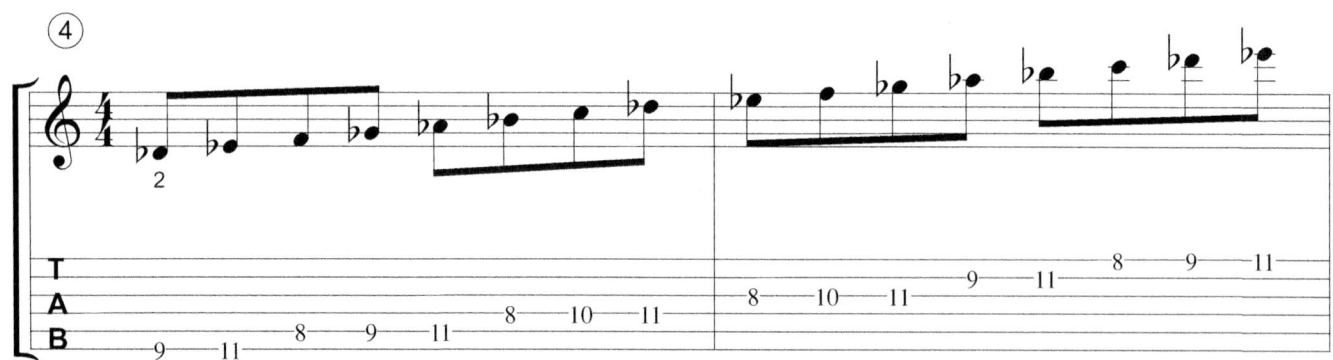

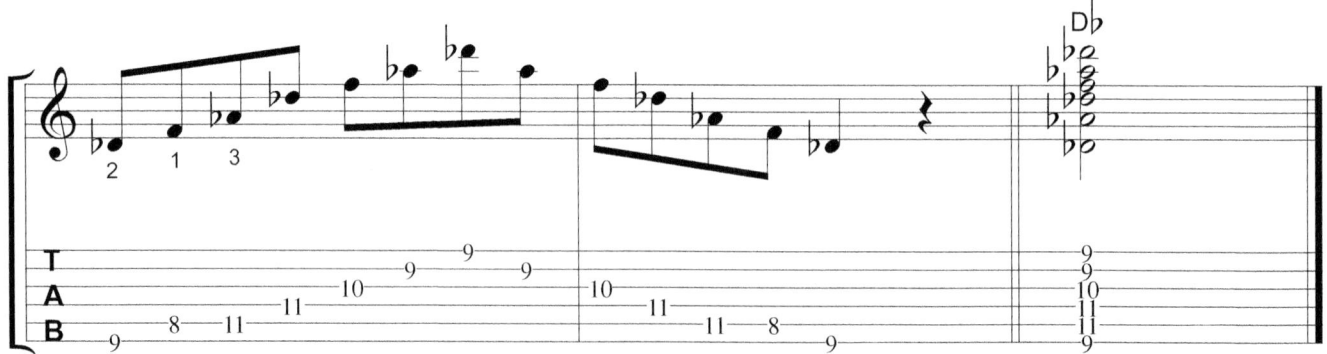

D♭ Major - 11th Position

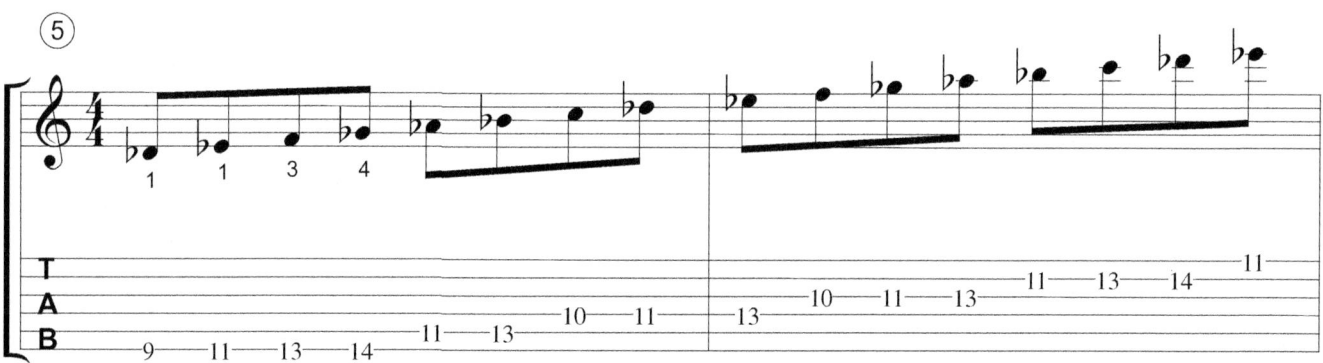
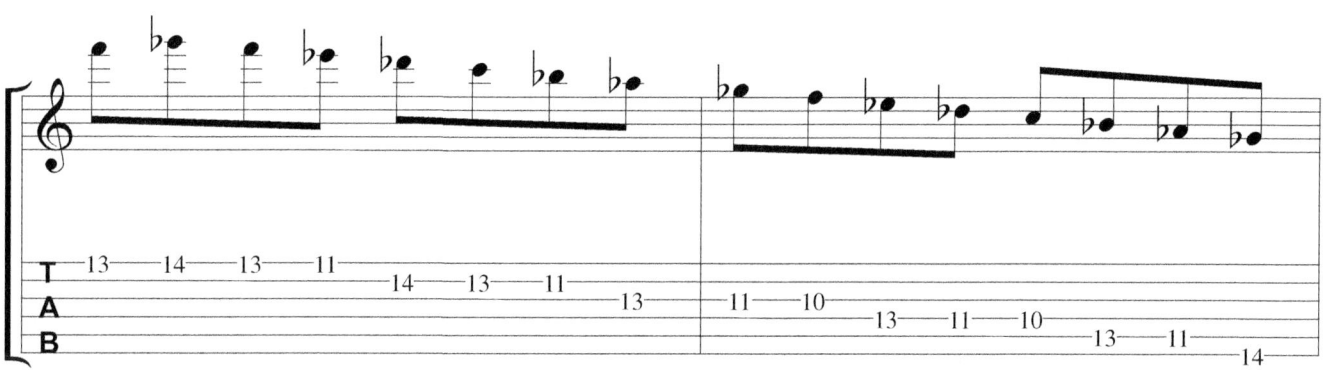
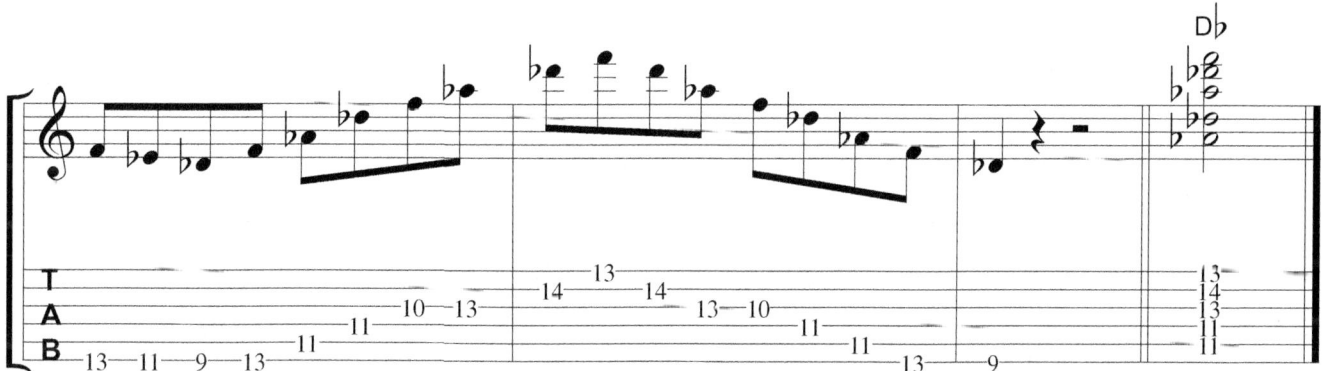

G7 Scales and Arpeggios

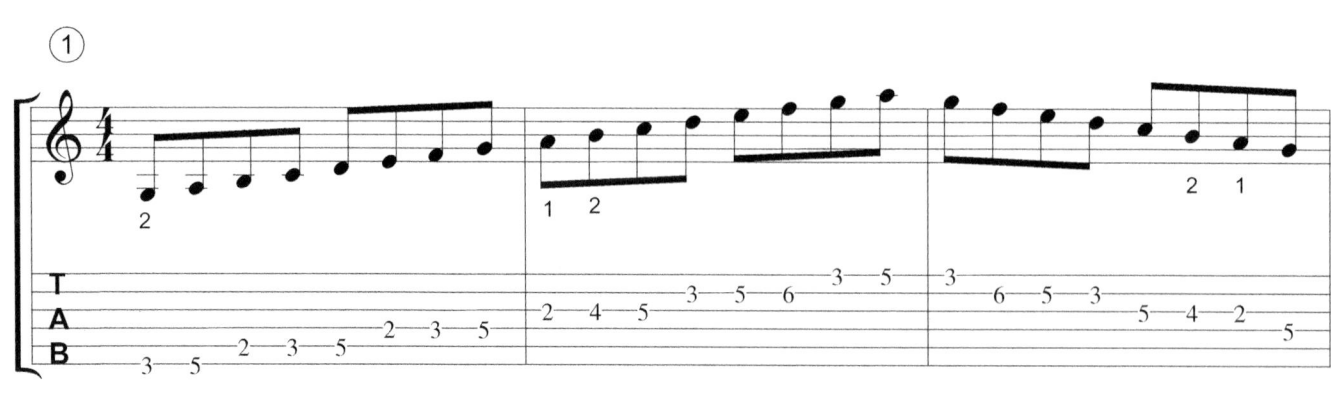

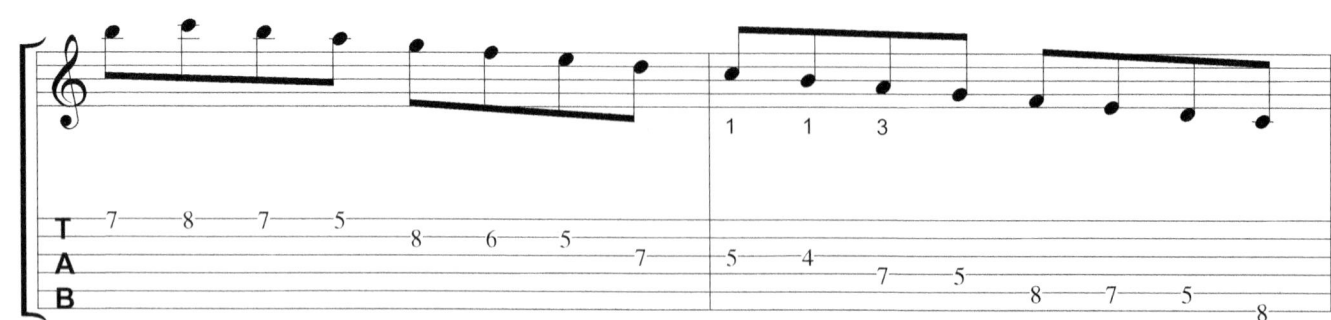

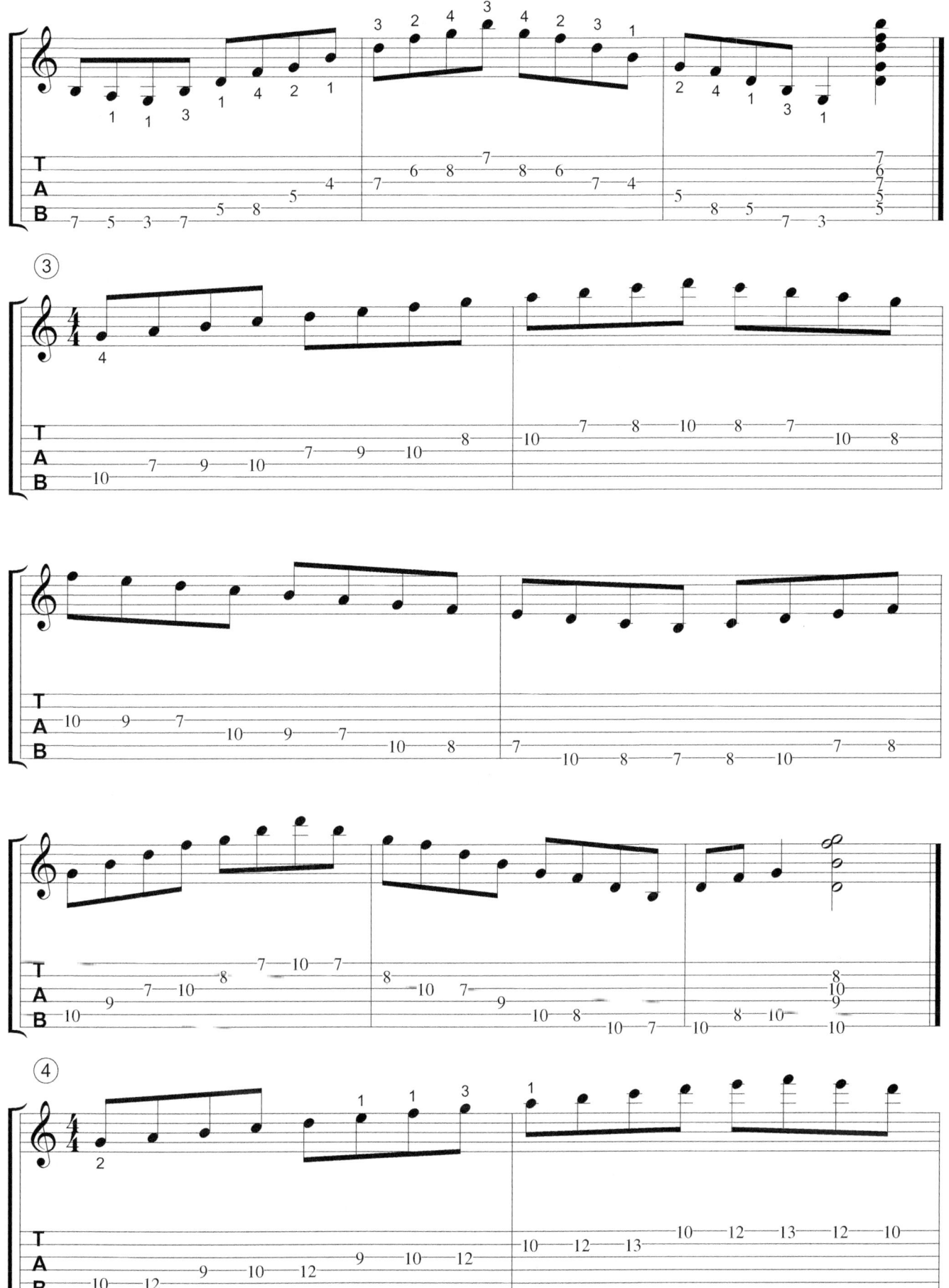

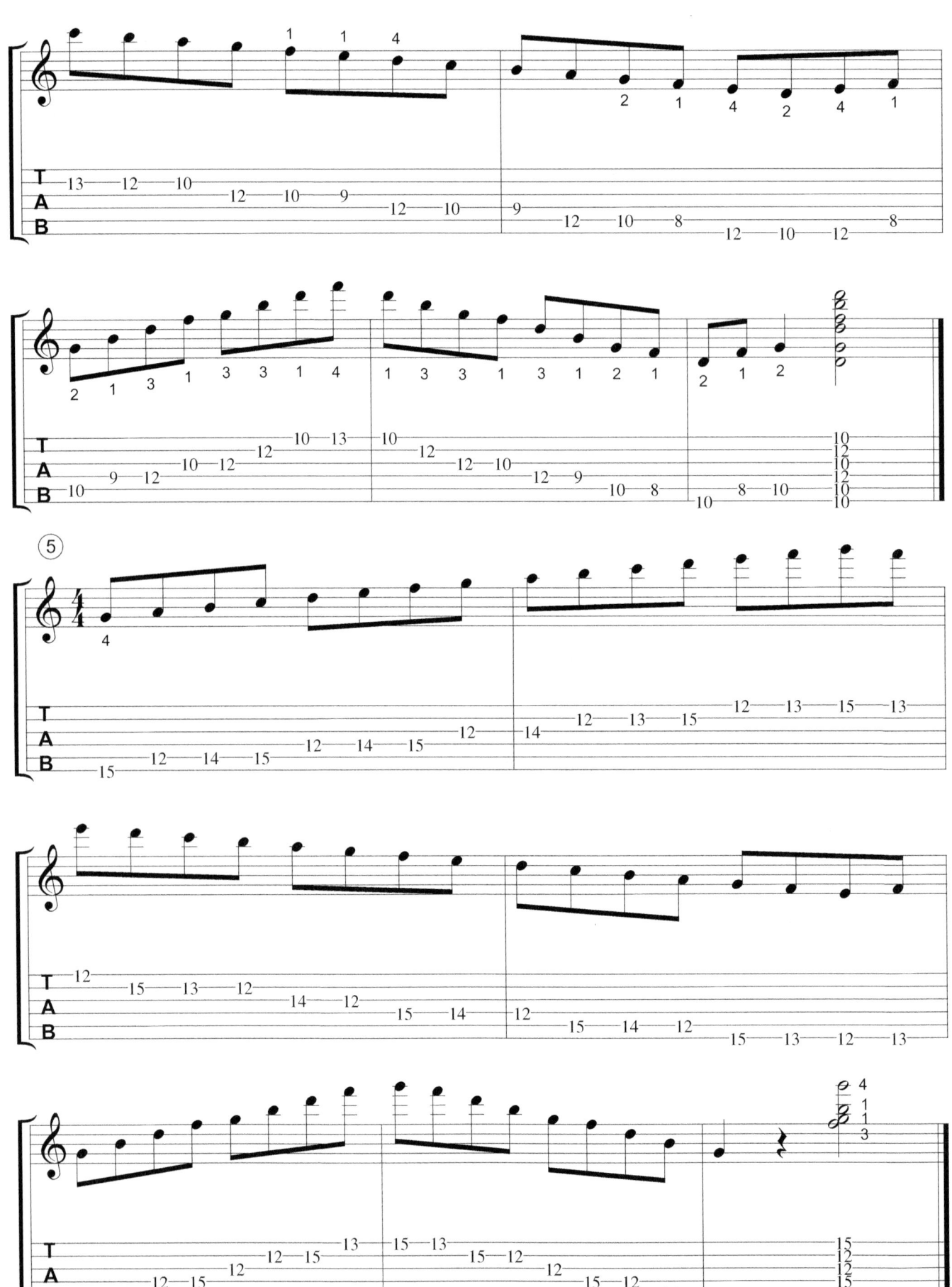

G Minor Scales, Arpeggios and Chords

Because there are different kinds of minor scales, many of my students have had problems trying to discover which minor chord is applicable to a certain progression.

The first five notes in all minor scales are the same. All minor scales have a minor third (the third tone of a minor scale is a half-step lower than it is in a major scale). The main difference between the different minor scales is with the sixth and seventh tones.

Scale #1 is a simple G major scale.

Scale #2 is a natural or pure G minor scale because it has the same notes as the relative major scale (B♭).

Scale #3 is a harmonic G minor scale. Notice the step and a half interval between the sixth and seventh tones.

Scale #4 is a melodic G minor scale. Notice the major 6th and major 7th ascending (same as a major scale), and the minor 6th and minor 7th descending (same as a natural minor scale).

> Jazz musicians identify the melodic minor scale only in the ascending aspect with the sixth and seventh notes always being

Scale #5 is a minor scale which is a G dorian mode (F major scale starting on the second tone G). This is the minor scale which I emphasize the most because it is the most applicable in jazz improvisation. The progression of a G minor chord (or Gm6, Gm7, etc.) to a C7 dominant type chord is the most common resolution in jazz improvisation involving a G minor chord. The C7 would then most likely resolve to an F chord. The C7 and the F have the same scale as the G dorian mode.

In determining the correct scale for a minor chord, you must consider the parent scale of the next chord. Sometimes the inclusion of a minor sixth is preferable to the major sixth. That is a consideration when the minor chord is the tonic or when the minor sixth is a chord tone of the next chord, (ex. Gm-E♭7 or Gm-Cm). But, for practical reasons, I teach the dorian minor because it will almost never sound wrong.

Scale #6 is a G dorian minor scale and arpeggio to be played in second and third positions with no open strings.

Scale #7 is played primarily in 5th position. Observe the fingering on the first two notes.

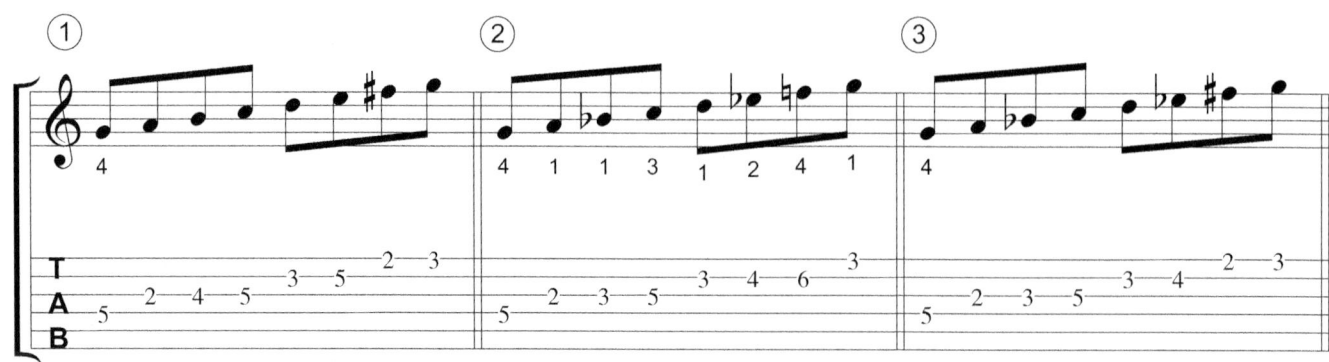

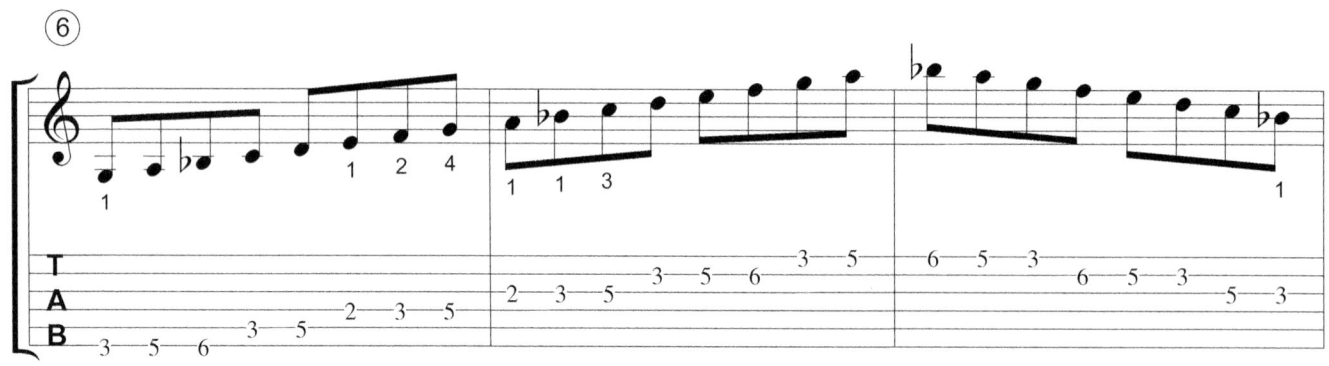
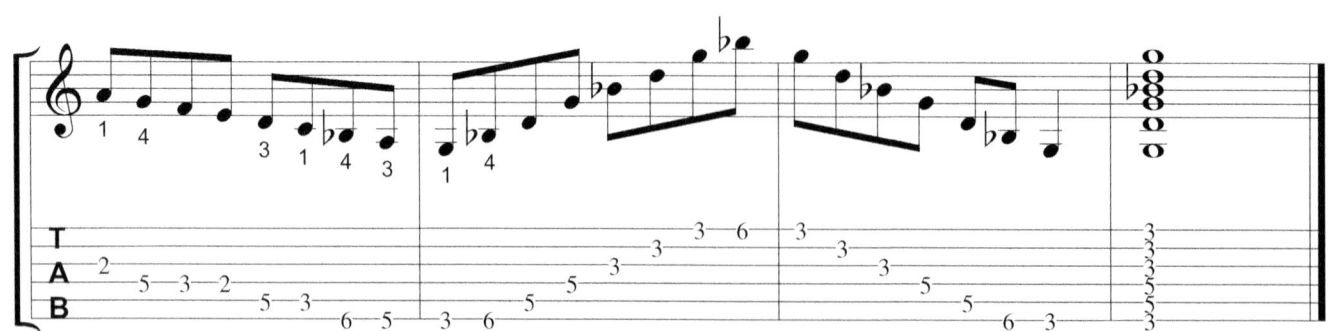

30

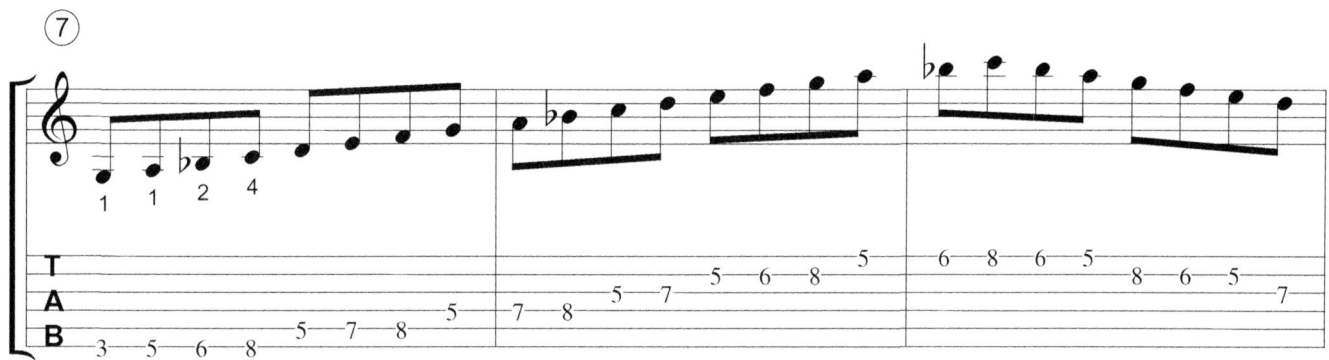
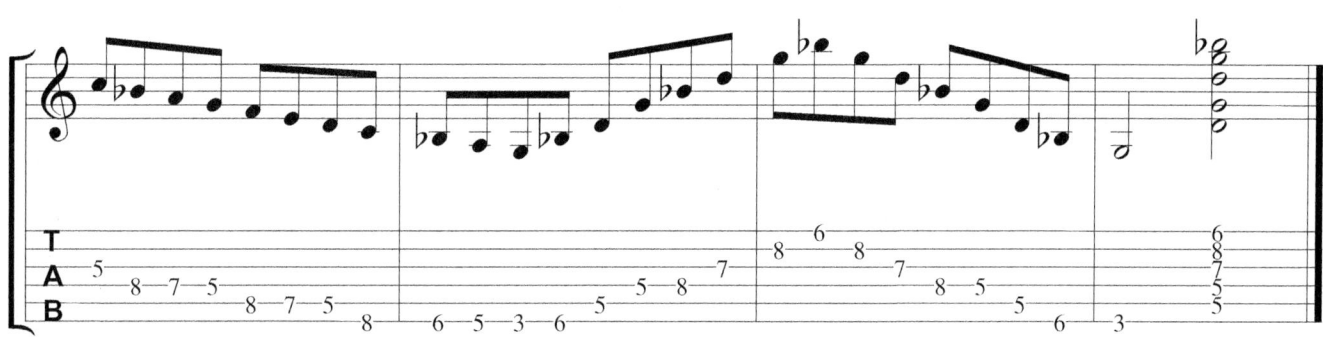
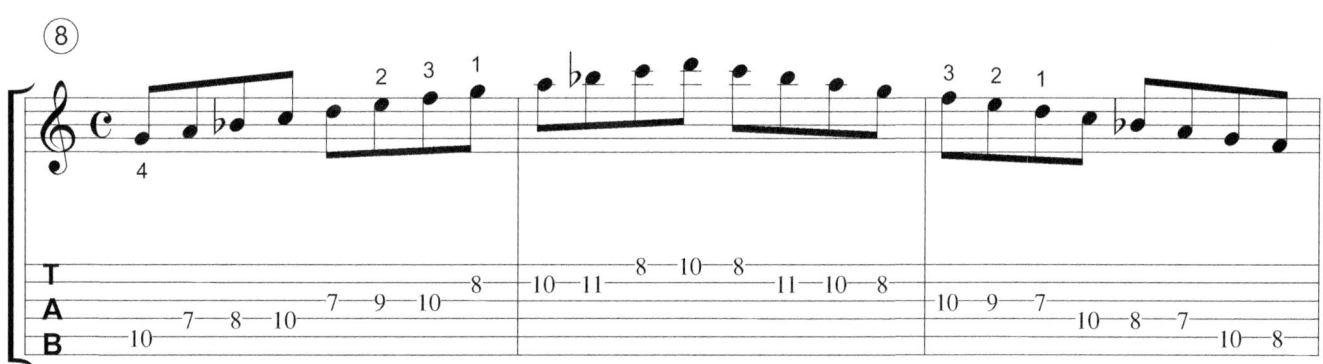
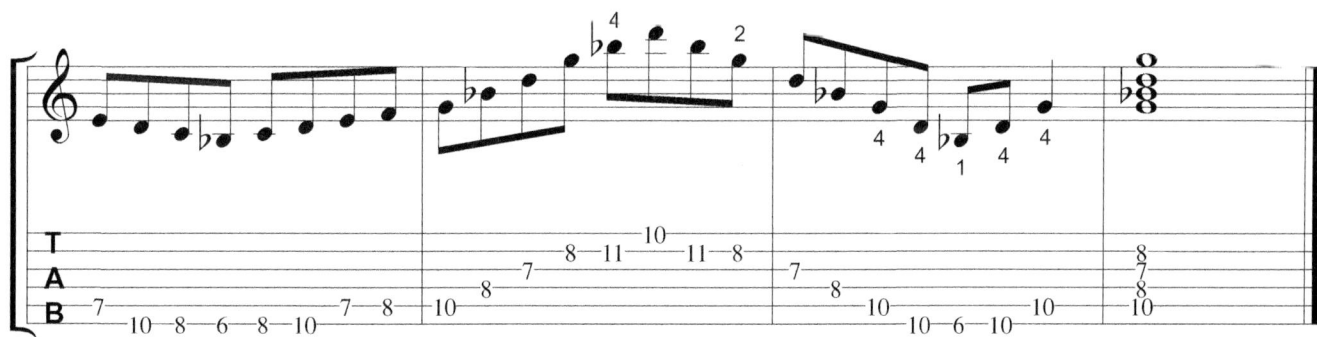

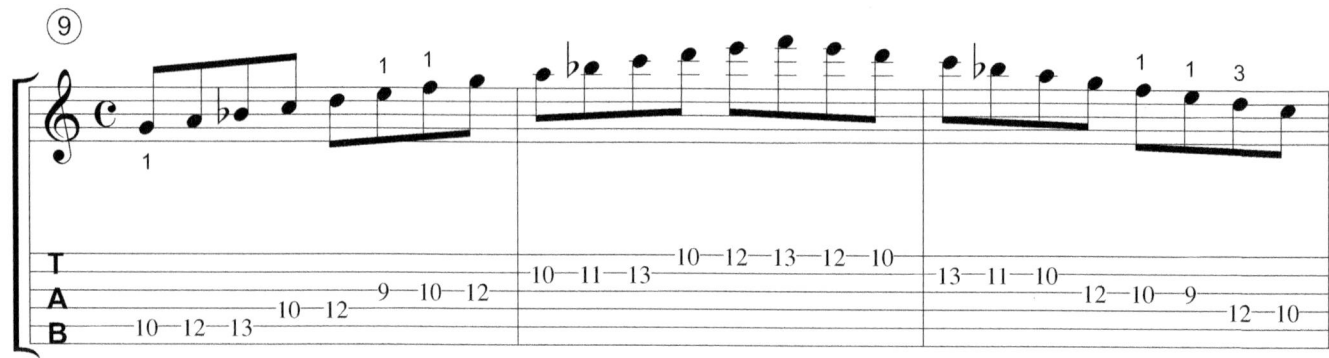
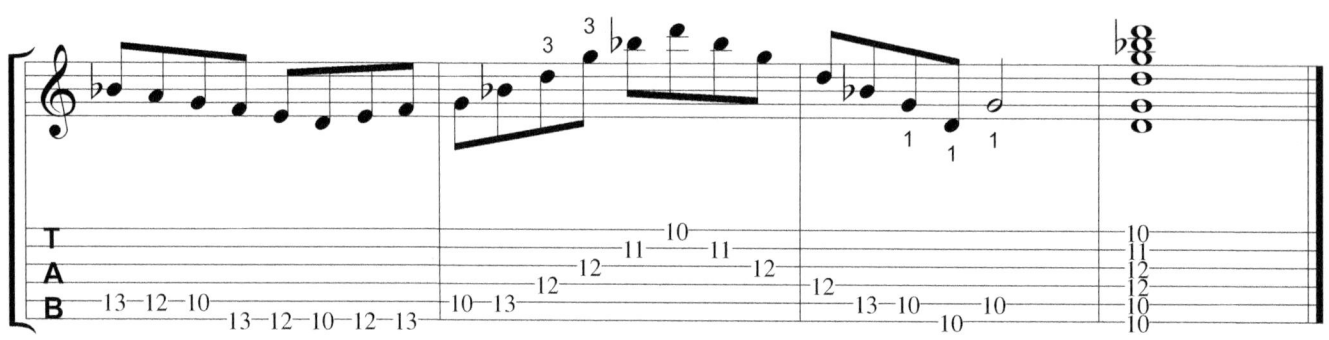
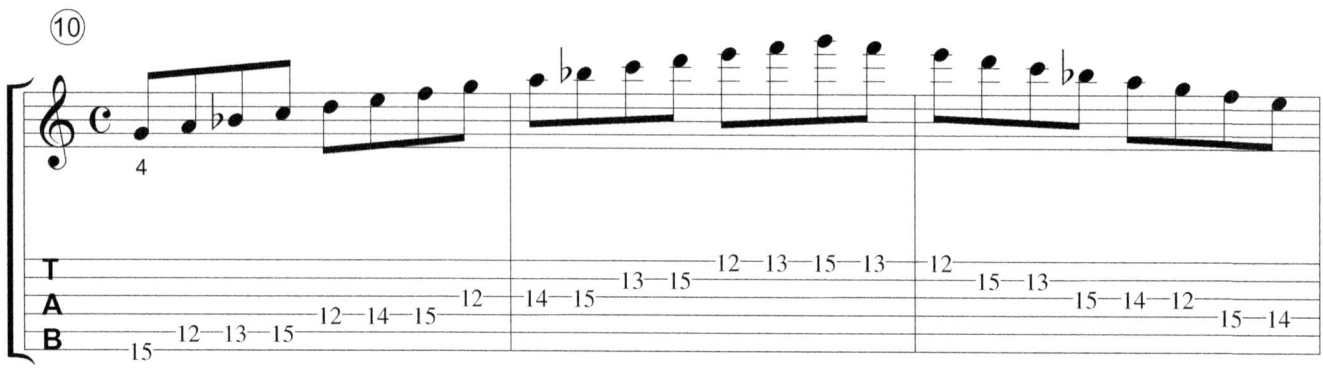
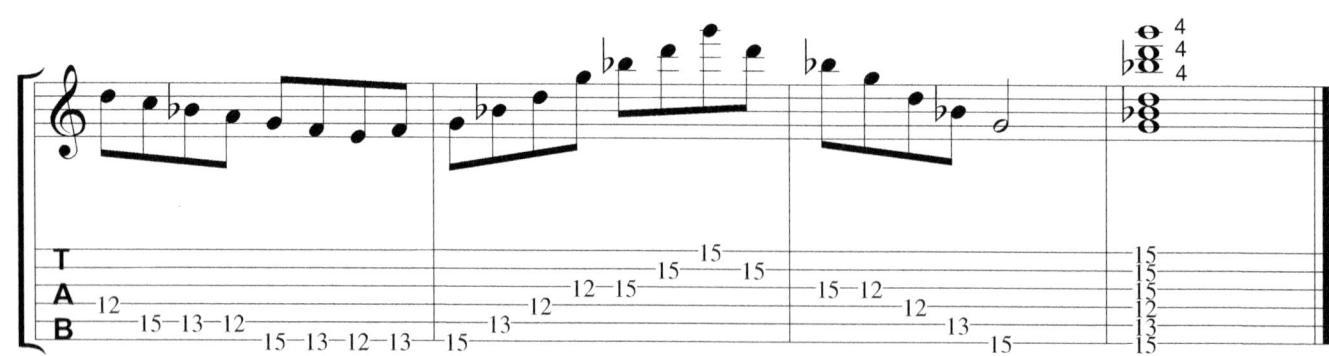

G Melodic Minor

Parent scale for altered dominant down a half step (F# altered dominant)
Parent scale for minor 7th b5 down a step and a half (E minor 7th b5)

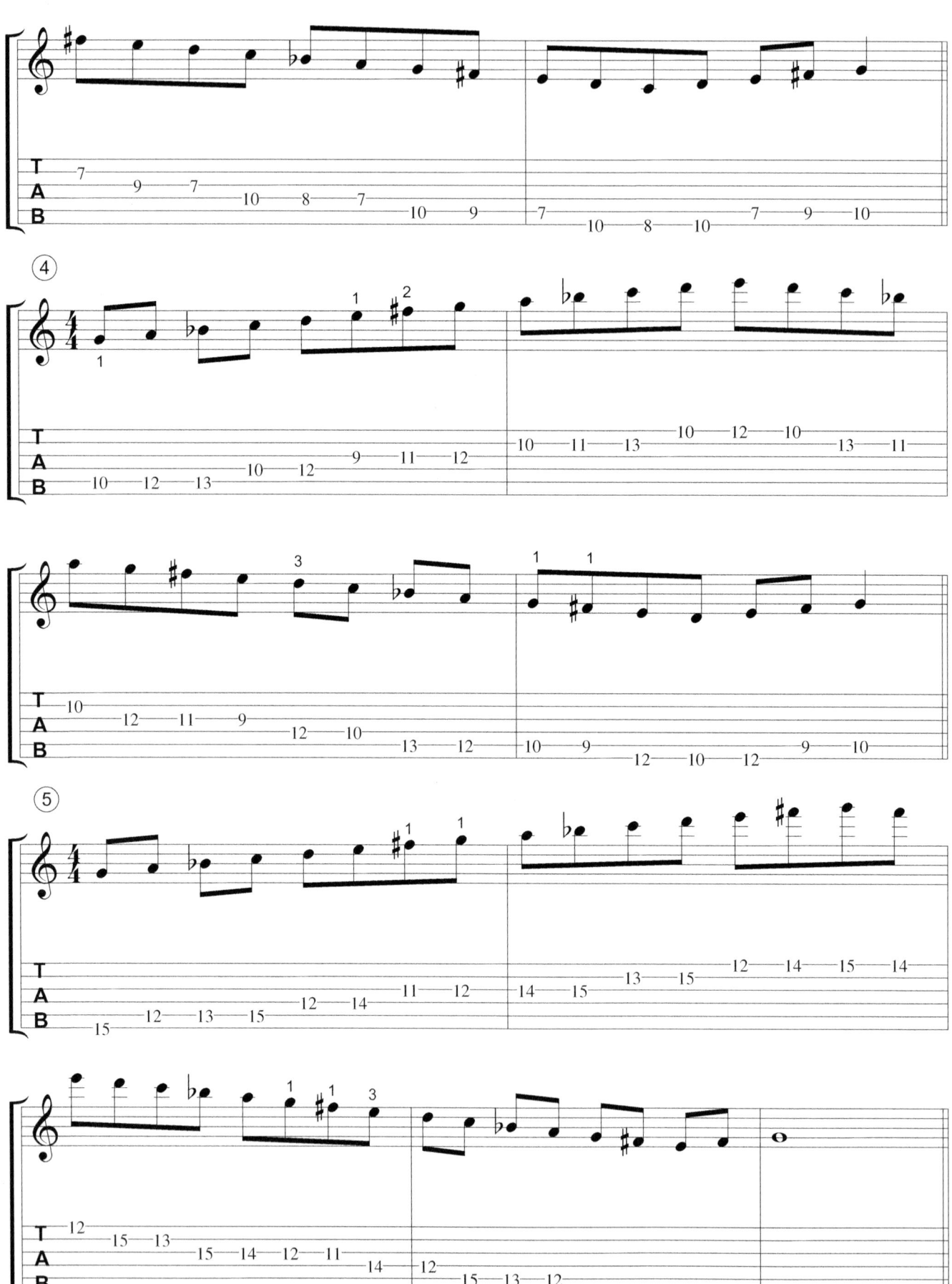

G Lydian

Parent scale for G major type chords.

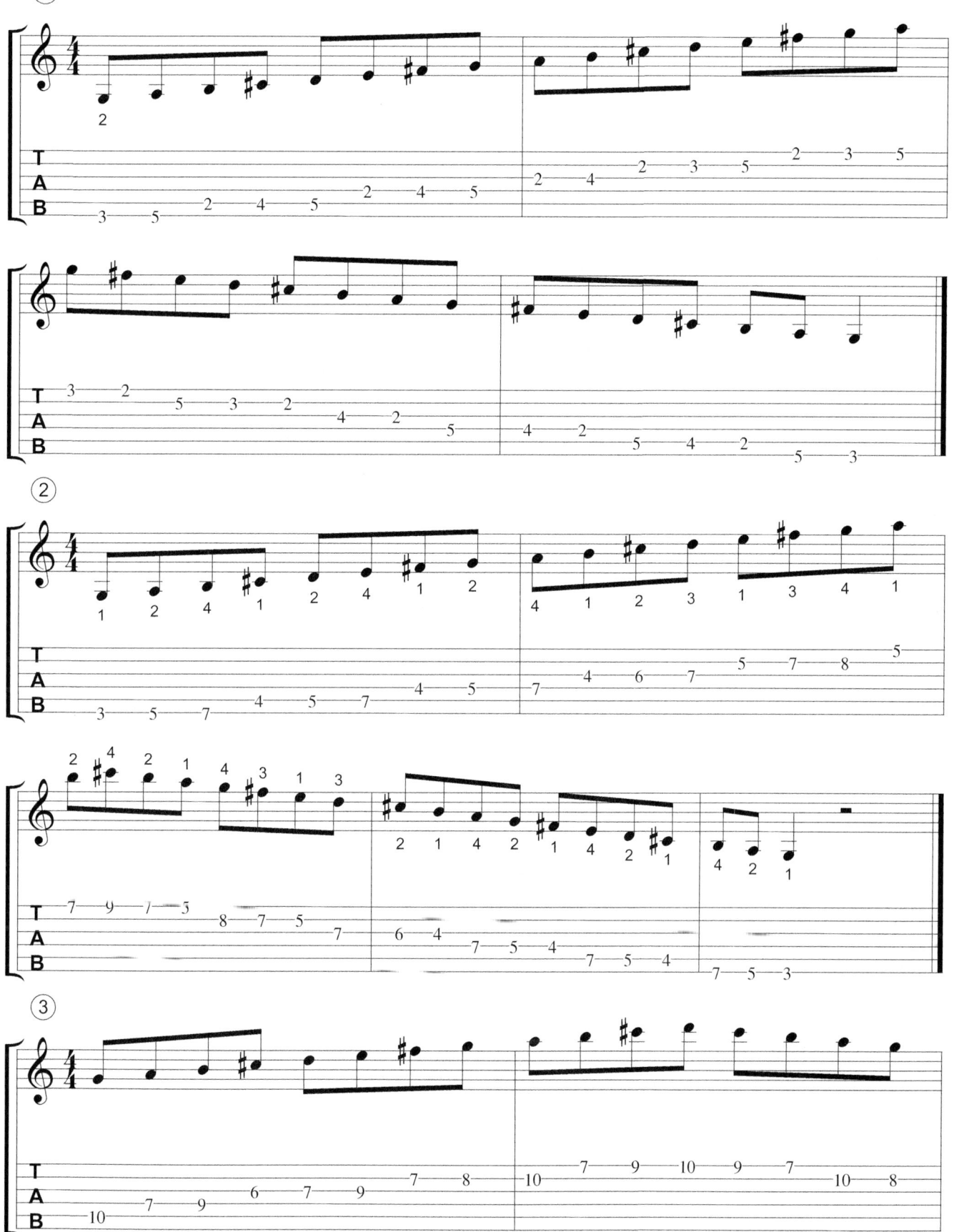

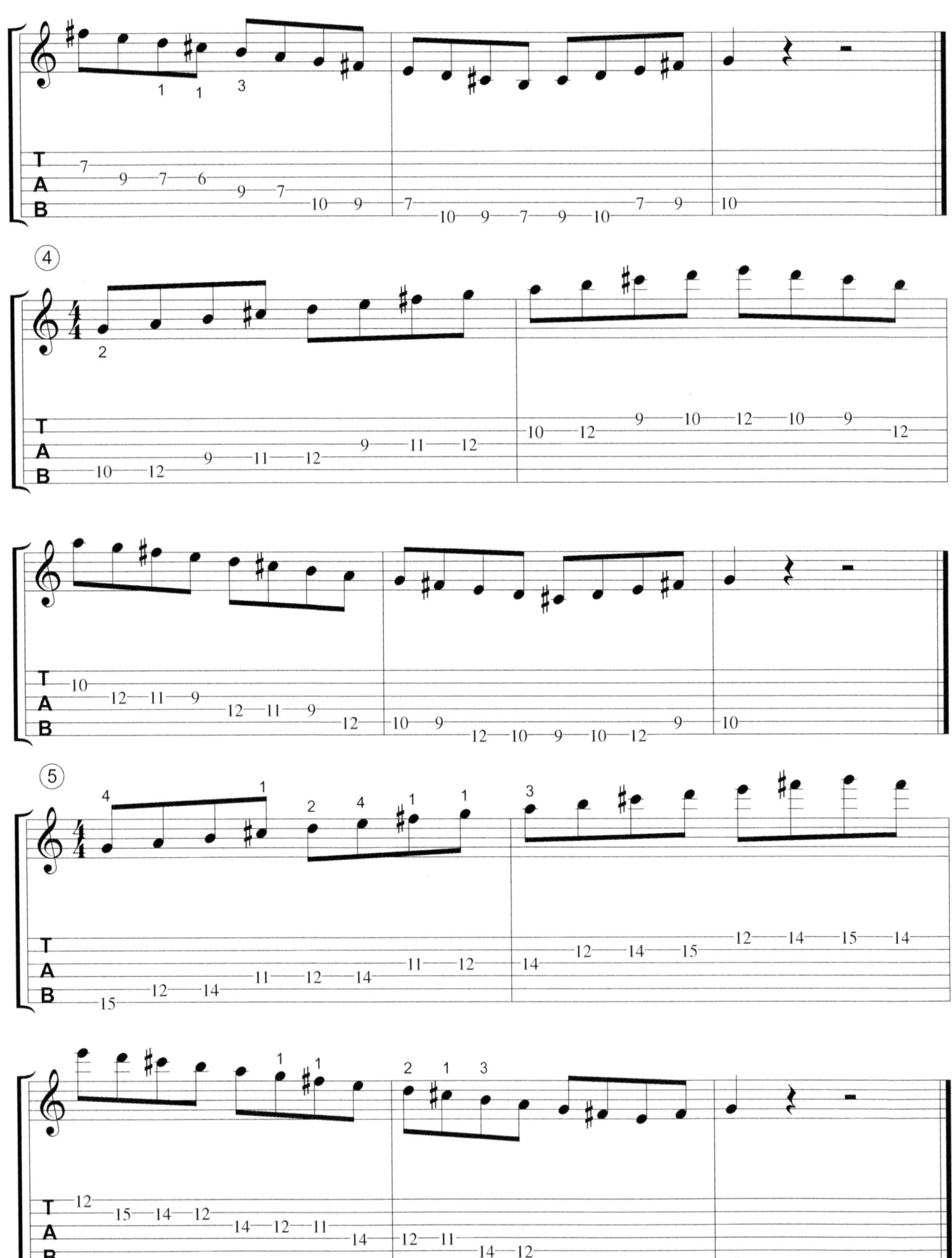

G Lydian Dominant

The 5th mode of the G Lydian dominant scale
is a D melodic minor scale.
Parent scale for G7 type chords (especially with a ♭5 or ♯11).

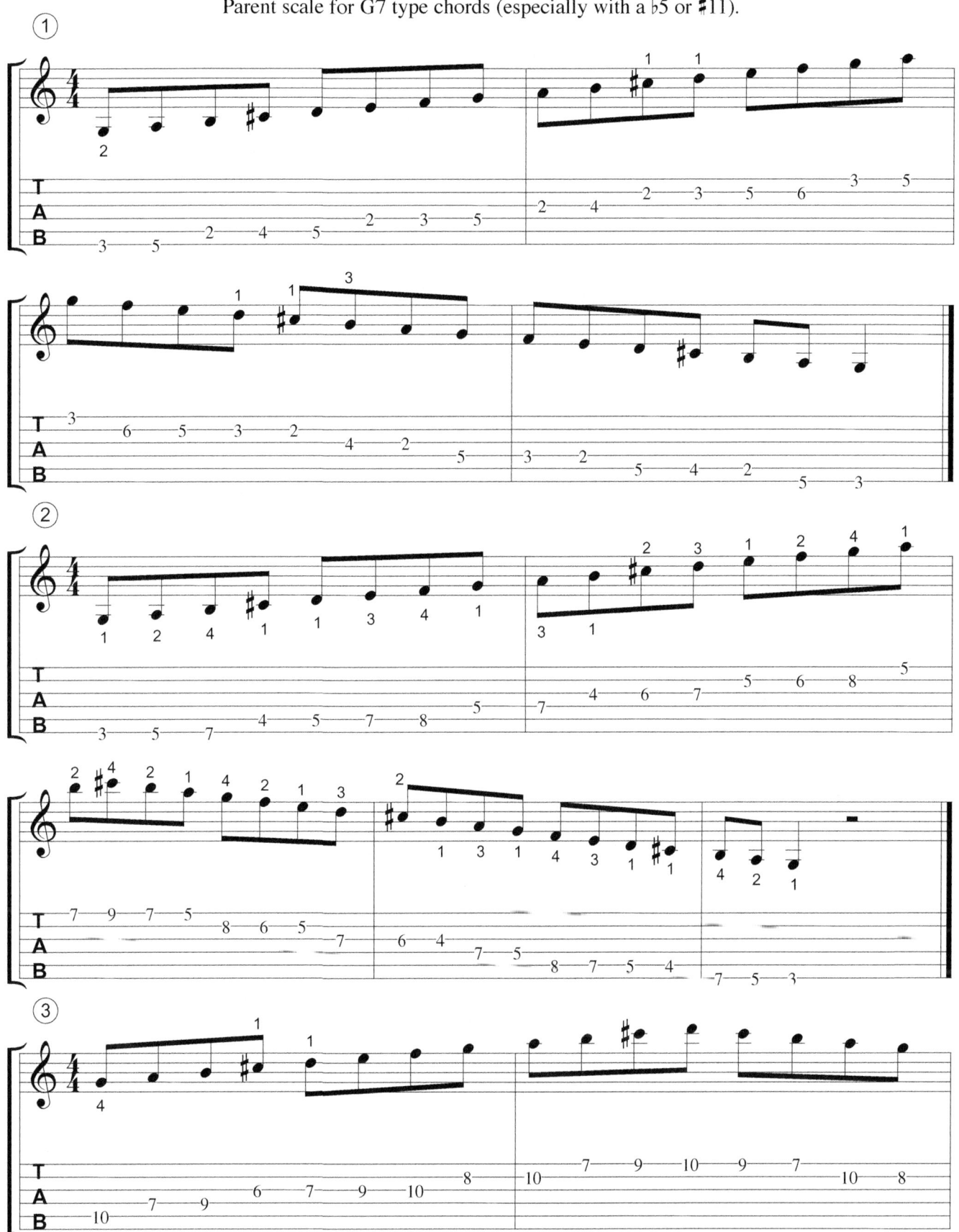

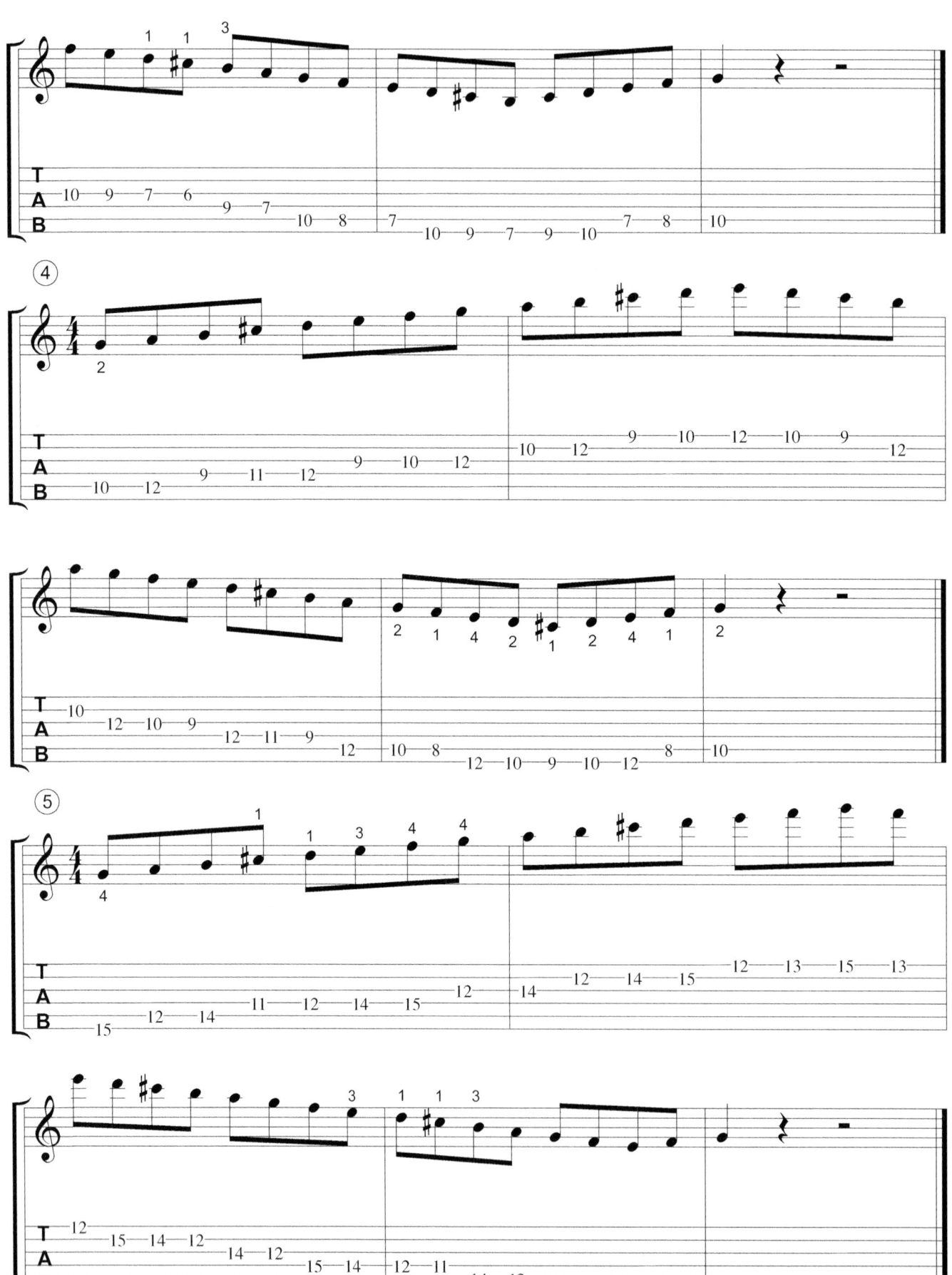

G Locrian

Parent scale for Gmi7♭5 chords.

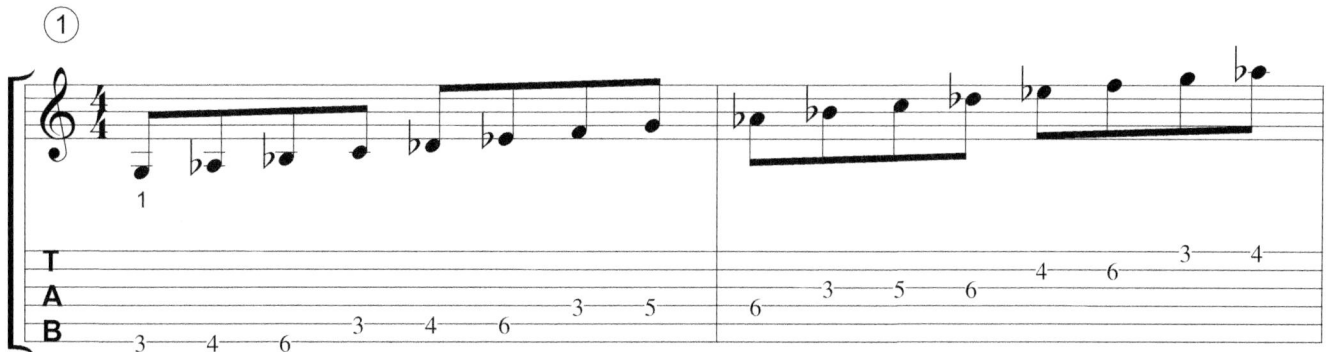

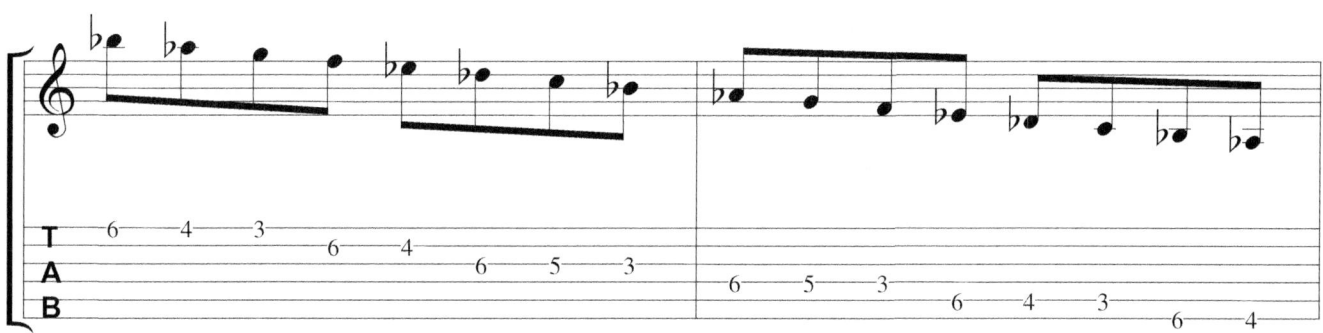

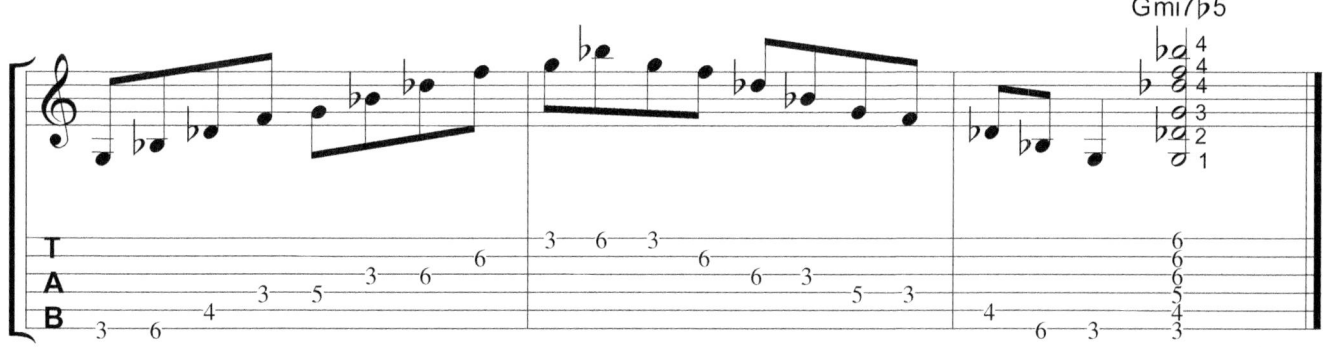

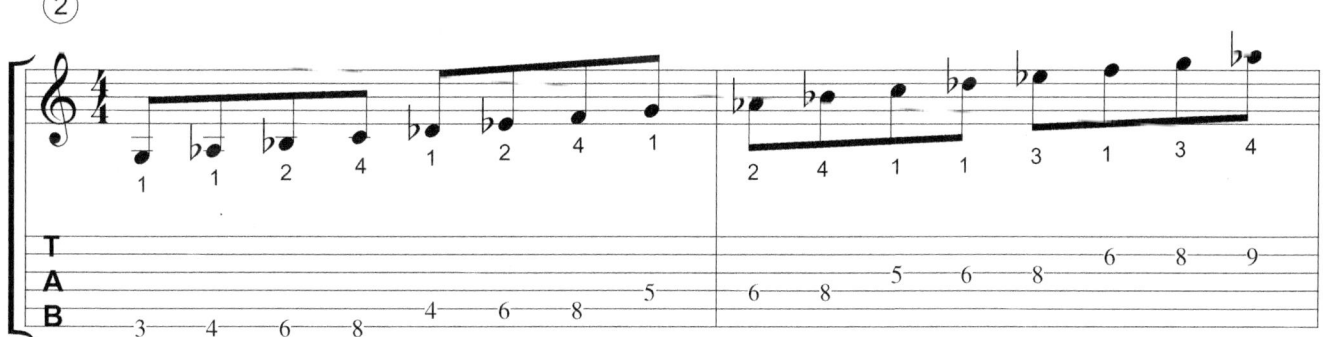

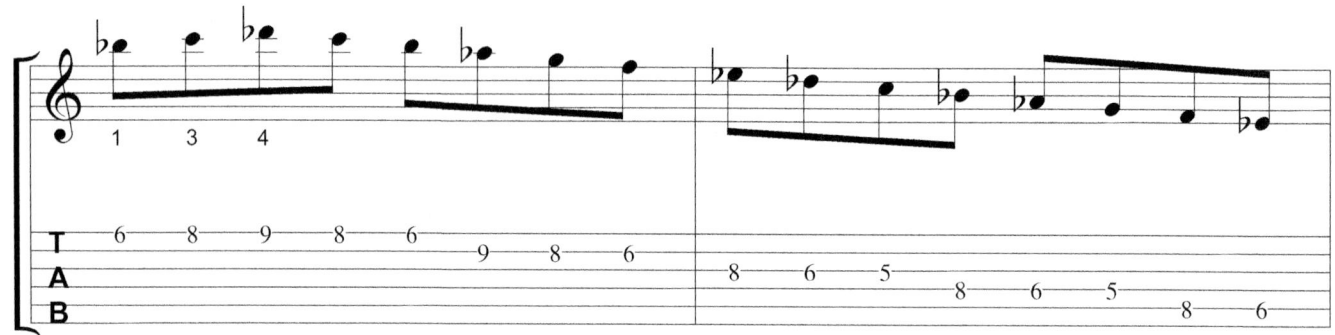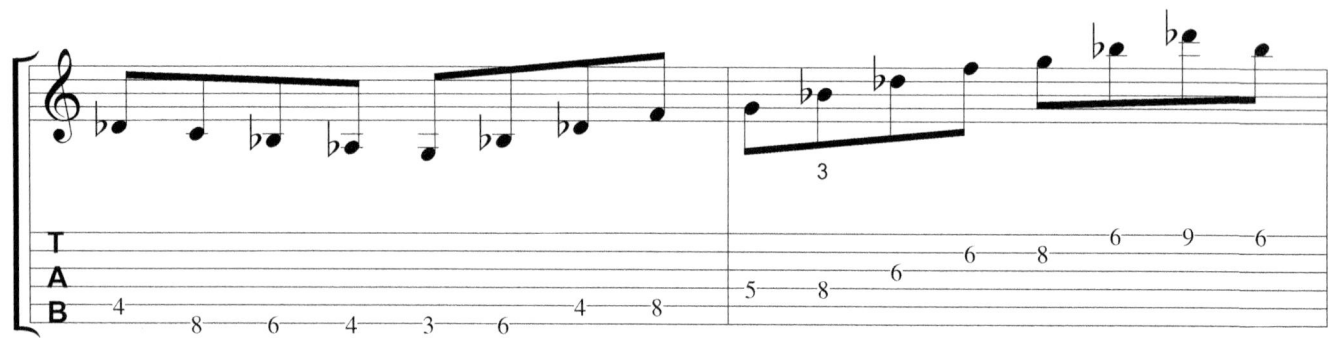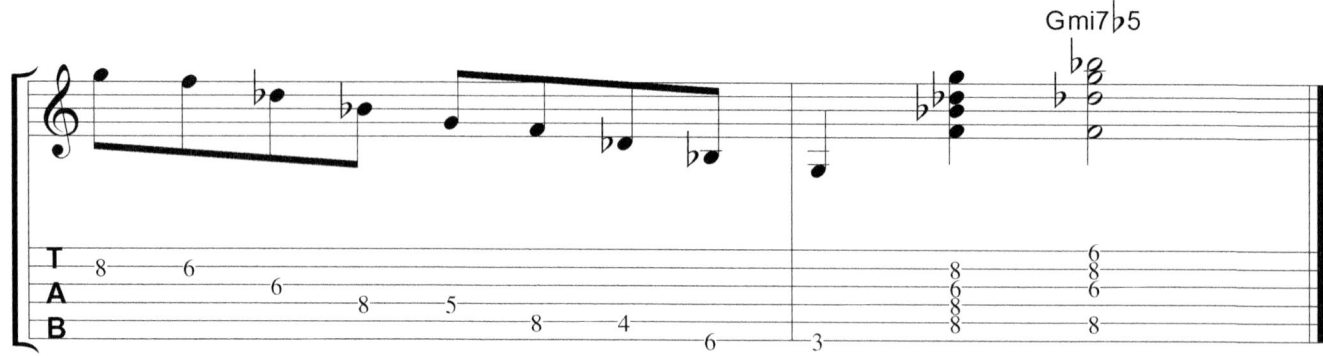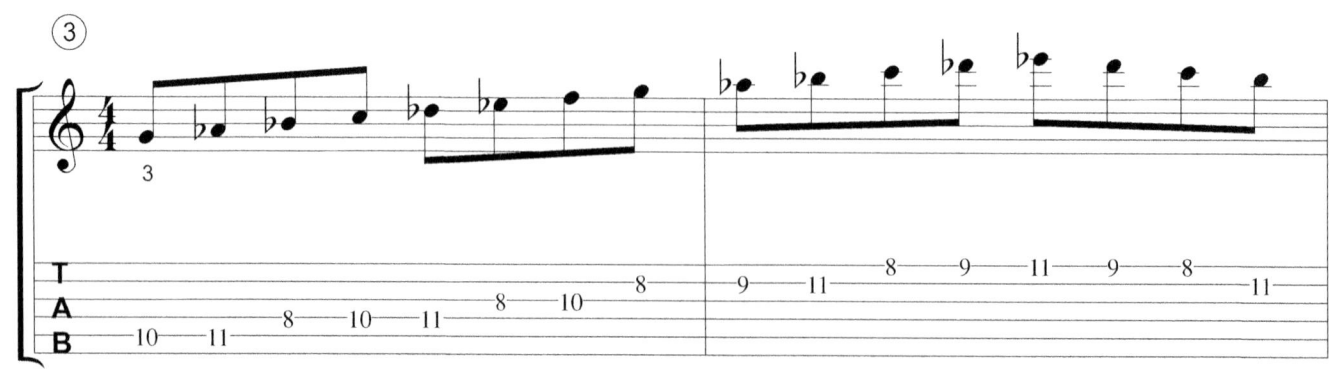

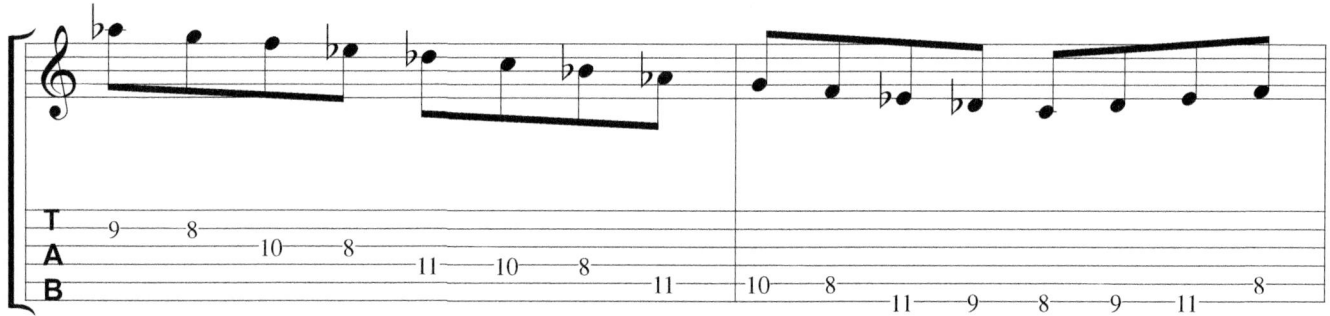

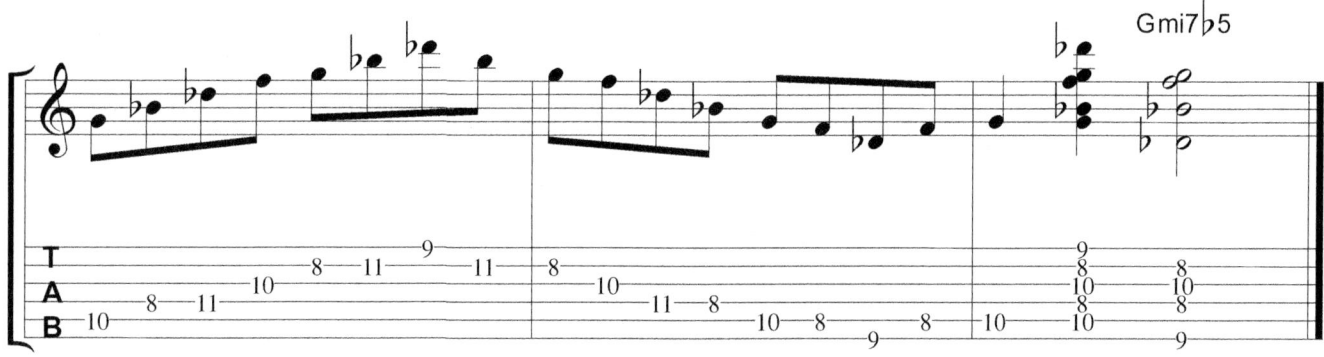

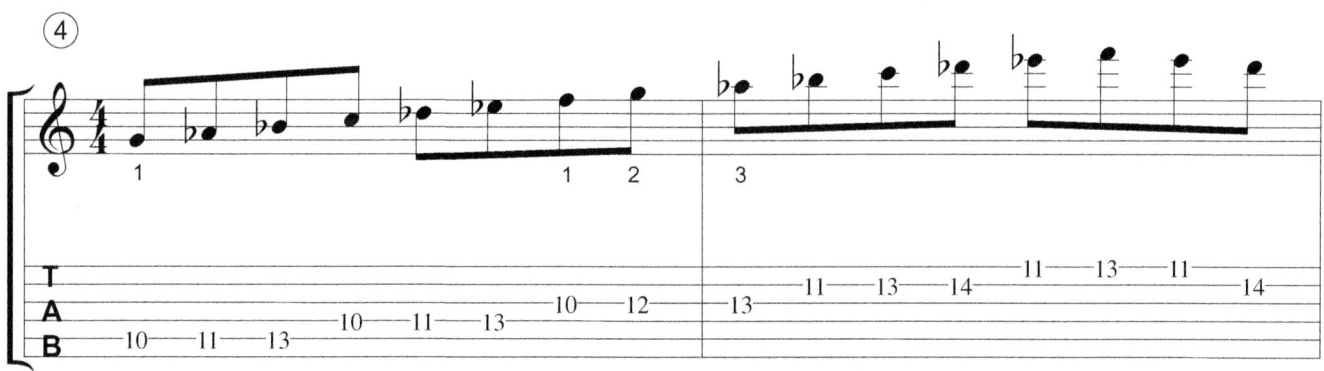

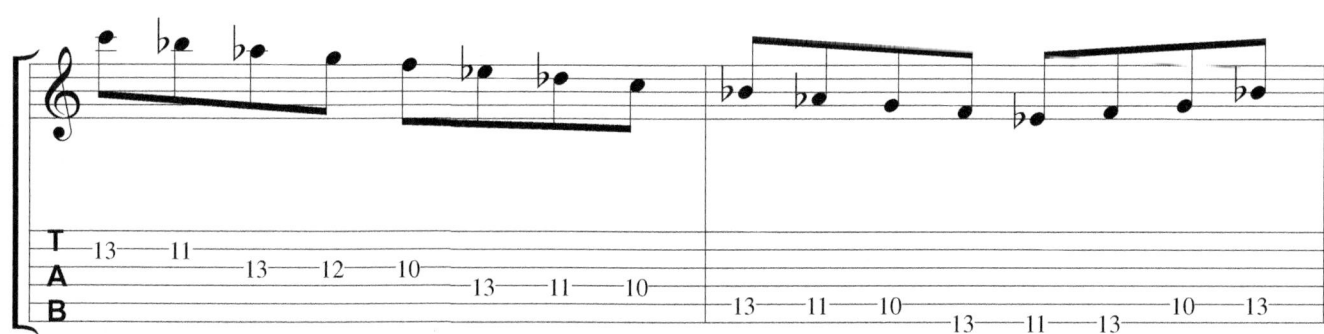

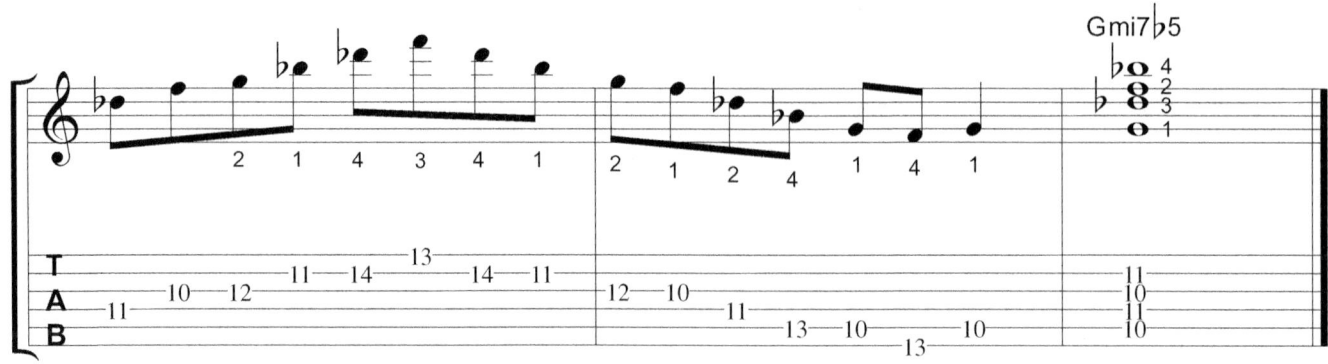

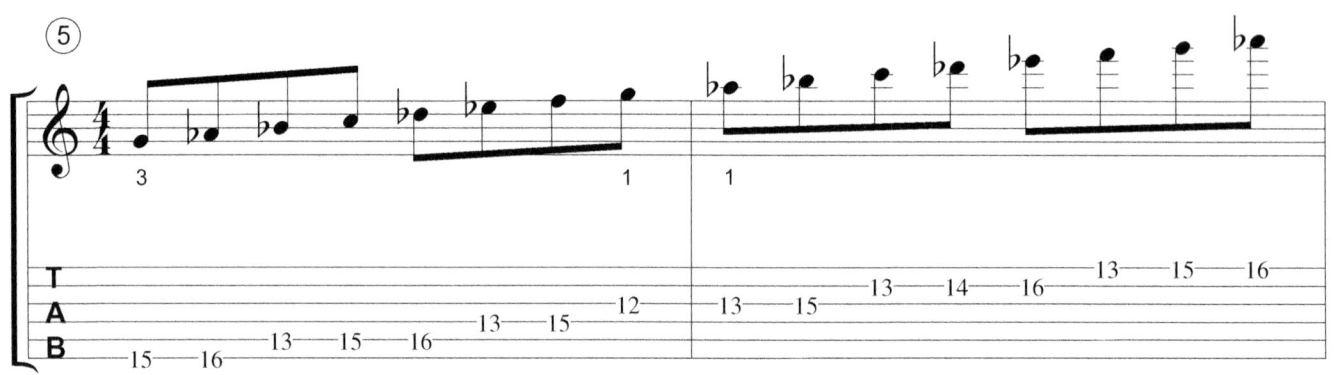

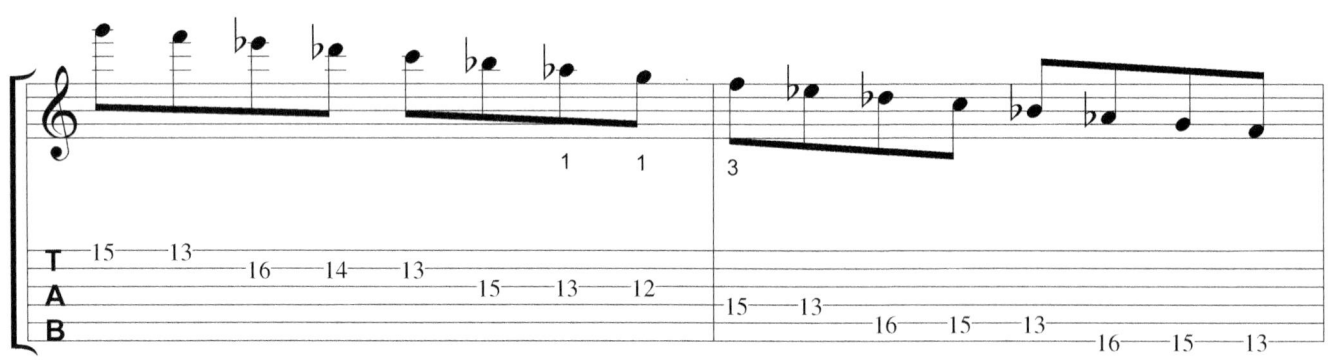

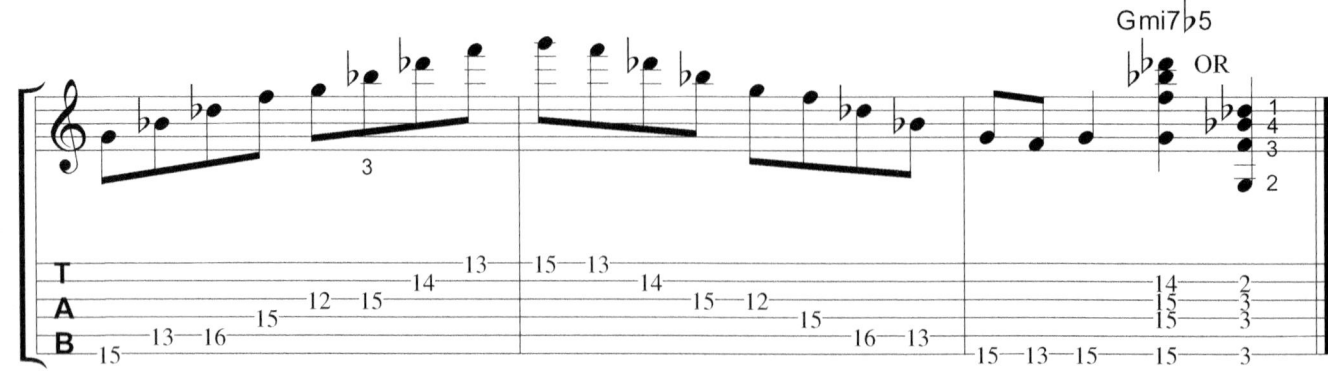

G Altered Dominant

Parent scale for G7 chord with an altered fifth and an altered ninth.
The 2nd mode of the G altered dominant scale is an A♭ melodic minor scale.

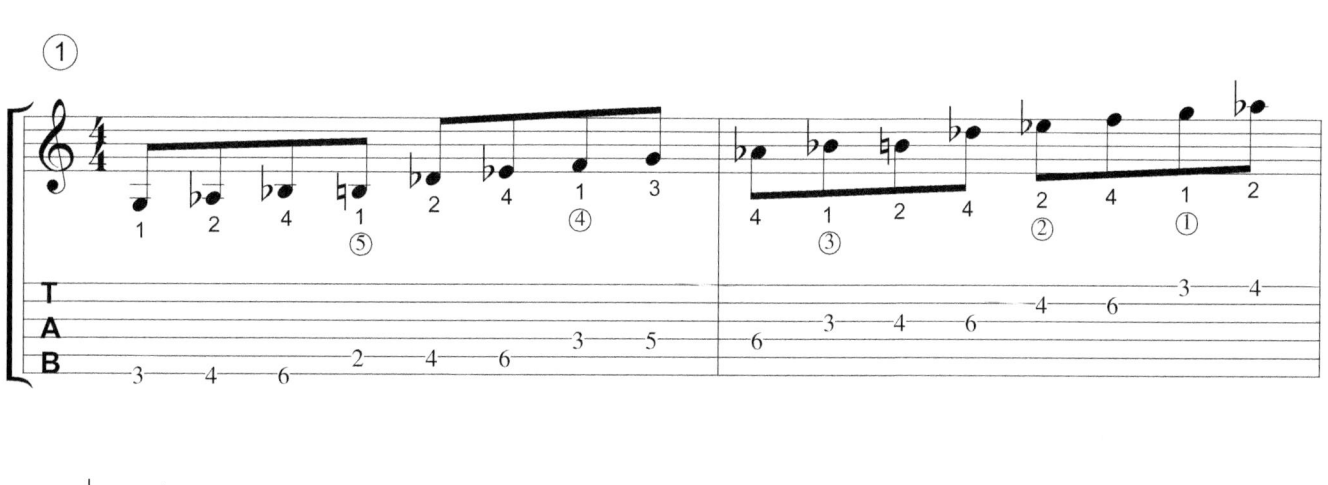

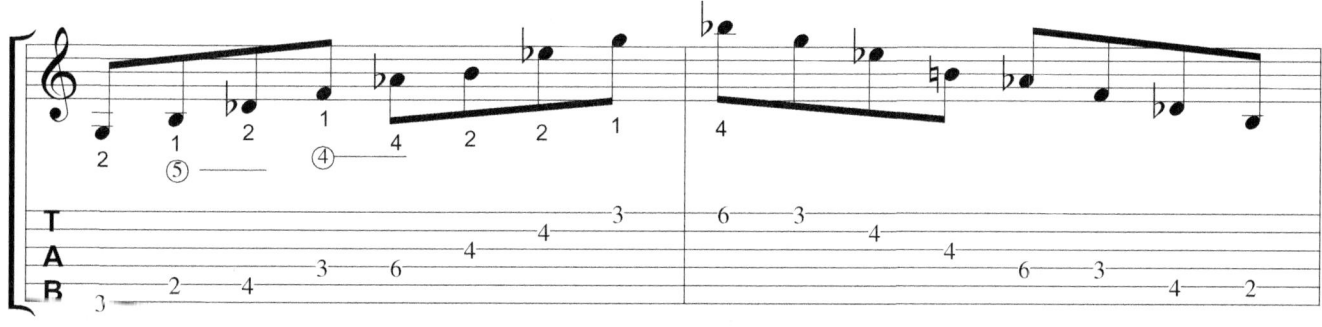
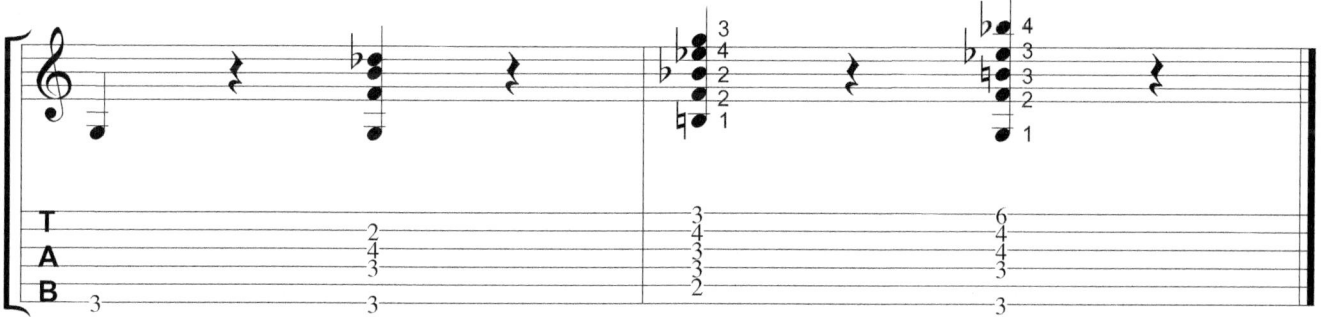

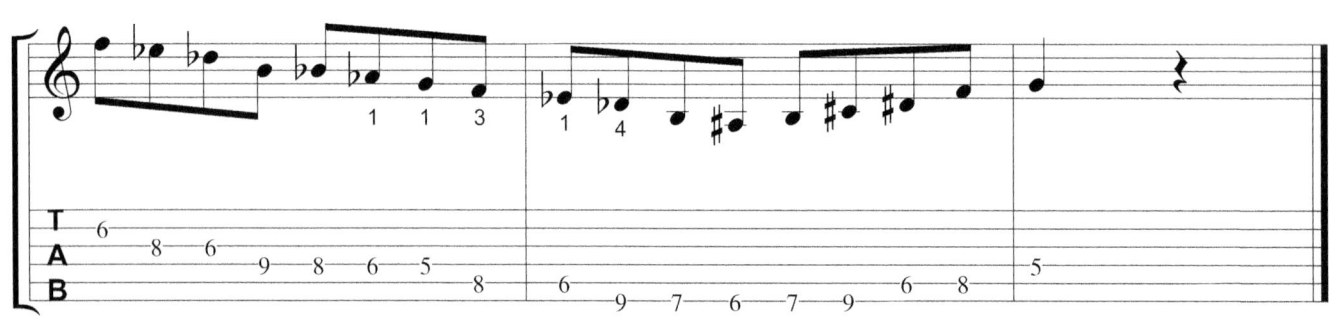
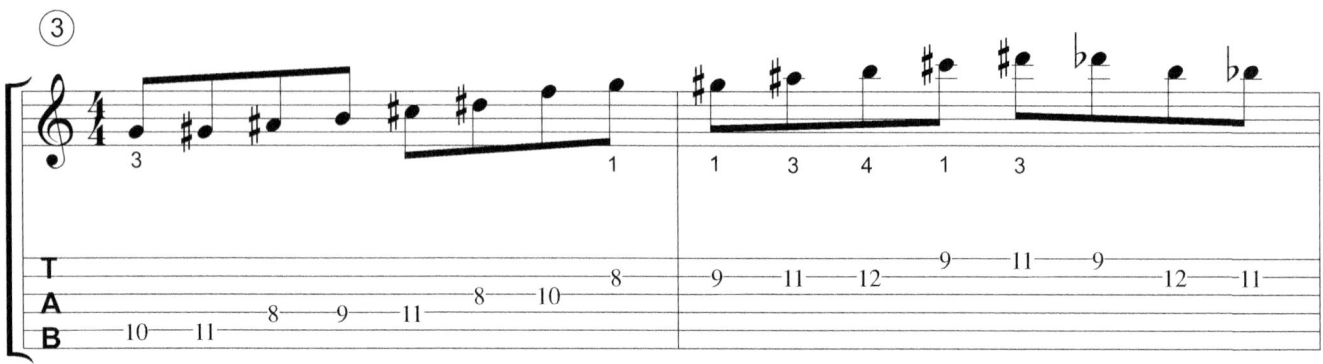
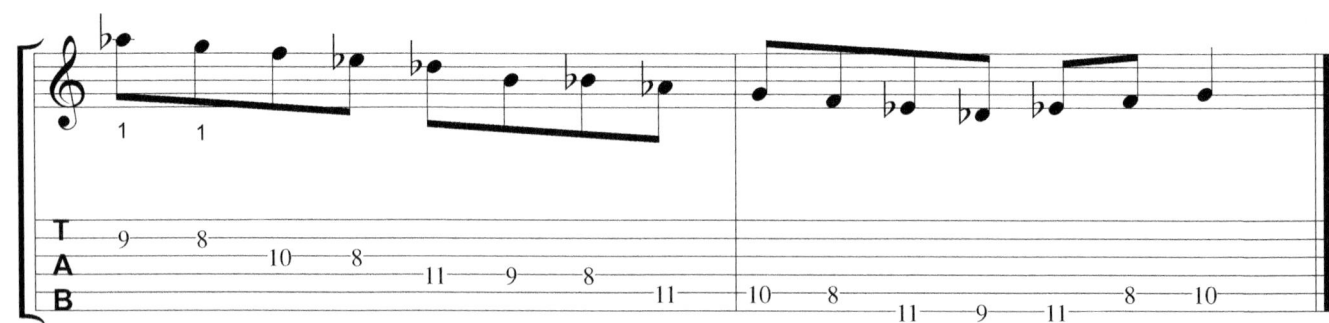

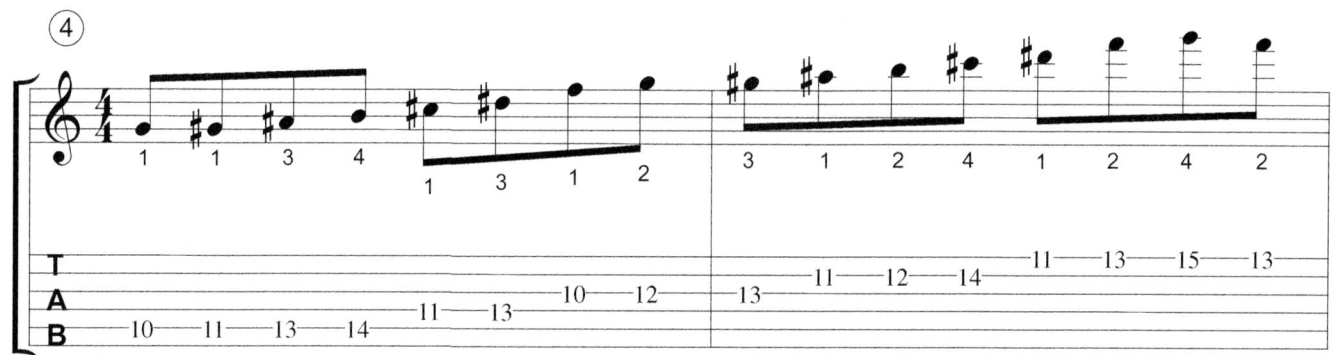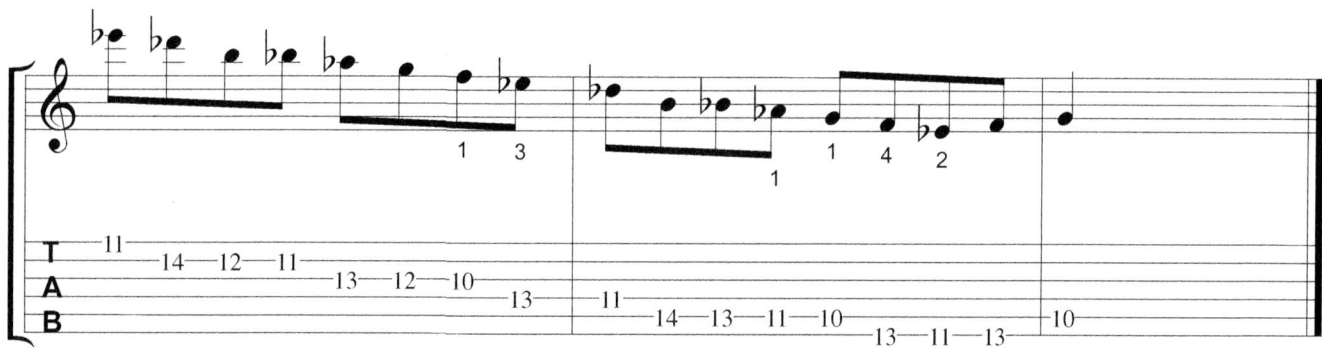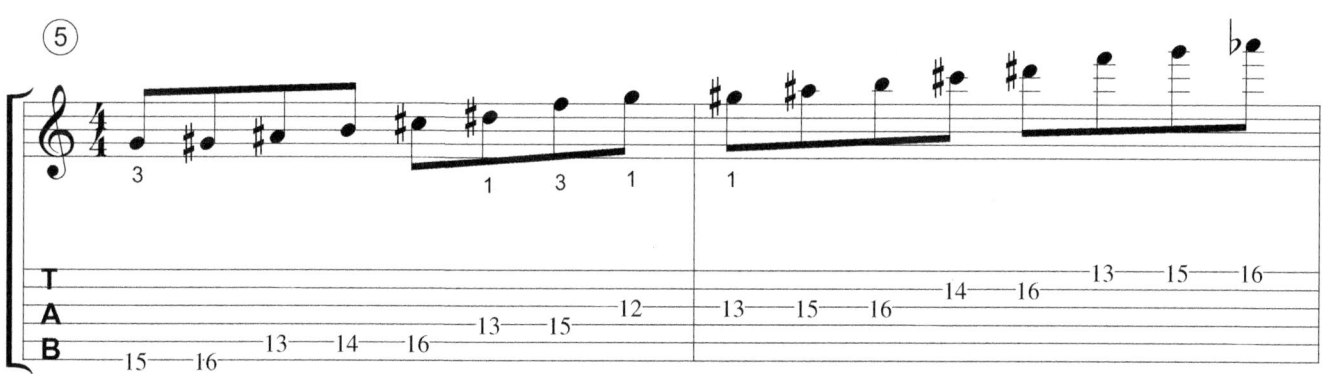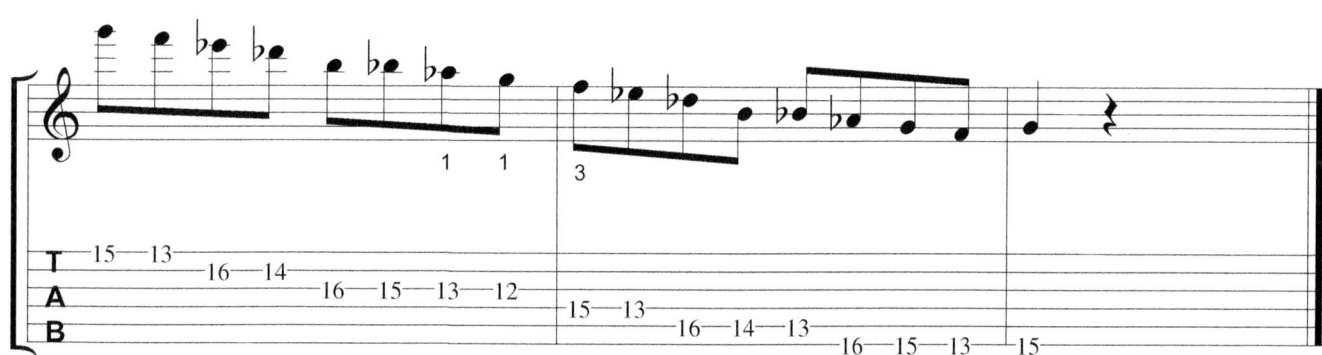

G Major Extended

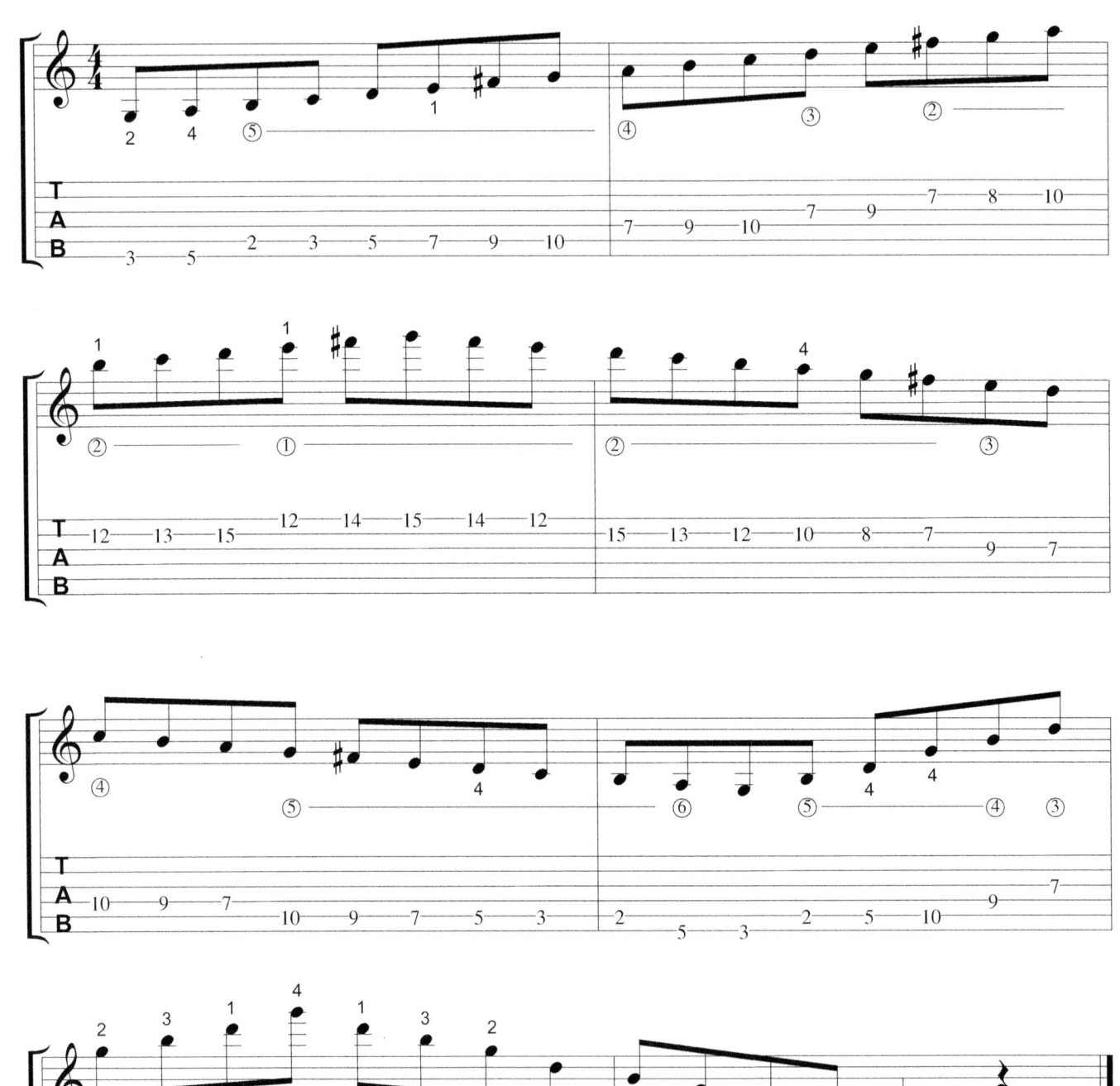

C Major Extended

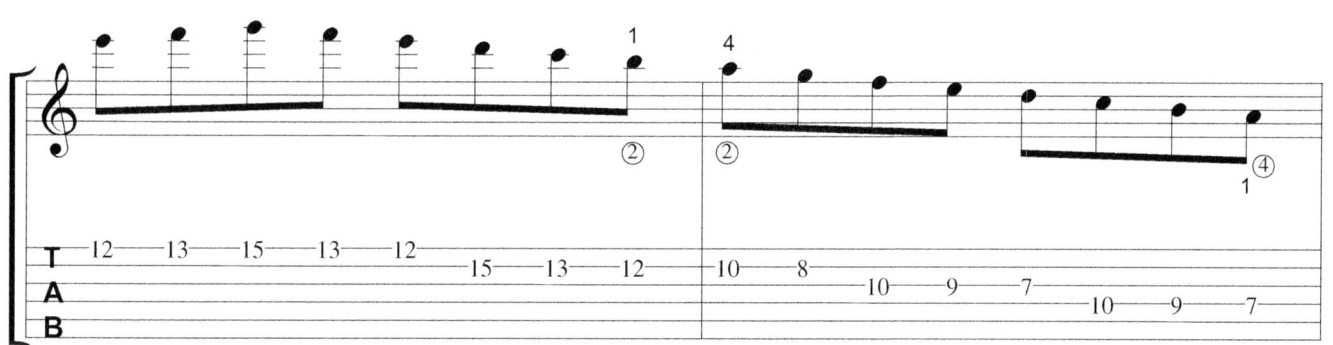
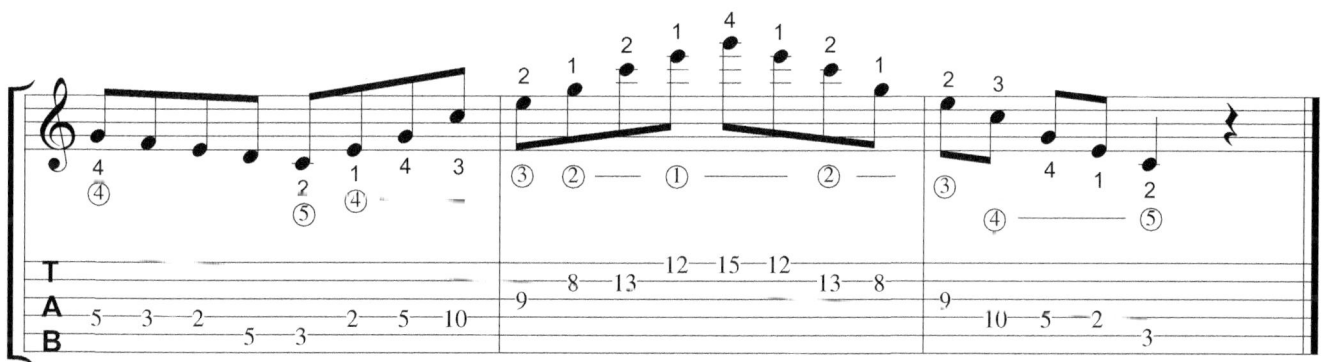

Diminished Scales and Arpeggios

Diminished scales are characterized by formulas containing repetitive patterns. The formula for a diminished scale is whole-step, half-step, whole-step, half-step, etc. Every other note in a diminished scale could be considered a root. Therefore, all diminished chords and scales repeat themselves every three frets (whole-step and a half-step), which means that there are only three diminished scales.

The primary function of diminished chords (and augmented chords) is to serve as passing or connecting chords. A degree sign (o) is used to indicate a diminished chord. A diminished chord includes a minor third ($\flat$3rd), diminished fifth ($\flat$5th) and a diminished seventh ($\flat\flat$7) which is the seventh enharmonic equivalent of a major sixth.

All scales and arpeggios should be memorized and transposed to the other keys and positions. Here are some diminished scales and arpeggios. Any of these could be used over a G°, B$\flat$°, D$\flat$°, or E°.

Diminished Scales and Arpeggios

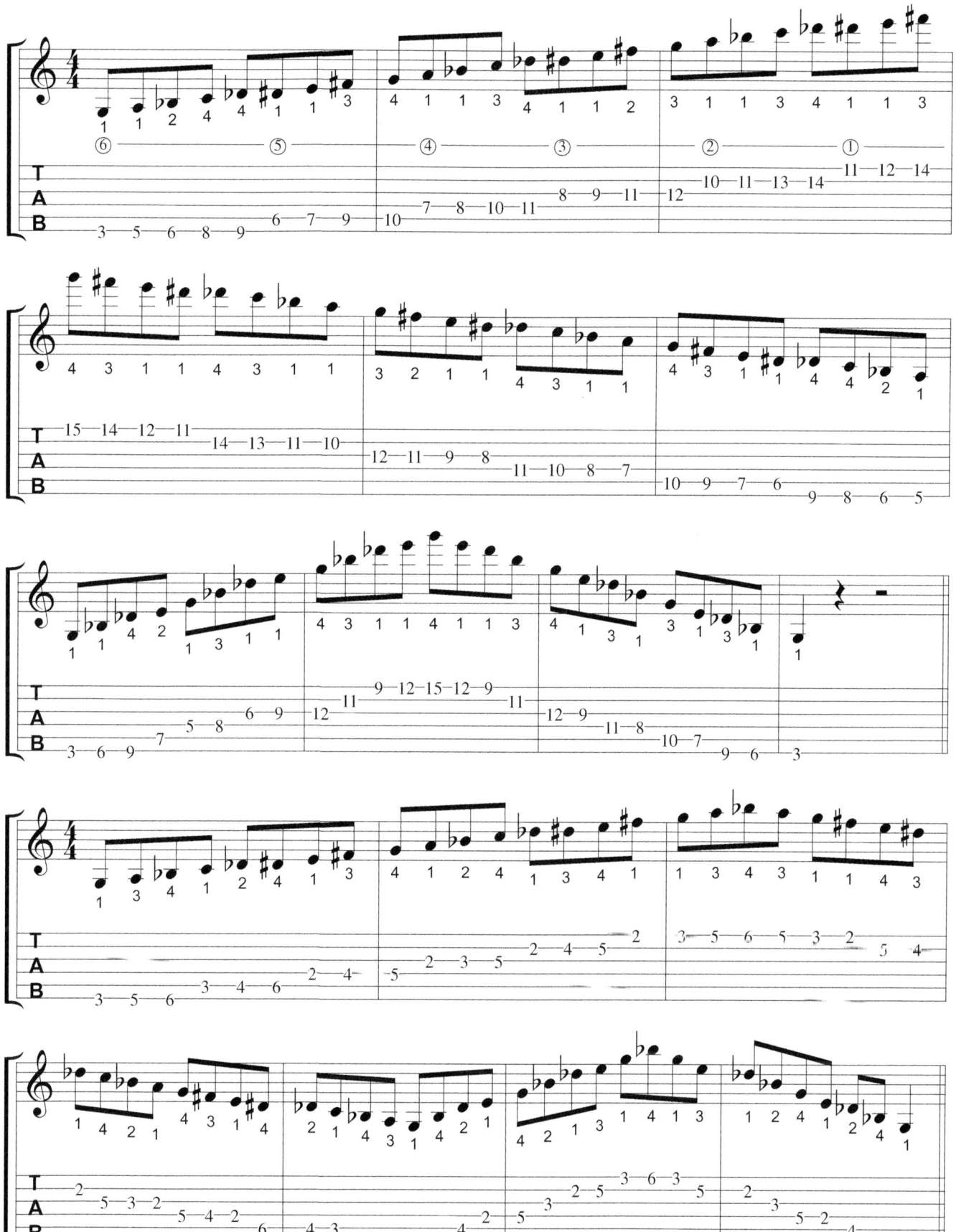

Patterns for Diminished Scales

Here are some patterns derived from a diminished scale, which may be played over a G°, B♭°, D♭°, or E°. Many of these, such as pattern 1, have been used by great jazz musicians, not only over diminished chords but also over dominant 7th (♭5♭9) type chords, such as F♯7, A7, C7, and E♭7.

There are many subtle ways in which the notes of these patterns can be rearranged. Patterns 1, 2, 3, 5 and 9 have repeating interval patterns which could be extended to other positions. Experiment as much as possible and try to uncover some of the great potential this scale has for improvisation.

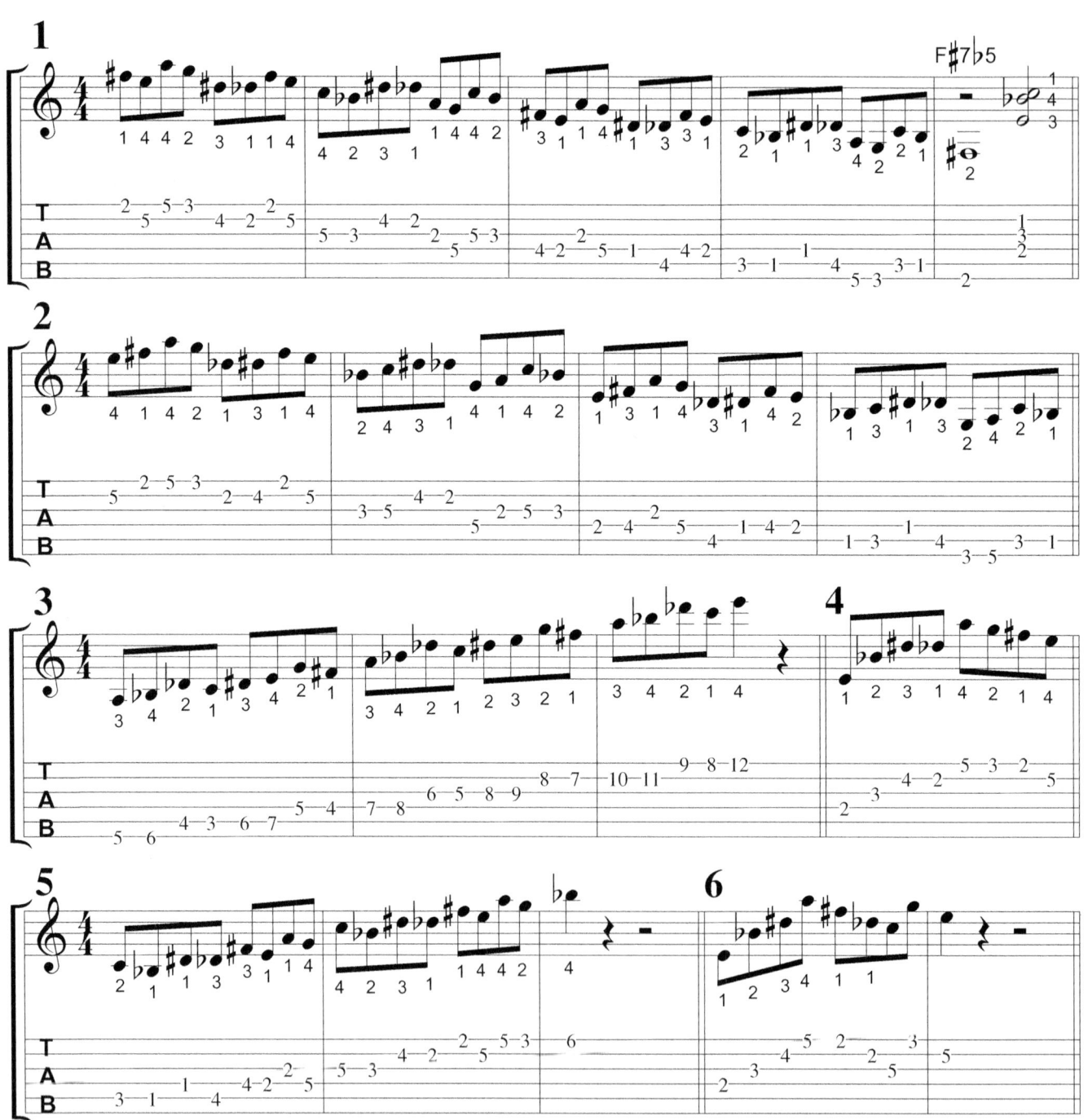

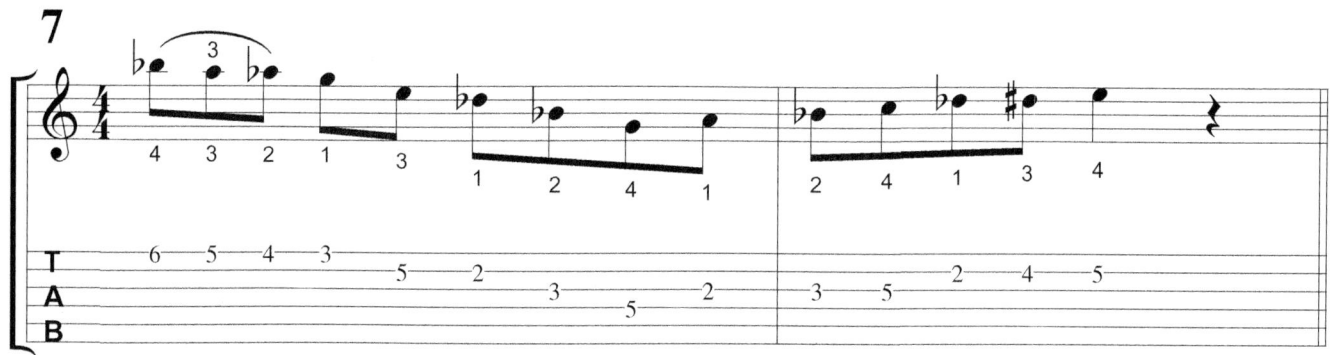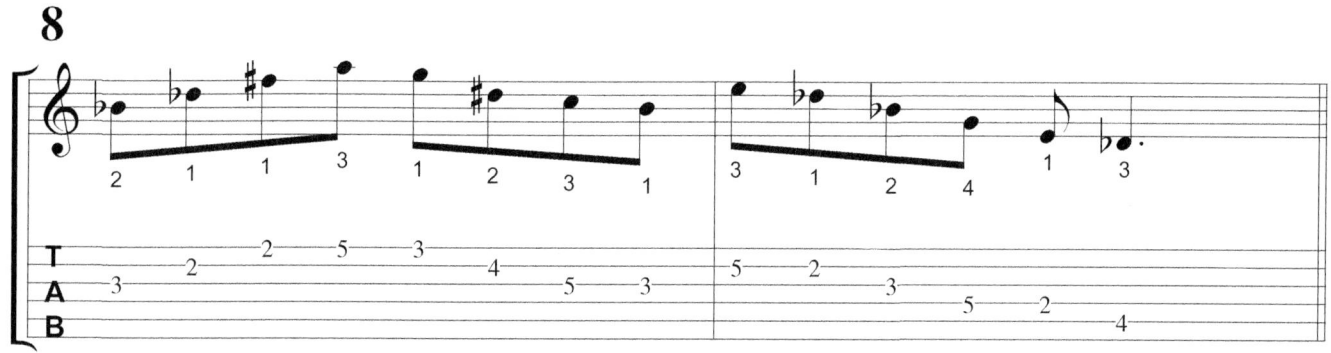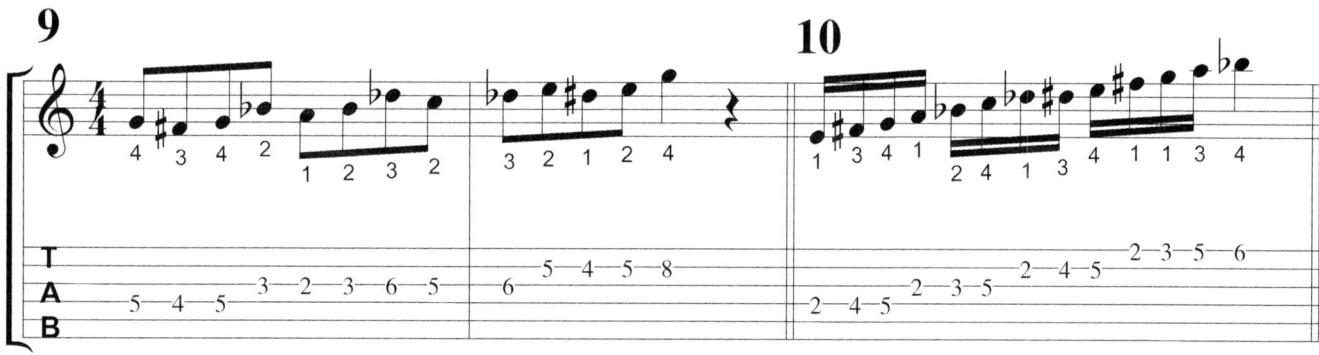

Whole-Tone Scales and Patterns

Whole-Tone scales are characterized with formulas containing repetitive patterns. The formula for an augmented scale is whole-step, whole-step, whole-step, etc. Since the whole-tone scale is a continuous line of whole-steps, any note in the scale could be considered the root of the scale. Each augmented scale has six different notes (roots). If you take a whole-tone scale and move it up a half-step, the combination of the two scales will encompass every note in a chromatic scale (12 notes). Therefore, there are only two whole-tone scales.

A plus sign (+) is used to indicate an augmented chord. An augmented chord has a raised fifth. The spelling of a G+ chord is G - B - D♯. Here are some whole-tone scales, arpeggios and patterns. Scale #1 moves up and down the fingerboard. Notice the similarity between scale #2 and scale #4, and also #3 and #5. Scale #6 combines the two different approaches of moving up and down, and moving across the fingerboard.

This entire section is down-up alternating picking with the exception of pattern 7 which is played on the 4th, 3rd and 2nd strings with down-down-up picking. I find this picking pattern much easier and faster than alternating picking, when picking three-string patterns. Pattern 7 should be played staccato so that the notes do not blend into each other. Pay close attention to the fingering in pattern 8. In pattern 9, notice how the first and second fingers are used to move up and down the fingerboard.

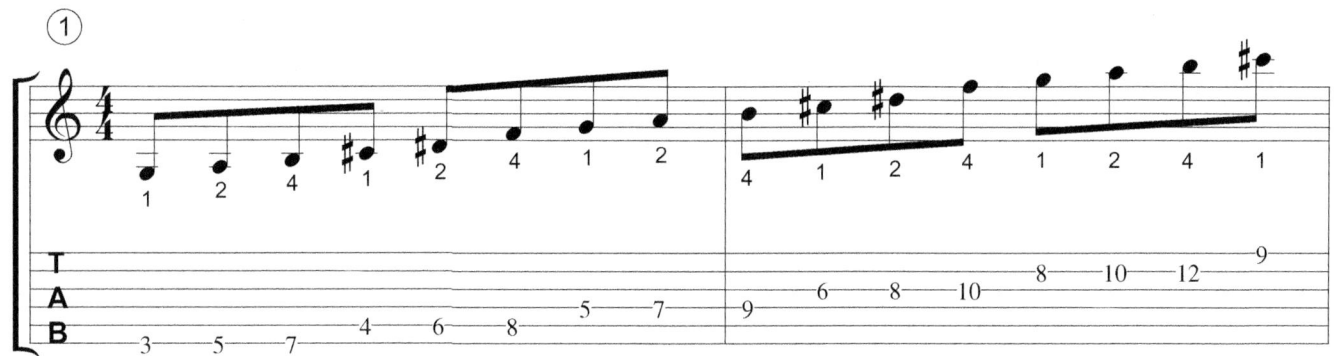
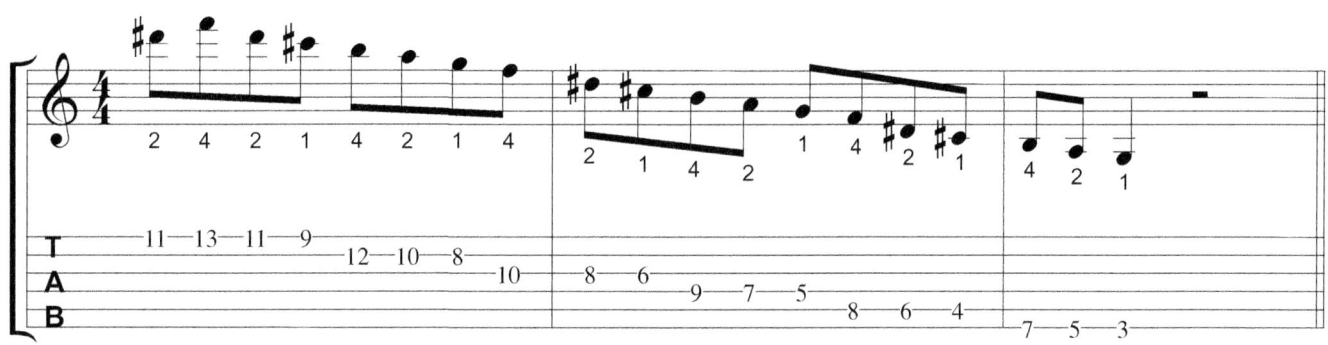
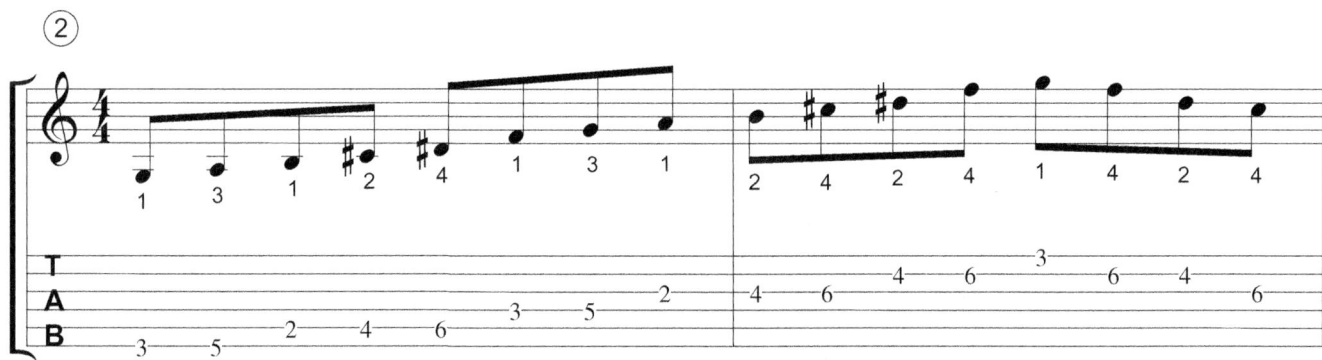
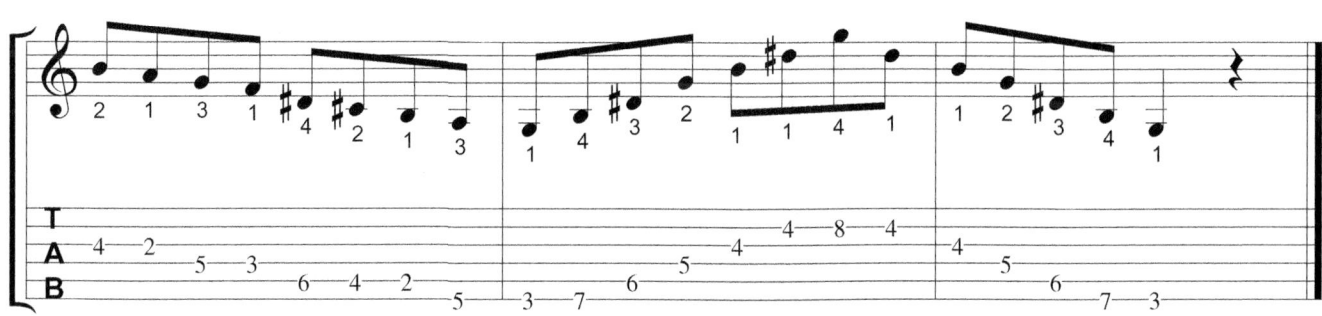

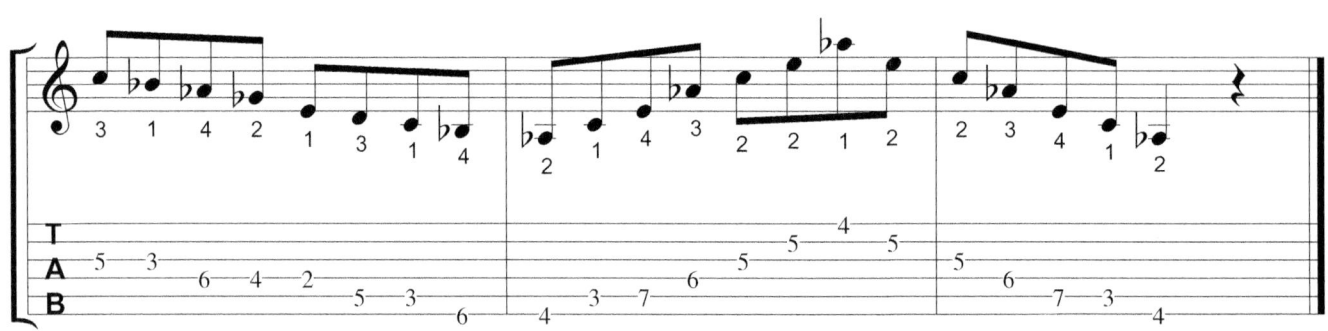

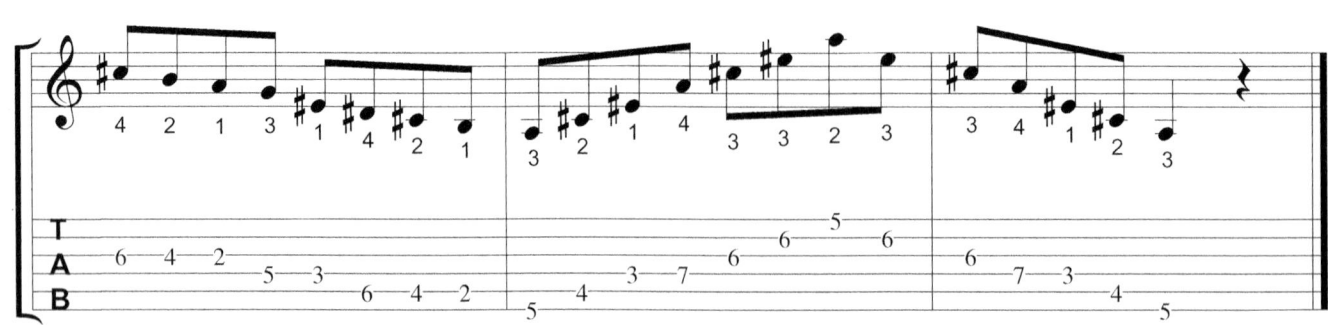

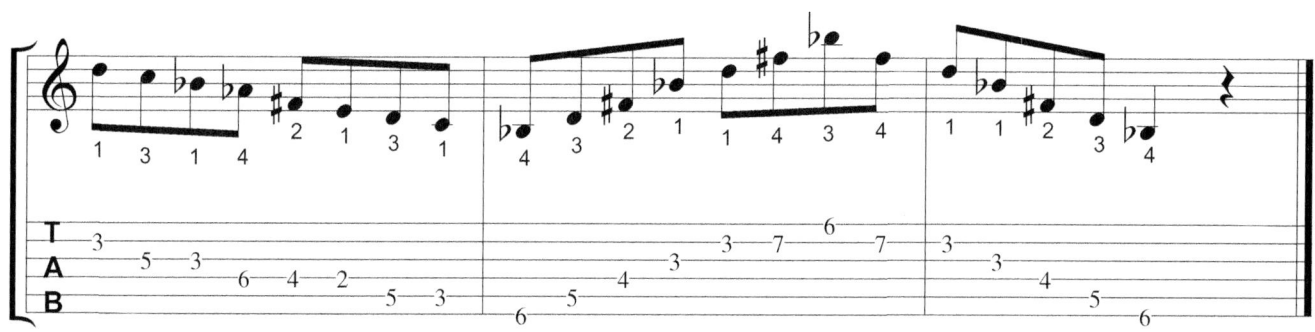
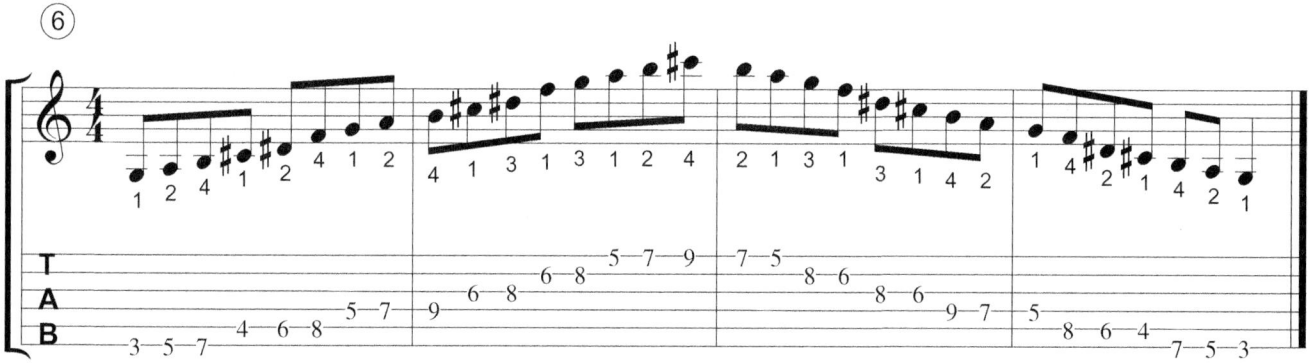
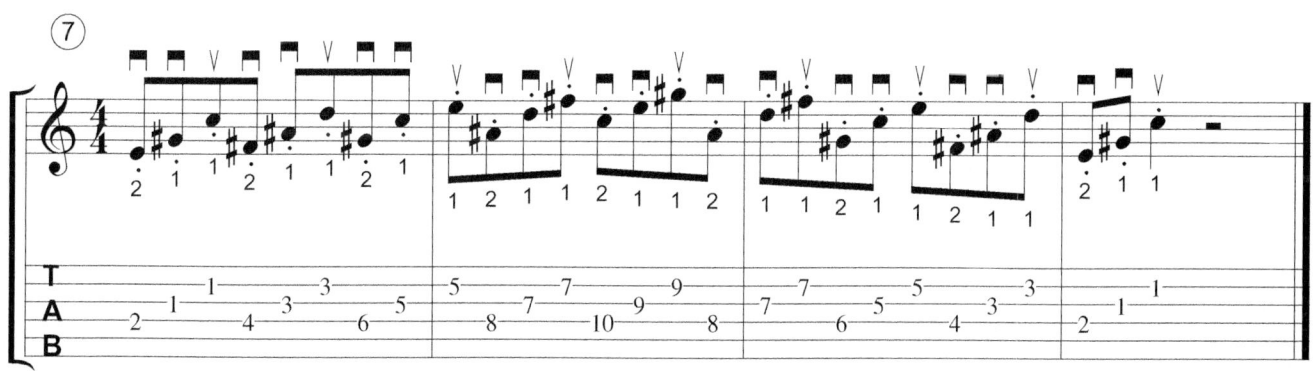

8
TAB
9
TAB
TAB
10
TAB
11
12
TAB

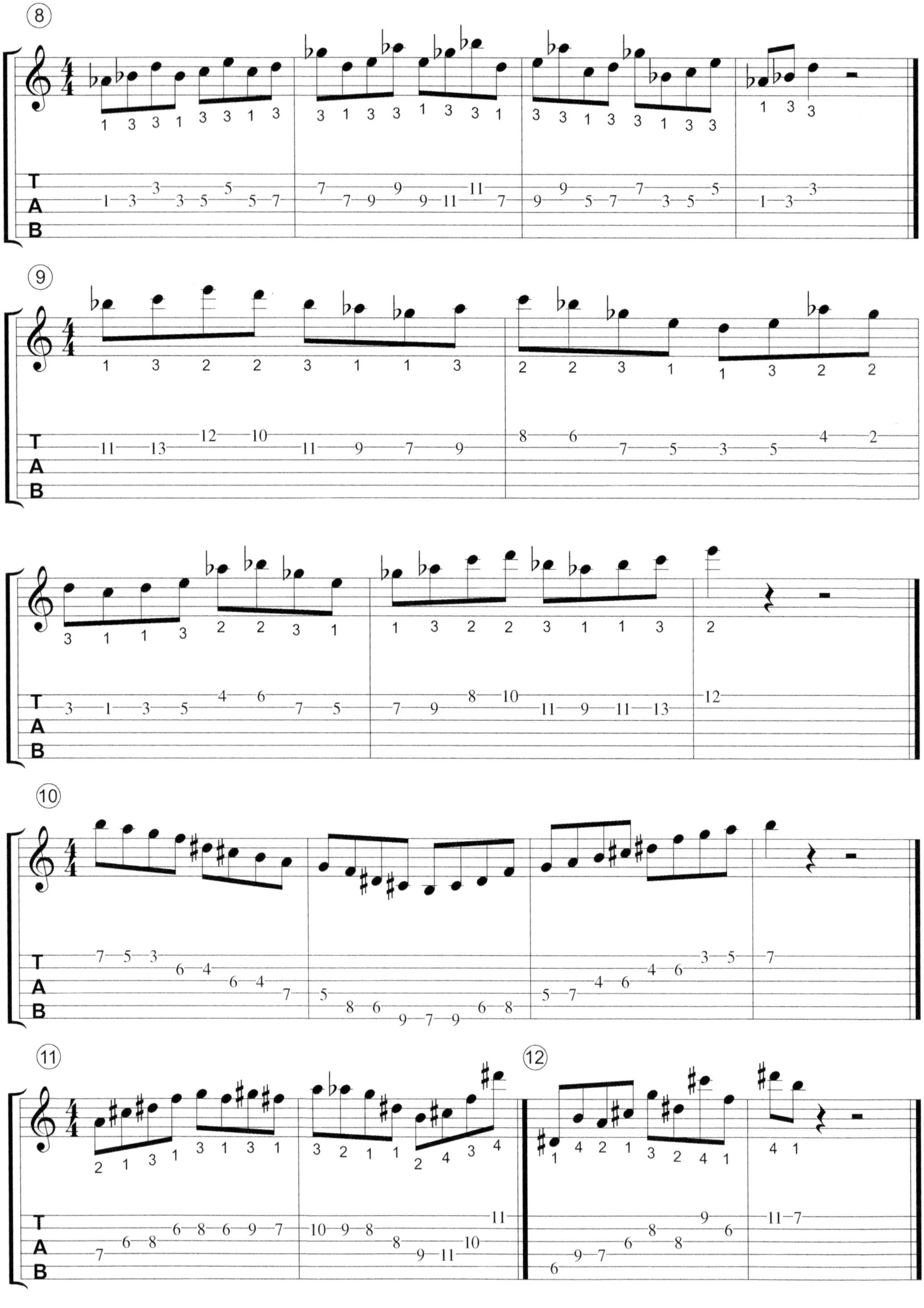

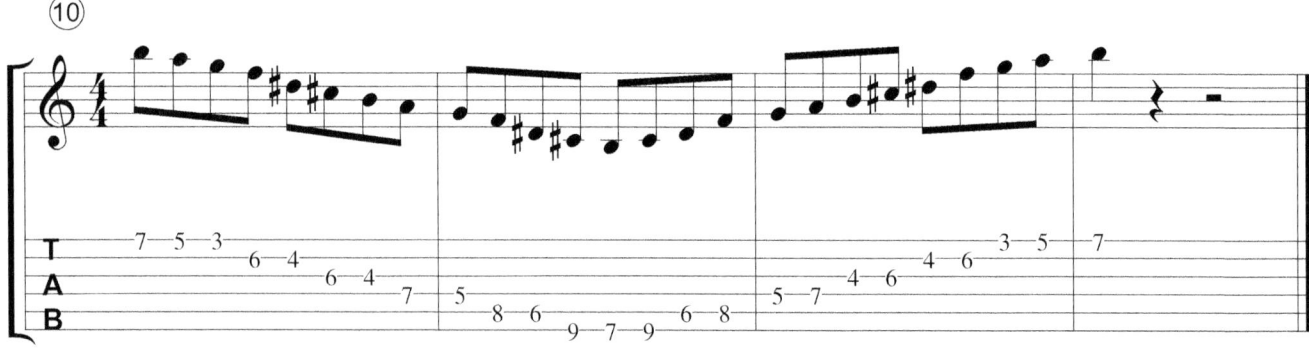

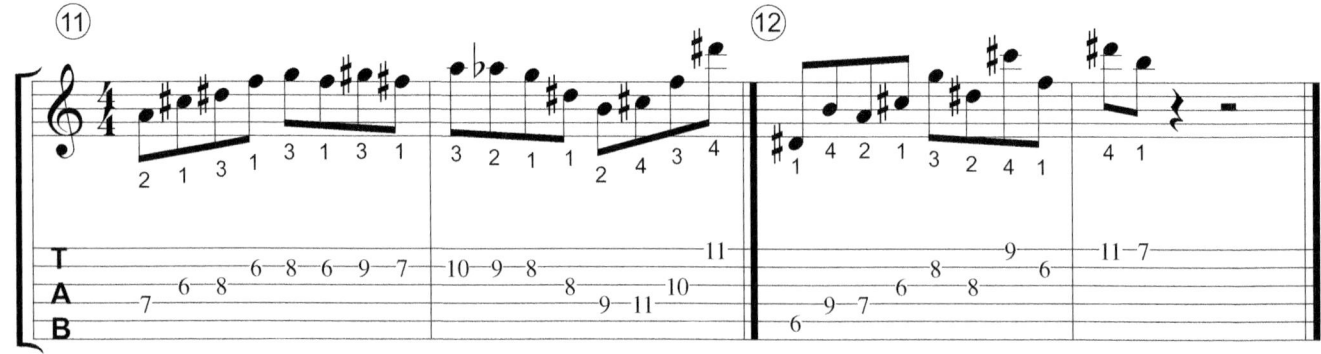

Cross-Picking Exercises

The following exercise is one of the best right-hand workouts I know; however, it is also very good for the left hand. Since flowing sounds are essential for a good guitarist, alternating picking is a must. You should begin each part of the exercise with a down-stroke. You should then pick down-up-down-up, etc. Then, repeat the same exercise beginning with an up-stroke, picking up-down-up-down, etc.

Your picking technique should be a combination of forearm, wrist and finger movement with an emphasis on the forearm. I would also suggest that you use heavy pick, which should give you much more control than a medium or light gauged pick.

The many variations available in this exercise should be explored. For example, try repeating notes seven through fourteen over and over, and then reversing the direction of the entire line. The first ten notes may be used to play over chords such as: A13♭5♭9, E♭13♭5♭9, G♭13♭5♭9, or C13♭5♭9.

This entire exercise is to be played in 5th position.

Chord Positions for Cross-Picking Exercise

Alternating Picking

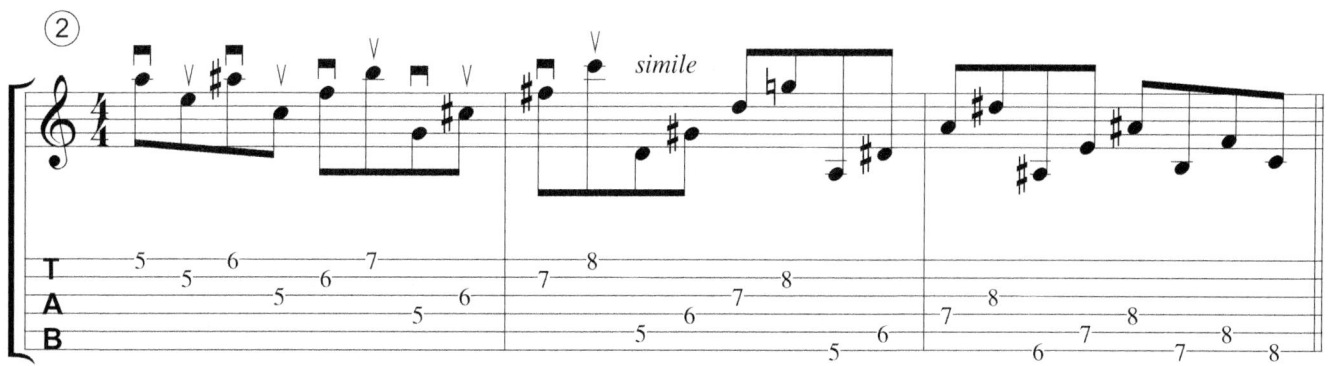
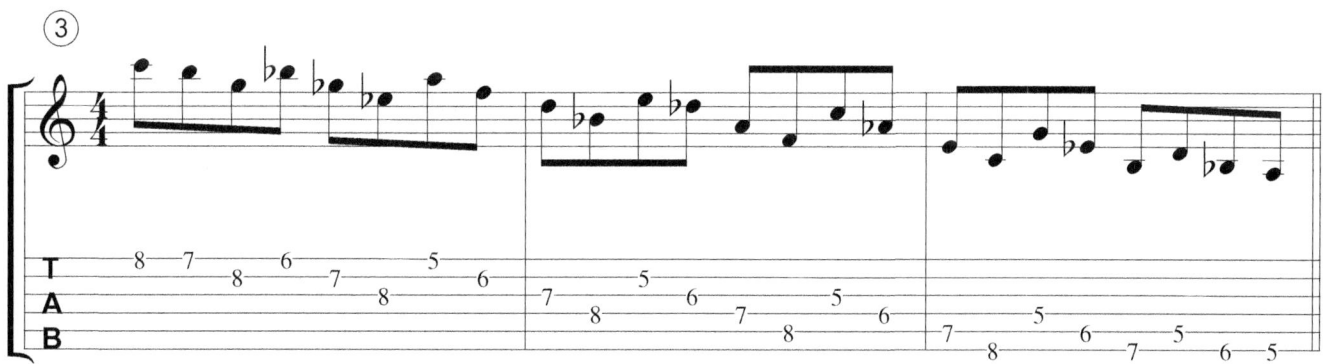
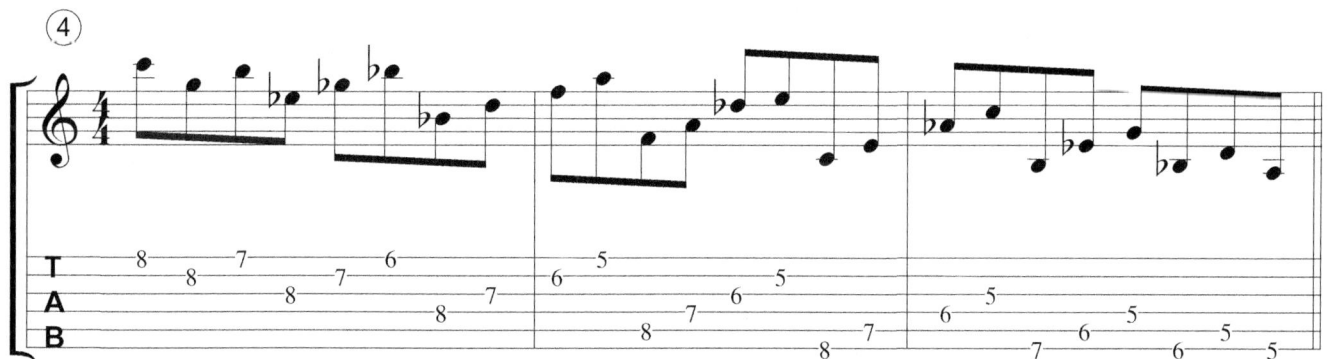

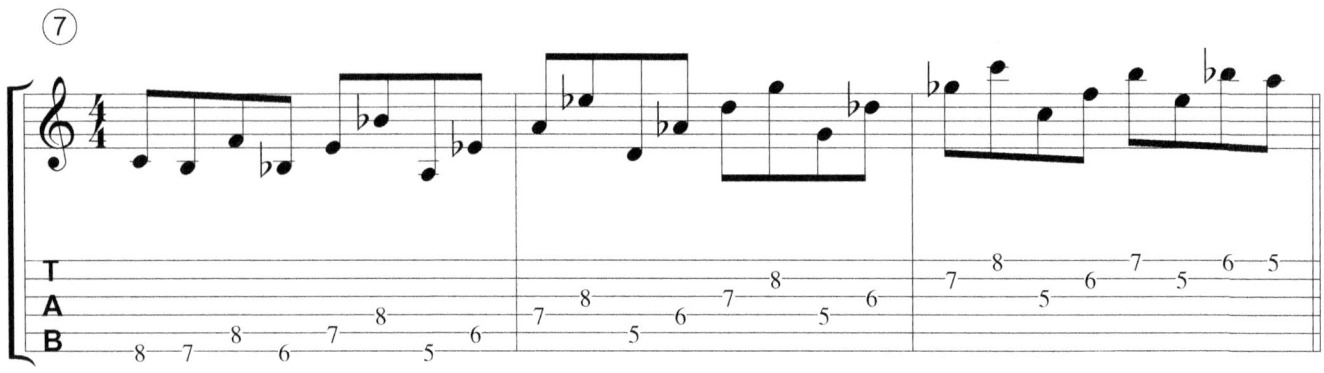

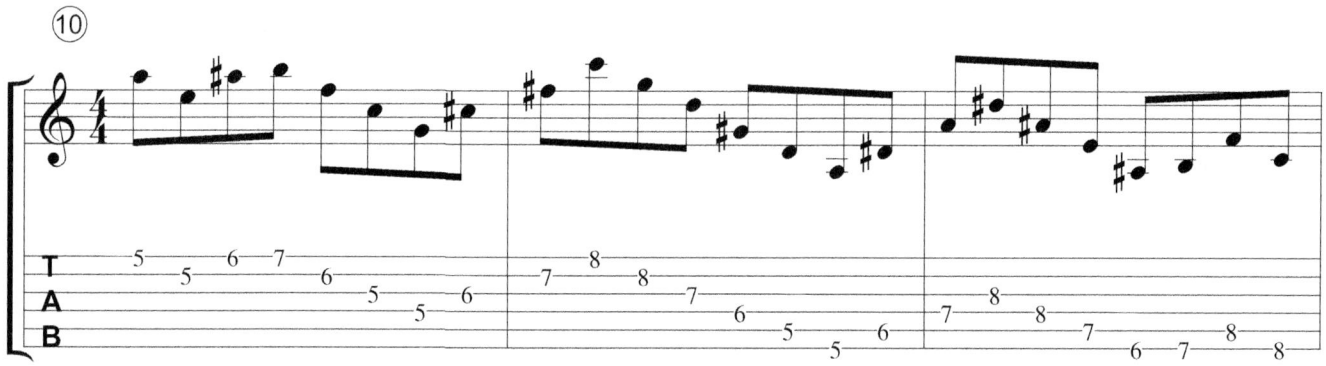
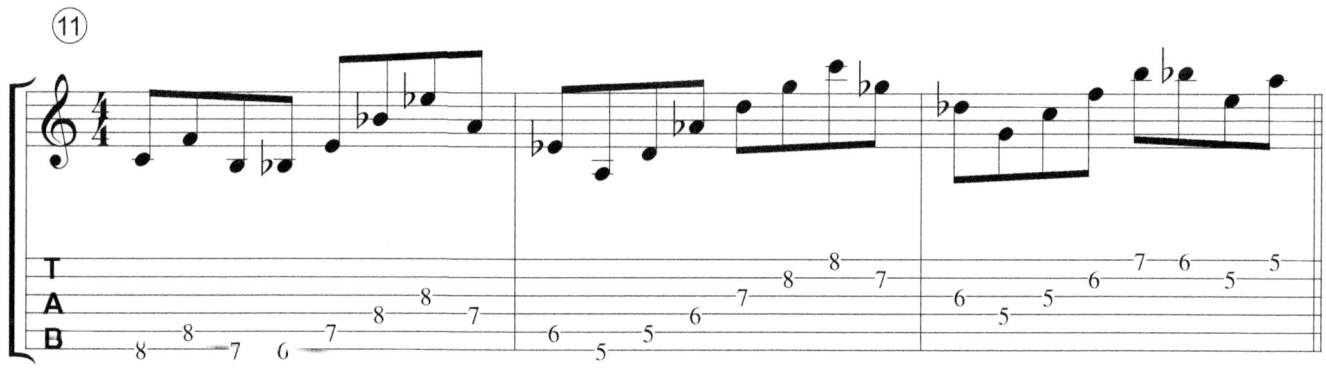

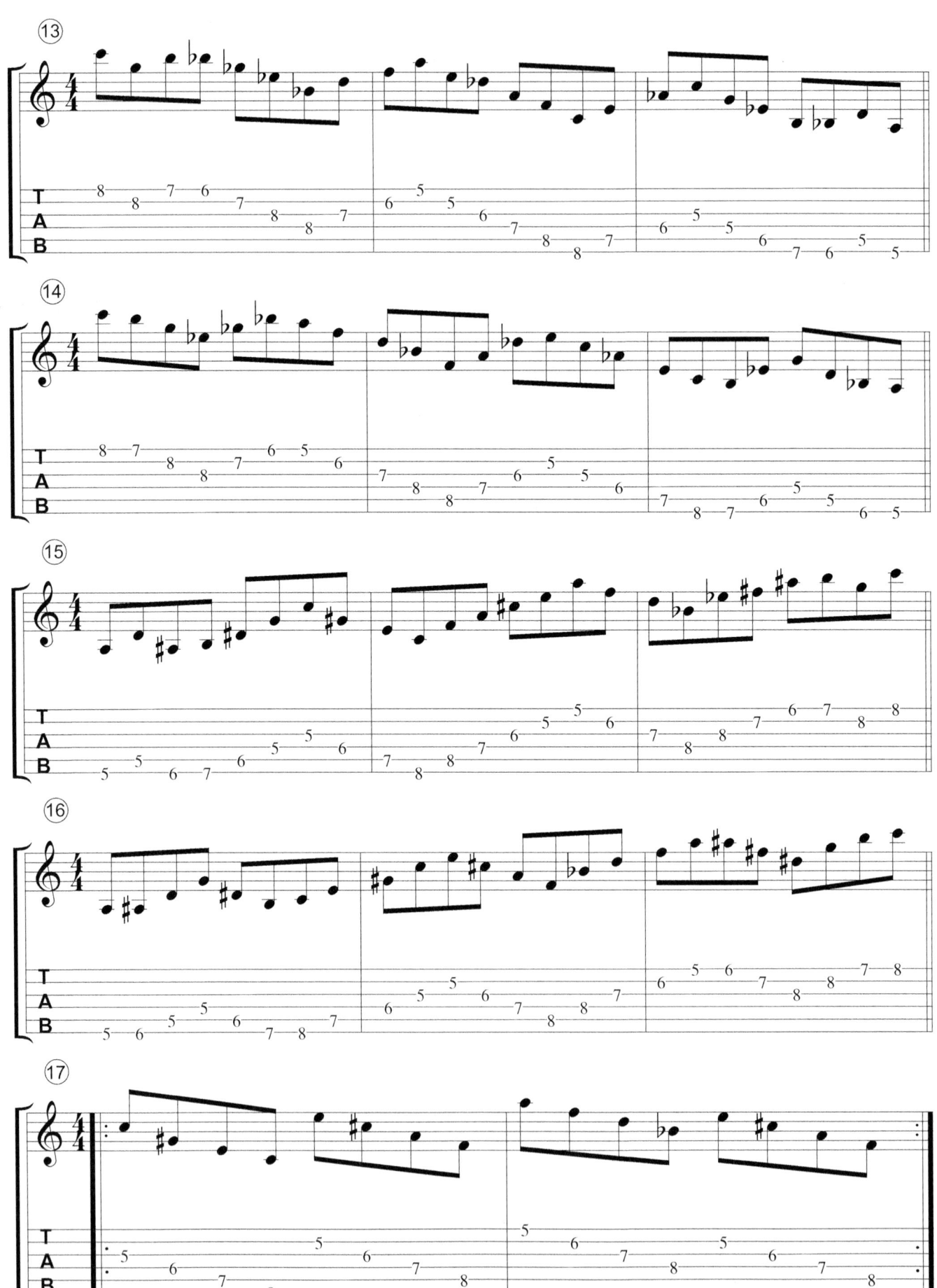

Cross picking Part II

I believe that regular use of a metronome during the daily practice session is one of the best habits a musician can develop. All exercises and scales should be practiced with a metronome for further of time awareness.

Exercise #1 can be repeated indefinitely. Exercise #2 may be practiced up and down the neck as far as you like. Exercise #3 should continue to move up the fingerboard and back down. Exercise #4 is played in the fifth position and should be practiced on all strings in a similar manner. When the same finger is used consecutively on two adjacent strings, the technique should be one of rolling the finger tip from one string to the other. If you are moving to a lower string in pitch (i.e. from the second to the third) you must start out with your finger almost flat on the fingerboard. It is also good to approach the string with your left-hand finger at a slight angle, as if coming from behind the fret. This entire section is to be played with alternating picking.

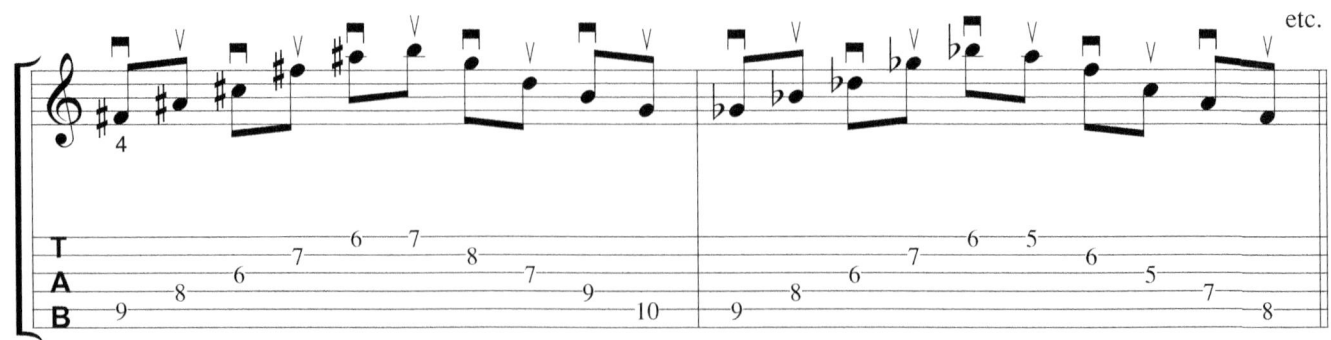

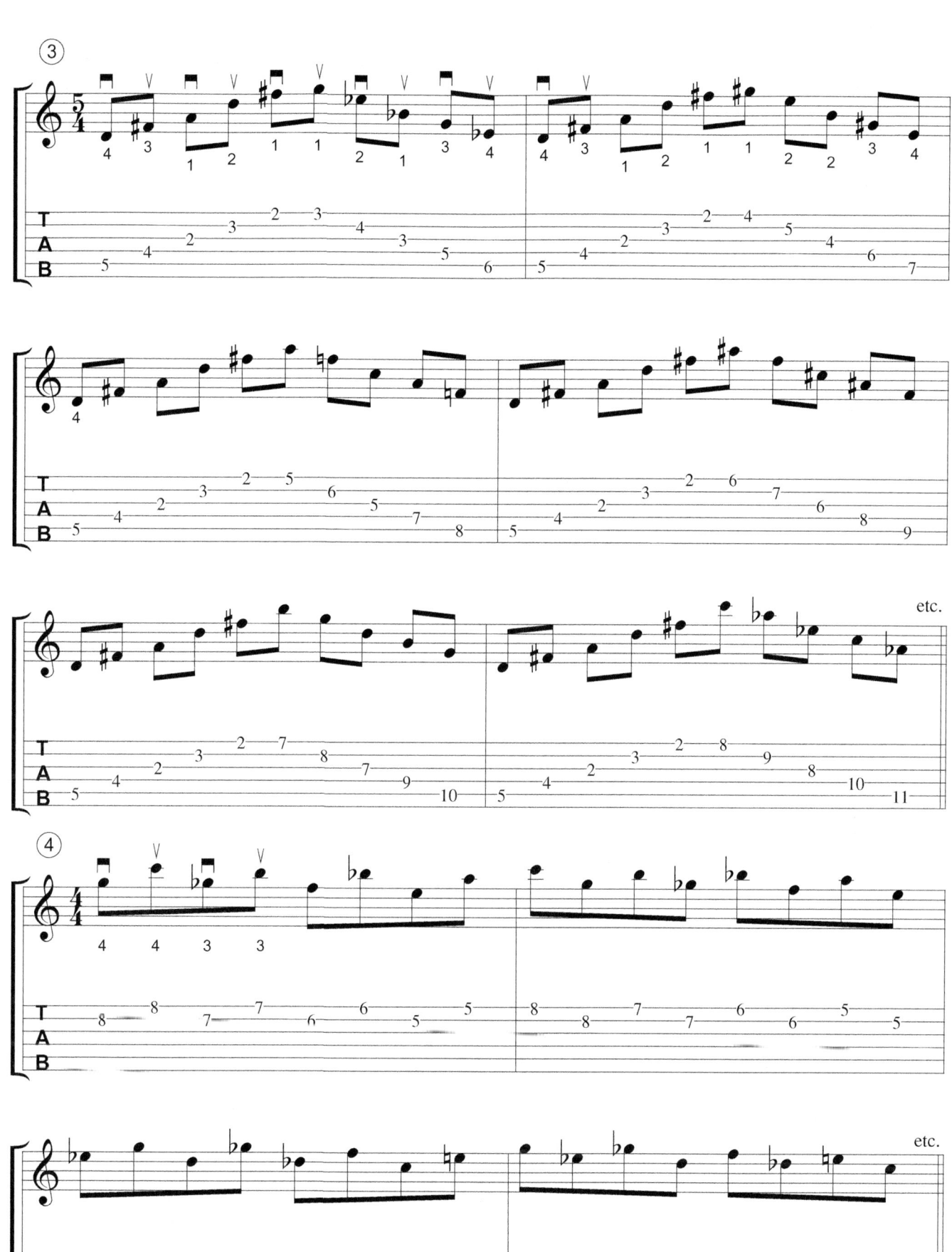

Seventh Position

Exercises #1, 2 and 3 should be played in the seventh position with the first finger of the left hand covering the notes on the sixth and seventh frets. The second finger never leaves the eighth fret. The third finger never leaves the ninth fret and the little finger never leaves the tenth fret. Alternating picking is a must for all of these single-string exercises.

Exercises #1 is derived from a C diminished scale. I have heard it called a double-diminished run. John Coltrane and other great jazz musicians have utilized this pattern in their playing. You may play this exercise over the following chords: C°, A°, F#°, E♭°, B7♭9♭5, A♭7♭9♭5, F7♭9♭5, and D7♭9♭5. Correct fingering in this exercise is very important.

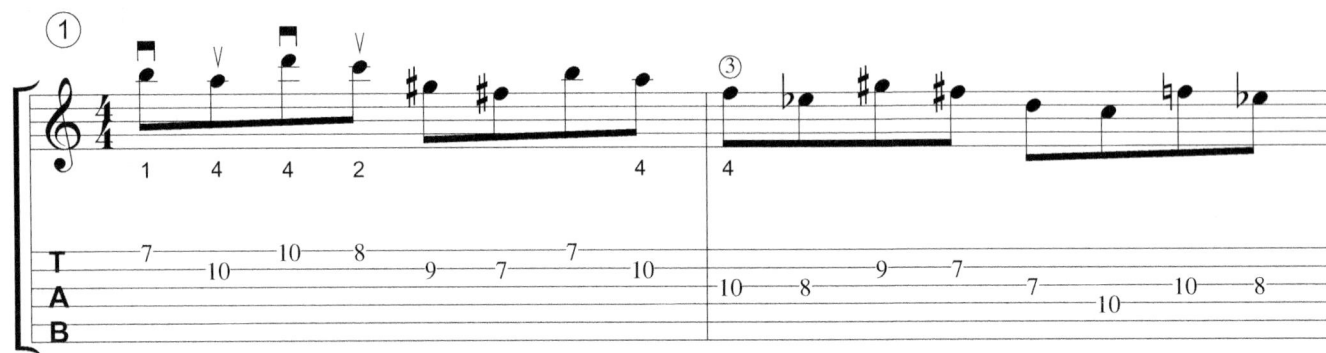

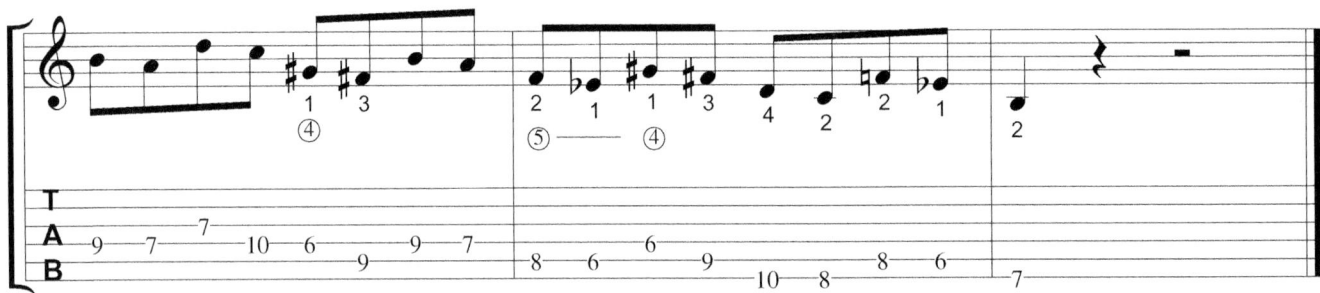

Exercises #2 is an exercise in thirds. Practice this exercise with alternating picking, starting with an up-stroke, and then beginning with a down-stroke.

Exercises #3 is a variation of exercise #2. There is an added note one-half step below the bottom note of each set of thirds. Watch the fingering.

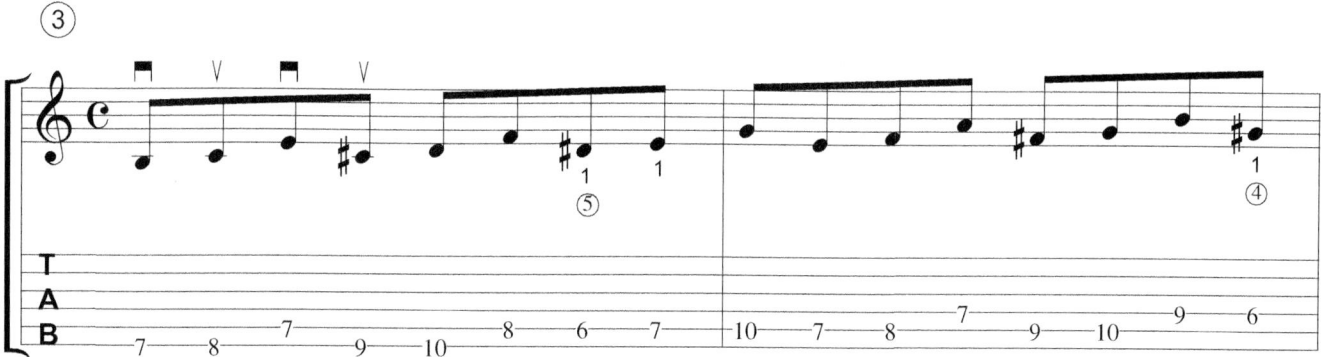

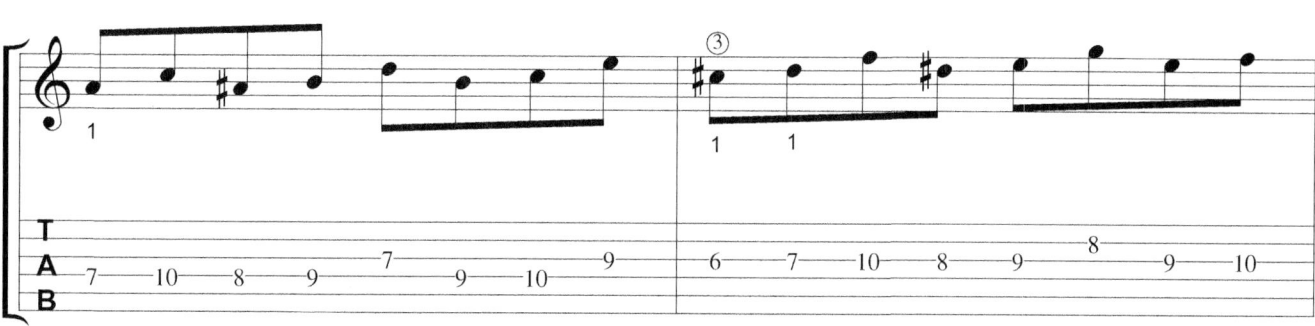

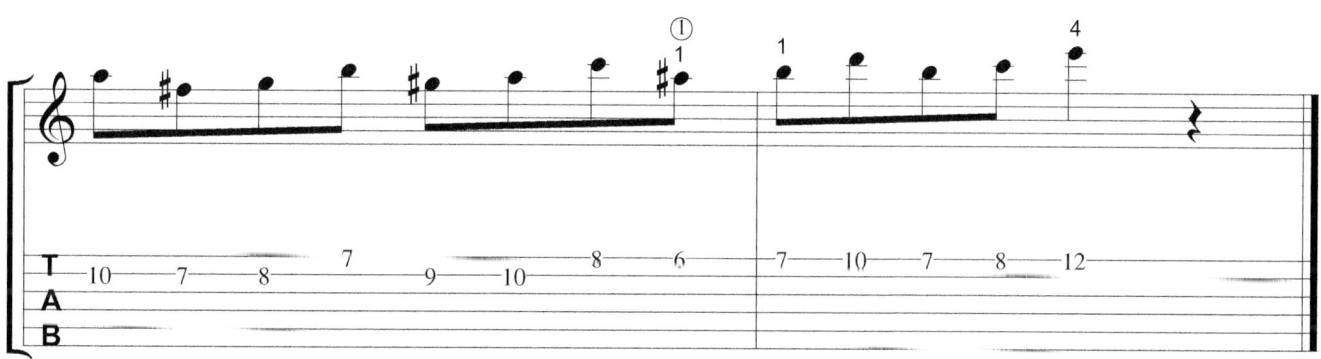

Alternative Picking Patterns

Exercise #1 should be practiced with the entire picking motion, originating at the elbow. Your pick should glide across the strings without a different picking action for each individual string. Your right forearm movement should be steady and even. Exercise #2 has been called the "mirror" exercise.

The "mirror" exercise can be played ascending as well as descending and can also be played on a different set of strings such as 2nd, 3rd and 4th strings.

To execute the slur at the end of every measure in exercise #3, use the same finger and slide into the note. Exercise #4 and #5 are primarily for development of the little finger. Be careful not to over practice these exercises, because it is possible to sprain your little finger. Exercises #6, #7, #8, and #9 are good basic exercises which should be practiced on all of the strings from the highest to the lowest and back to the highest string.

Exercises 12 through 16 can be played individually or collectively without repeat signs.

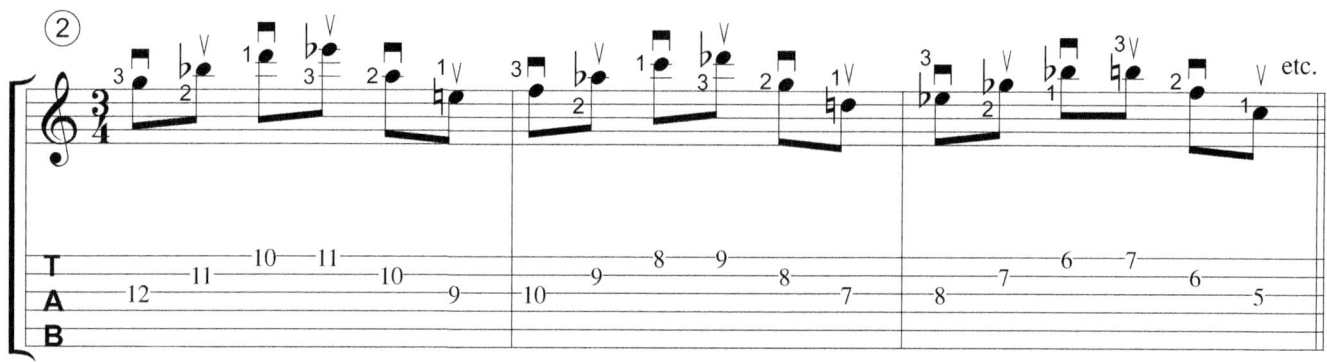
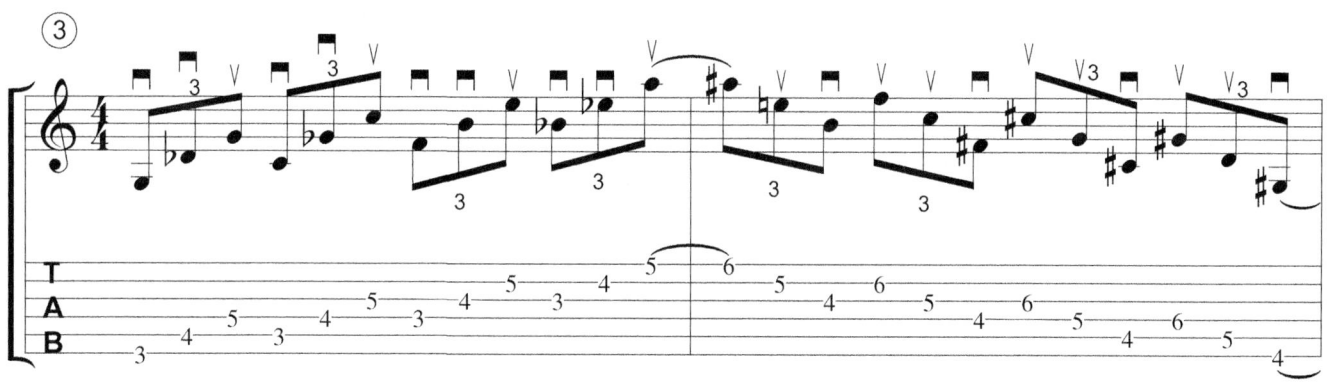
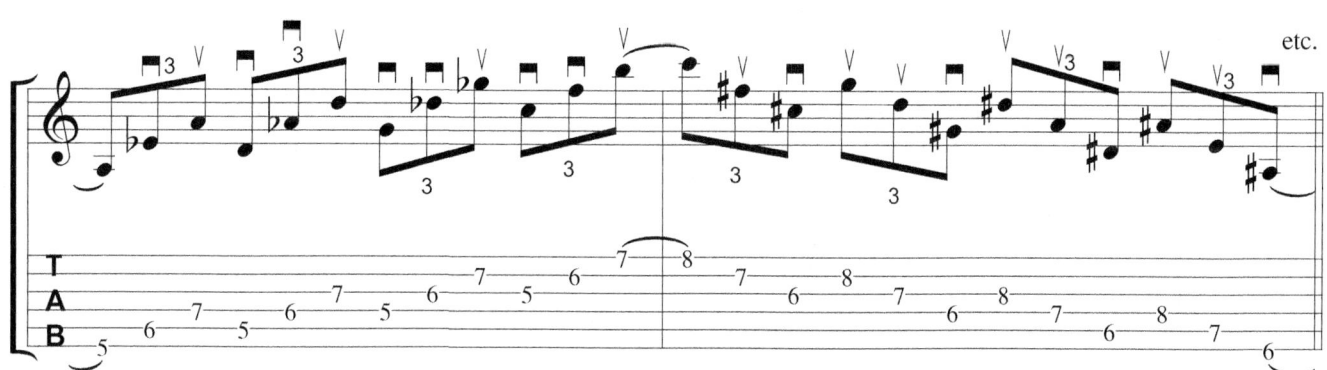

69

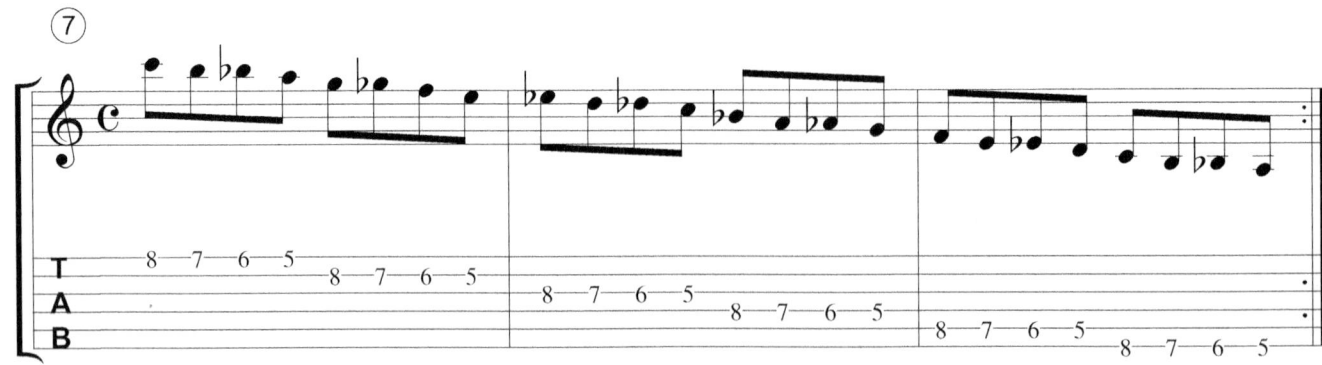

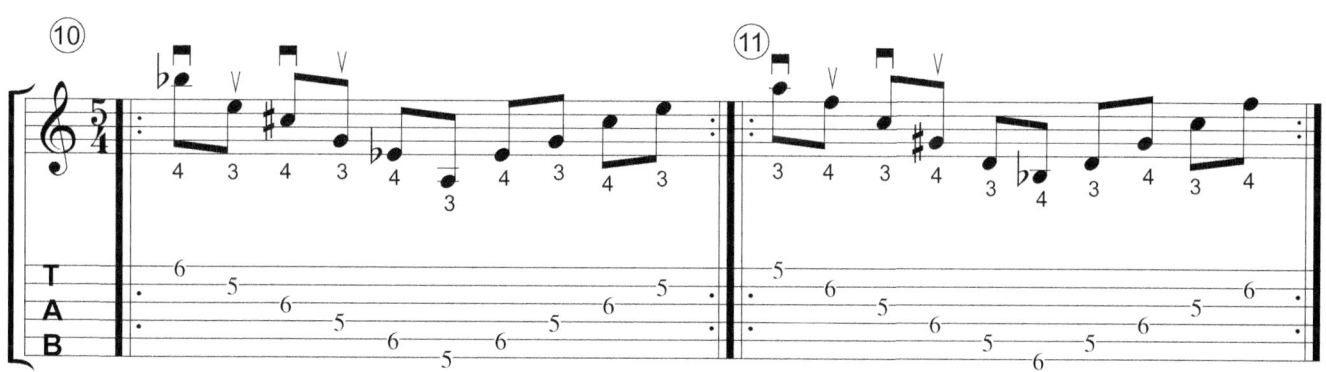
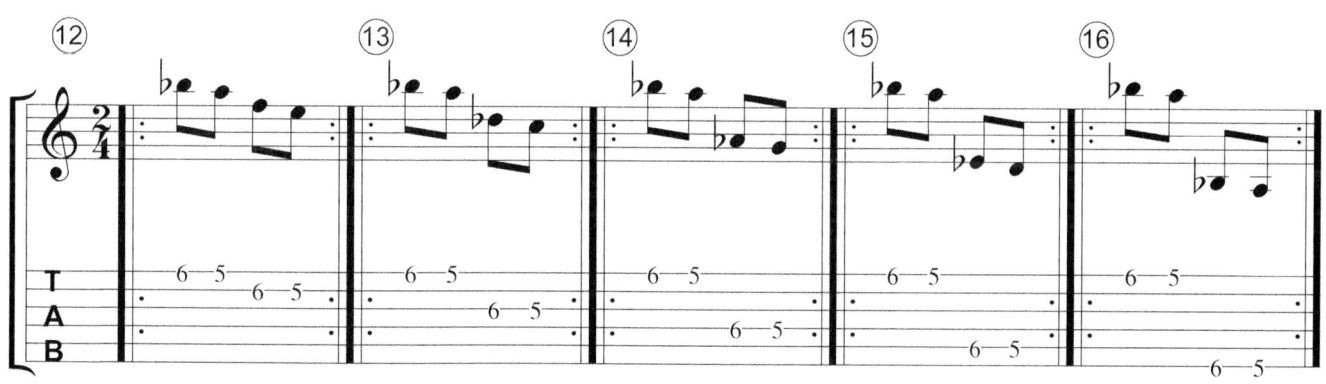

V7-I Patterns

Here are some patterns to be played over a V7-I progression in the key of C. I have instructed my students to memorize and record all of these patterns at least two times on tape. The sequence should change the second time. Play back each pattern on the tape one at a time and then play that same pattern on the guitar without referring to the music. This process helps develop your ear and your jazz concept. Study and analyze each pattern. Here are a couple of observations. Notice the use of leading tones (C# and F#) in the first measure and the motif established in the second measure of pattern #2. Thirds dominante patterns #7 and #11.

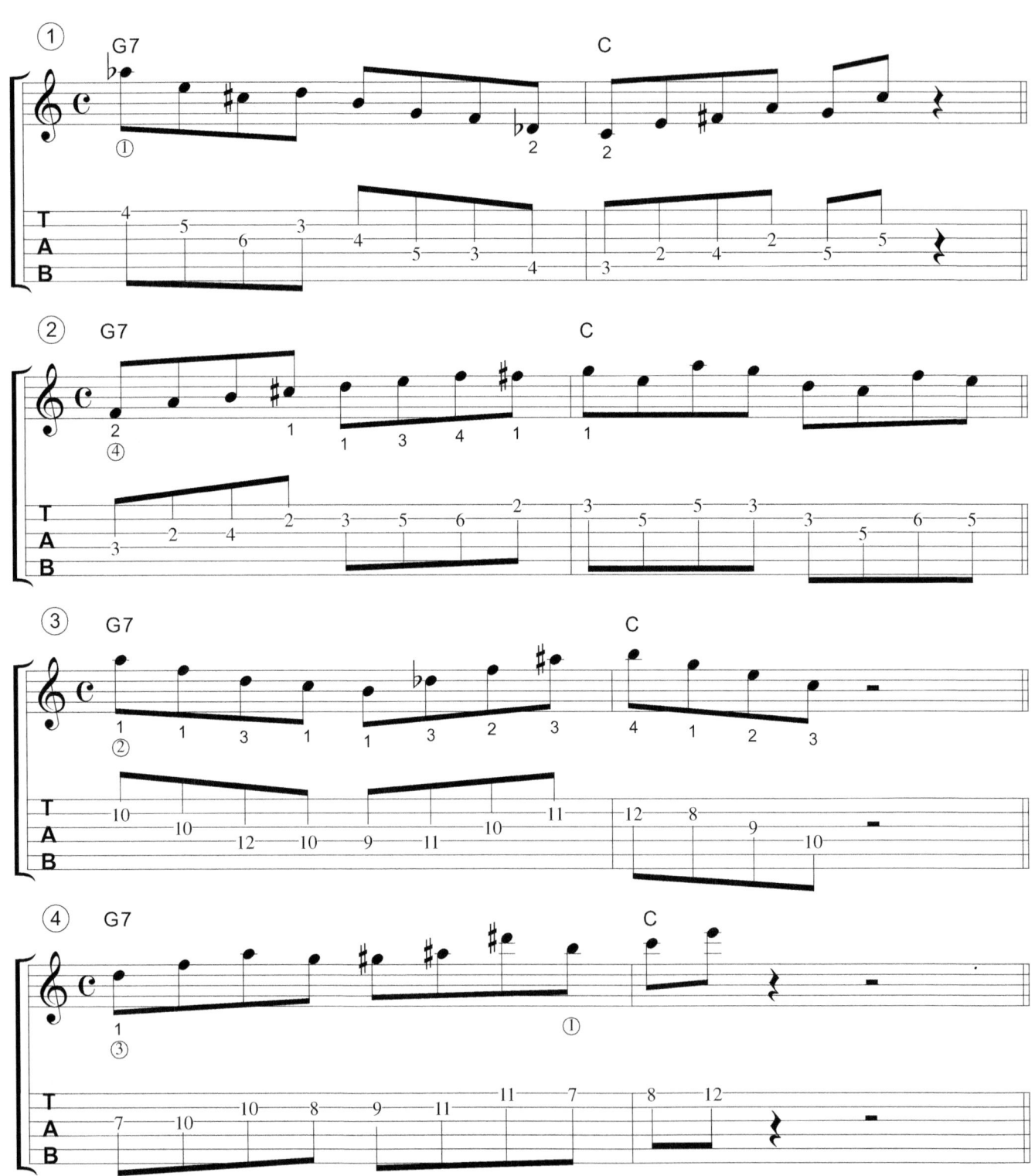

72

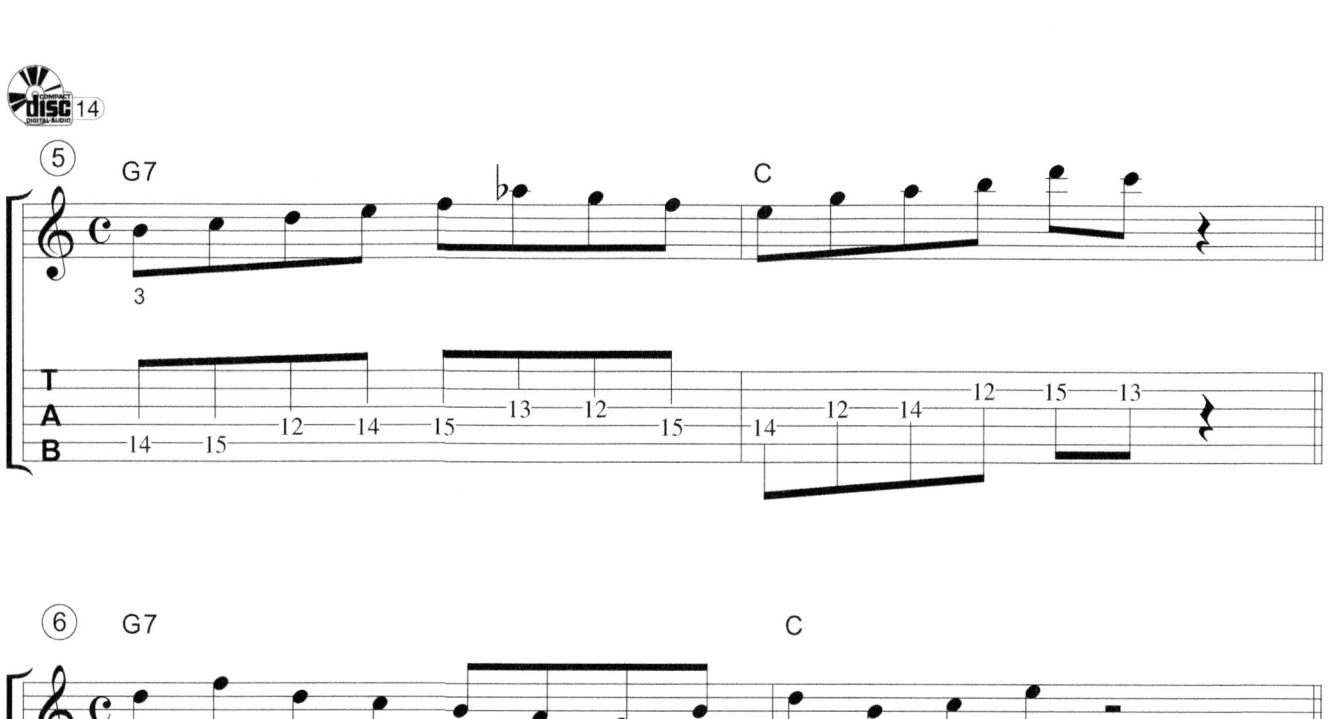
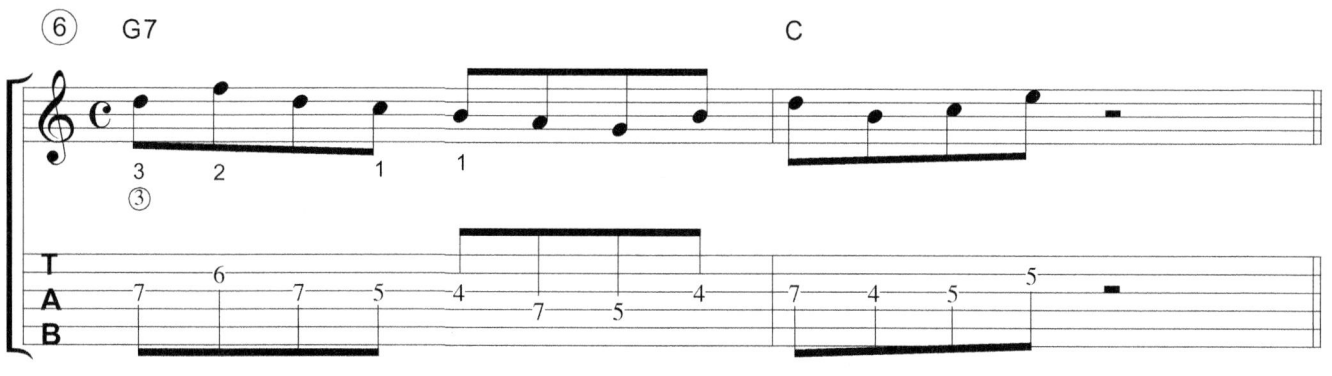
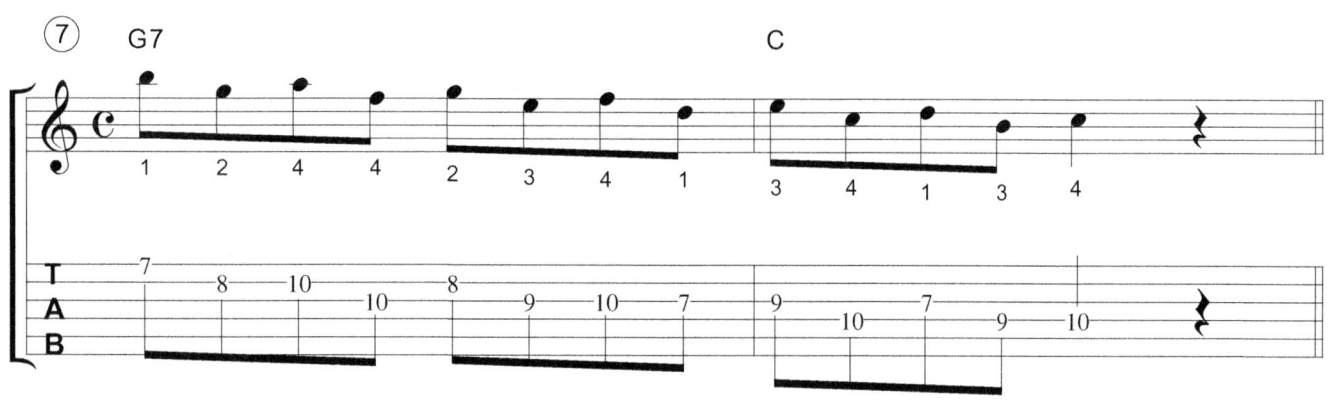
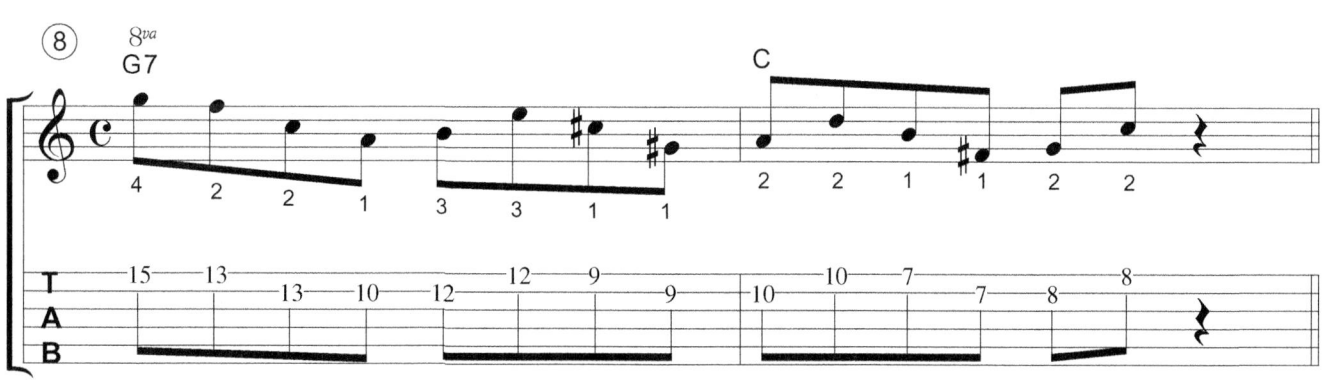

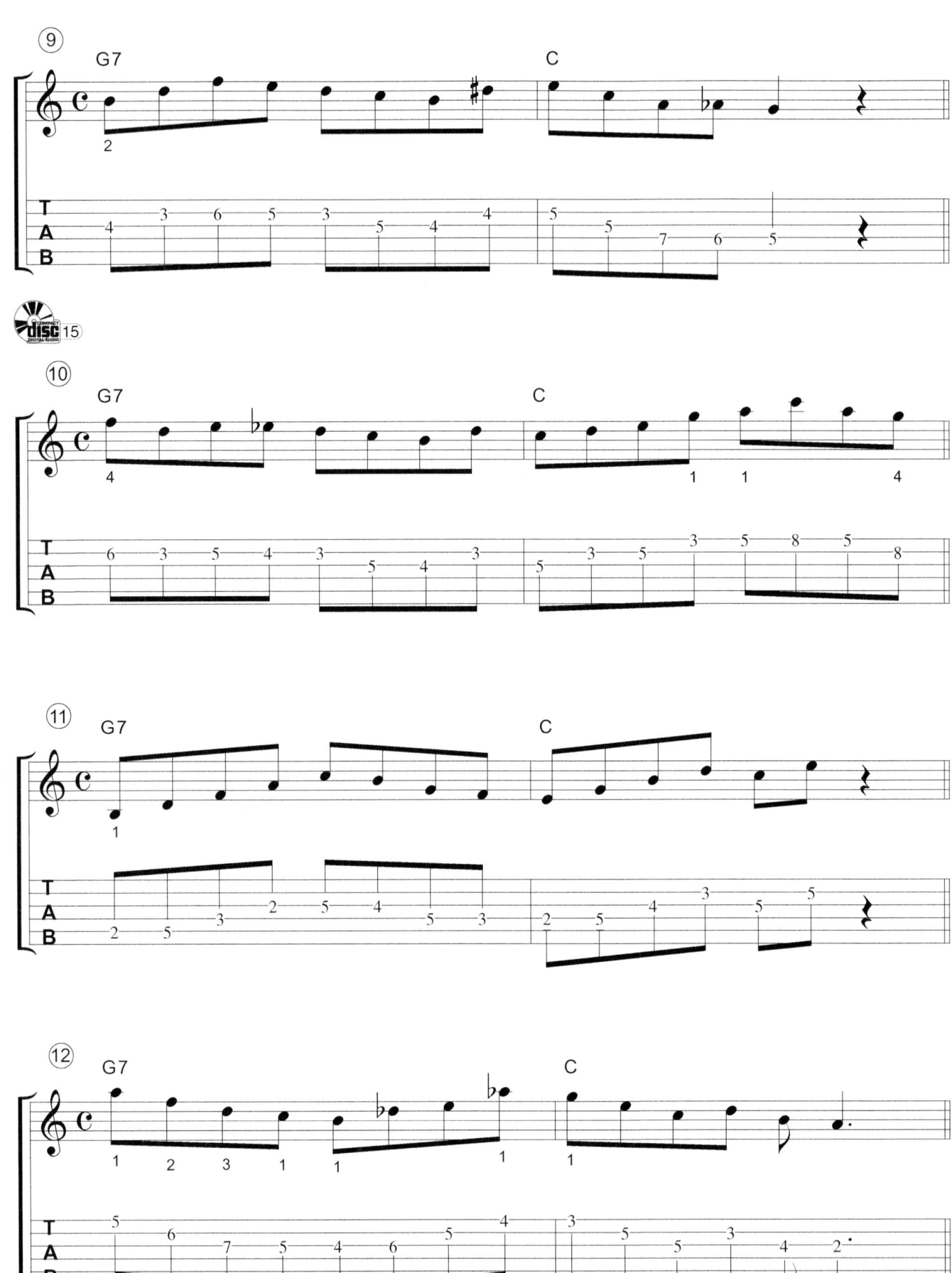

II7-V7 Patterns

This section is concerned with the II7-V7 progression in the key of C (Dmi7-G7). With the exception of pattern #12, all of the patterns are written in concert or actual pitch, therefore guitarists should refer to the tabulature and play an octave higher than usual. Notice the use of thirds in the second measure of pattern #1. The second and third notes of pattern #9 should be played with your second finger by rolling your finger from the first string to the second string without lifting it off the fingerboard. This entire column should be played with alternating picking. All of the notes on the down beat should be played with a down stroke and all of the notes on the up beat should be played with an up stroke.

Concert (Play one octave higher than regular guitar notation)

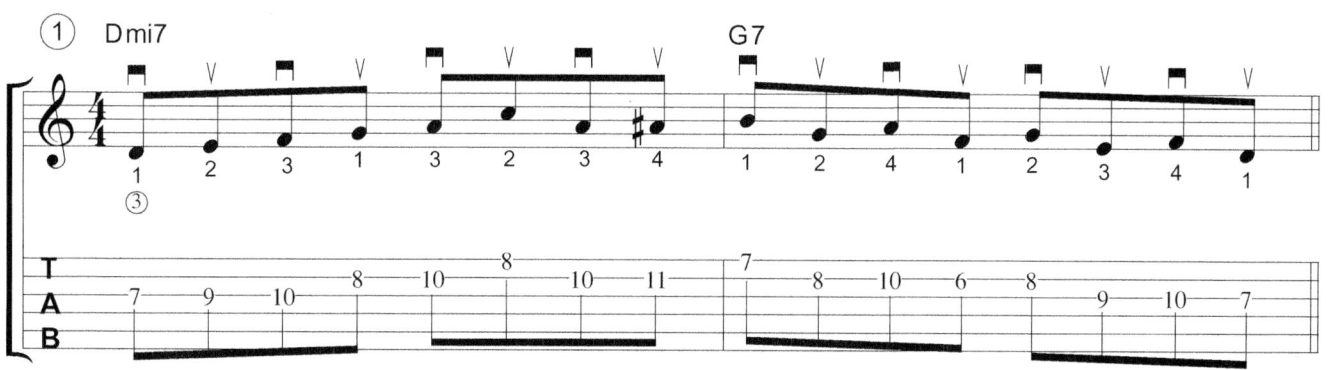

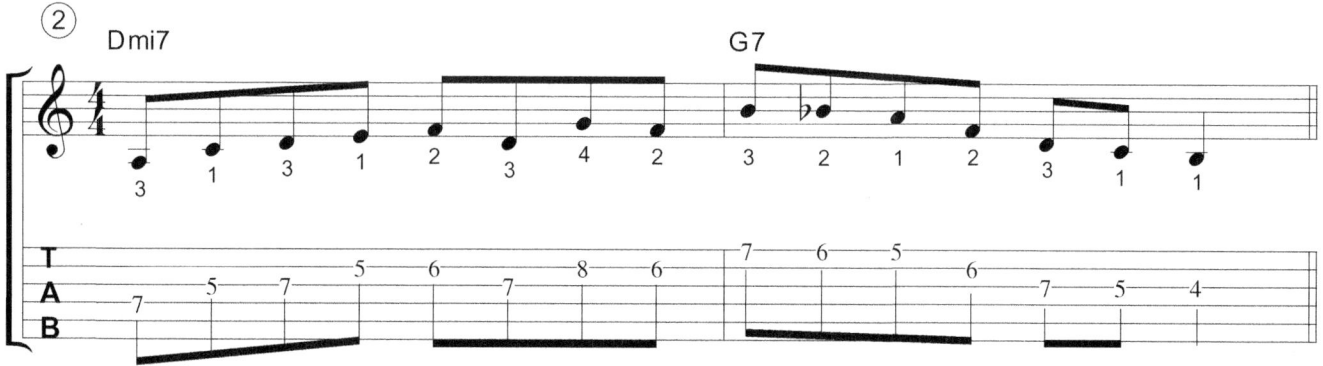

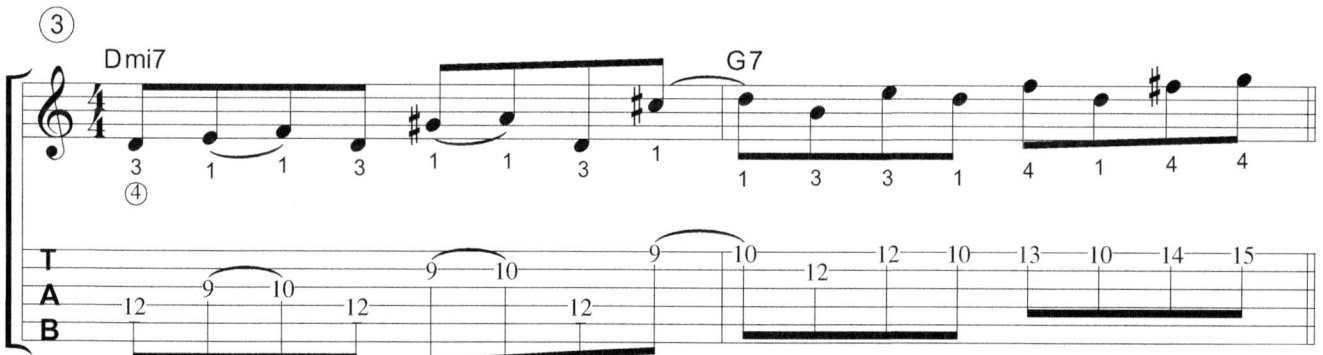

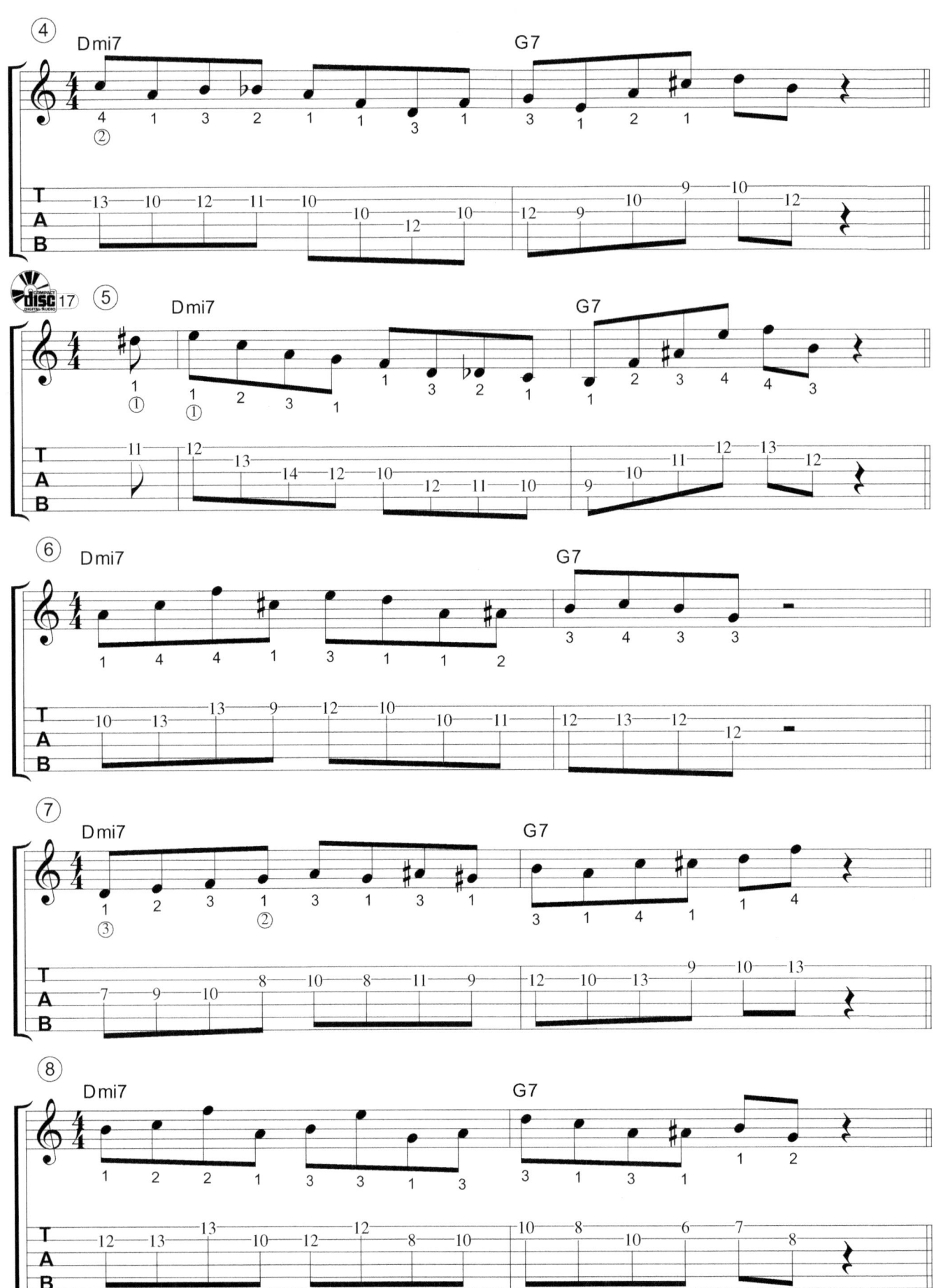

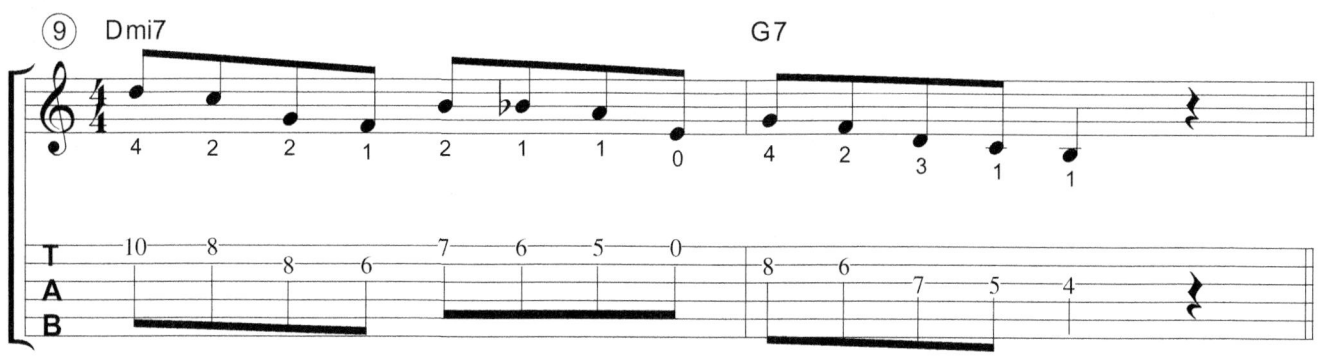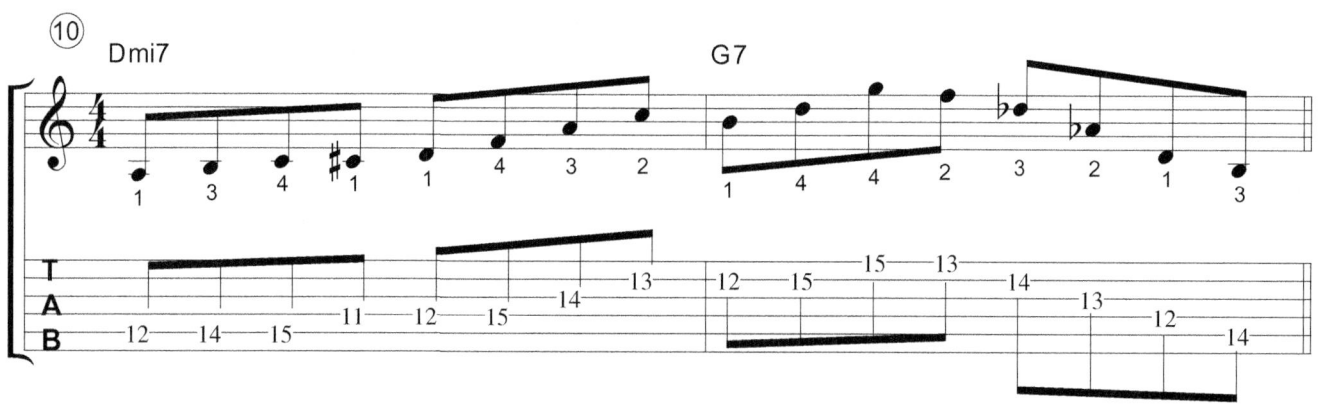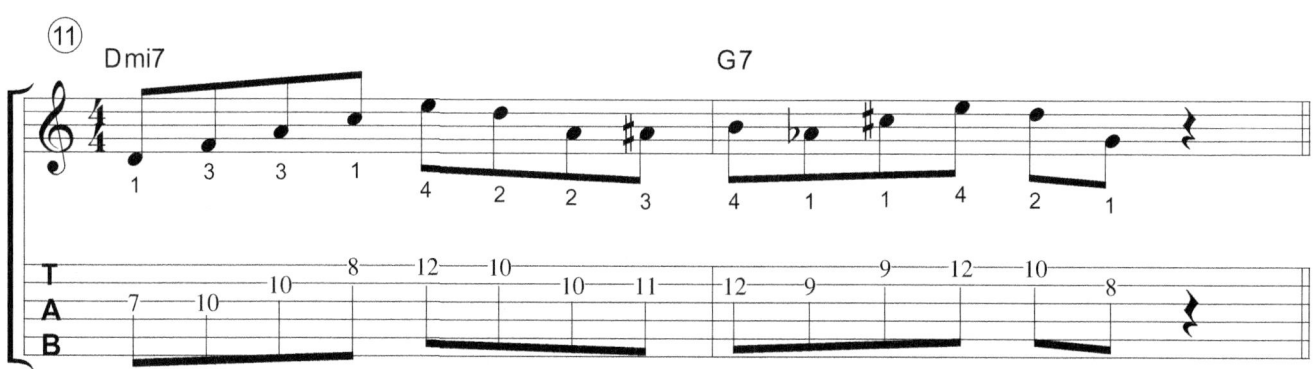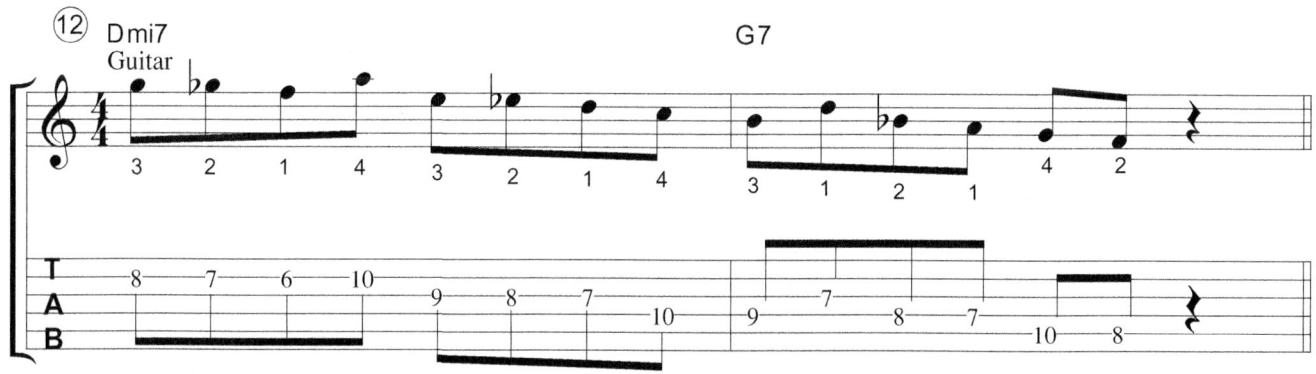

Bmi7♭5-E7 Patterns

My students often ask for tips on how to improvise over a minor seventh flat five chord. The parent scale for a Bmi7♭5 chord is a Locrian mode (C major scale starting and ending on B). A Bmi7♭5 chord has the same notes as a Dmi6 chord or the top four notes on a G9 chord. All of these chords have the same scale (C major) starting on different roots. Since most of us probably feel more comfortable improvising over a Dmi6 chord or a G9 chord, this knowledge becomes a source for ideas when improvising over a Bmi7♭5 chord. Bmi7♭5 - E7 will usually resolve to A minor (relative minor to C major). Patterns 9 through 12 are written in concert or actual pitch, therefore guitarists should refer to the tabulature and play an octave higher than usual. This entire column is alternating picking unless indicated otherwise.

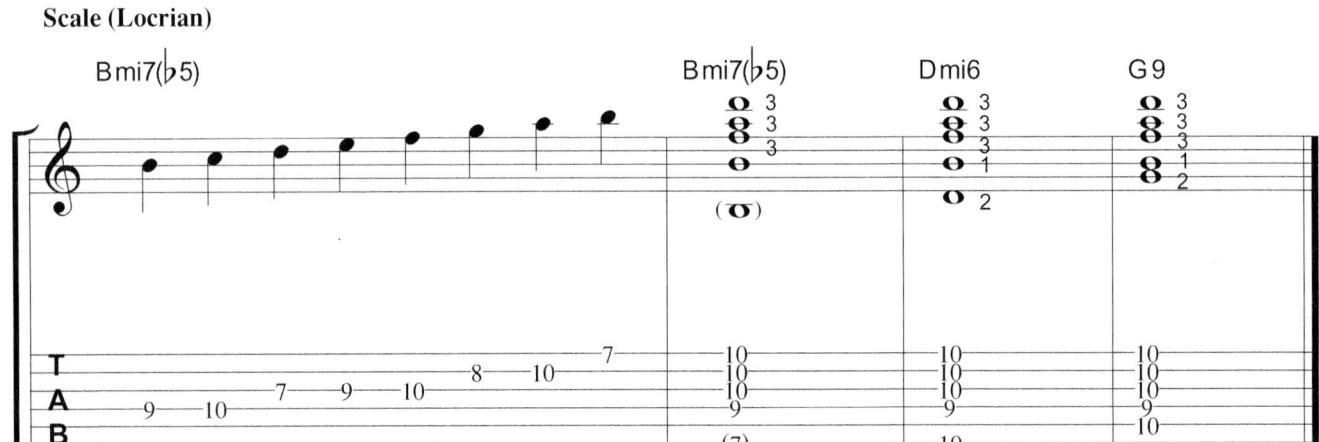

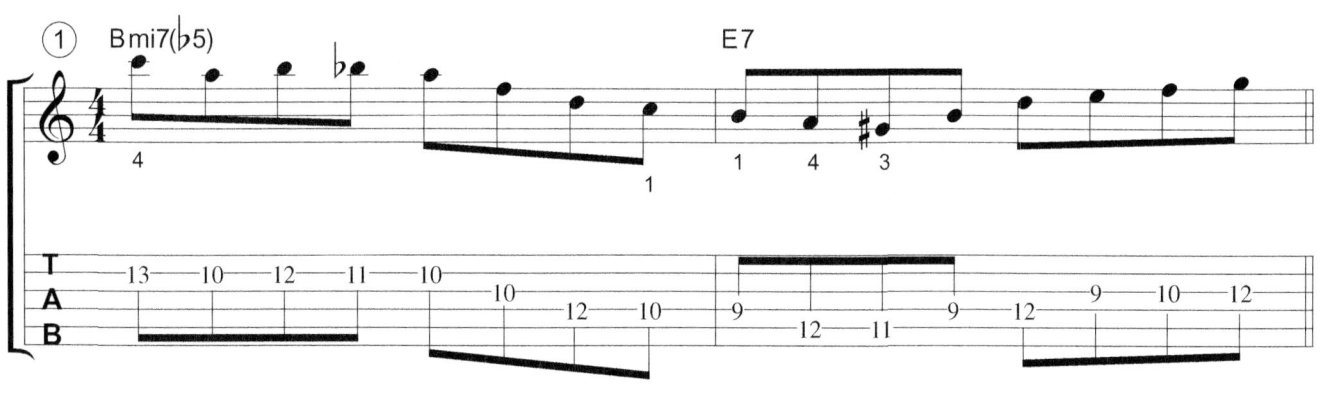
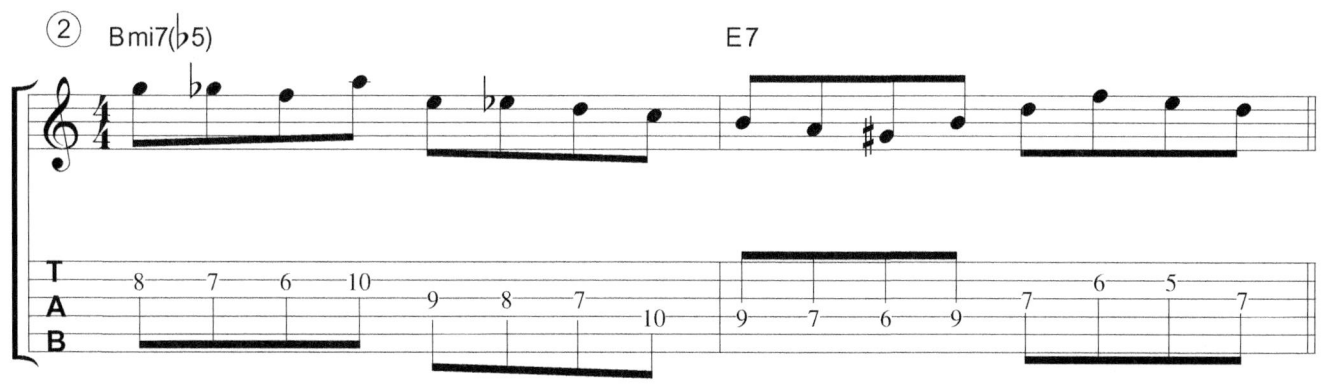
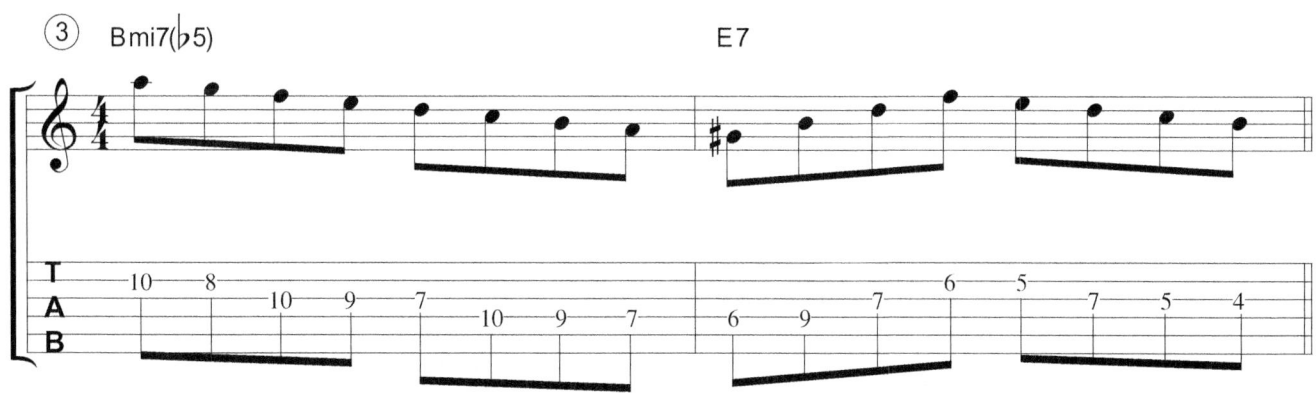
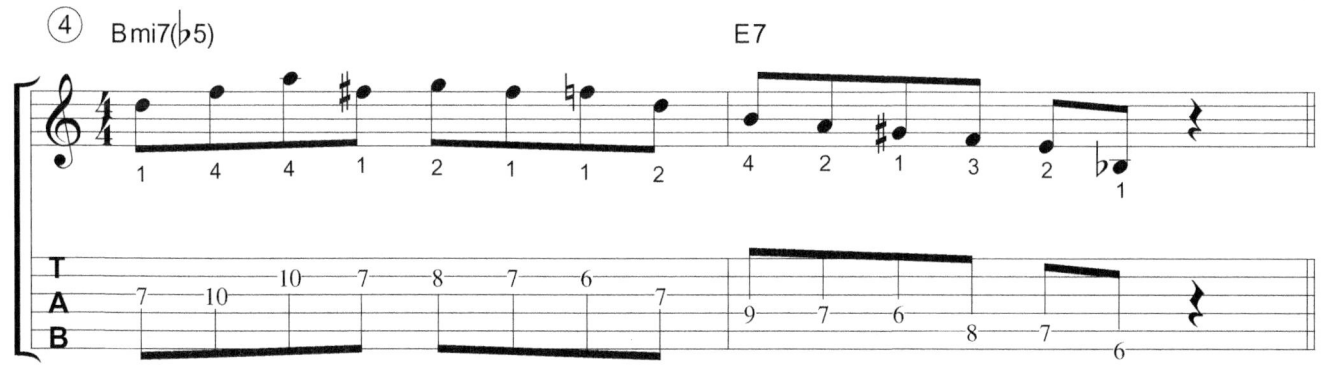

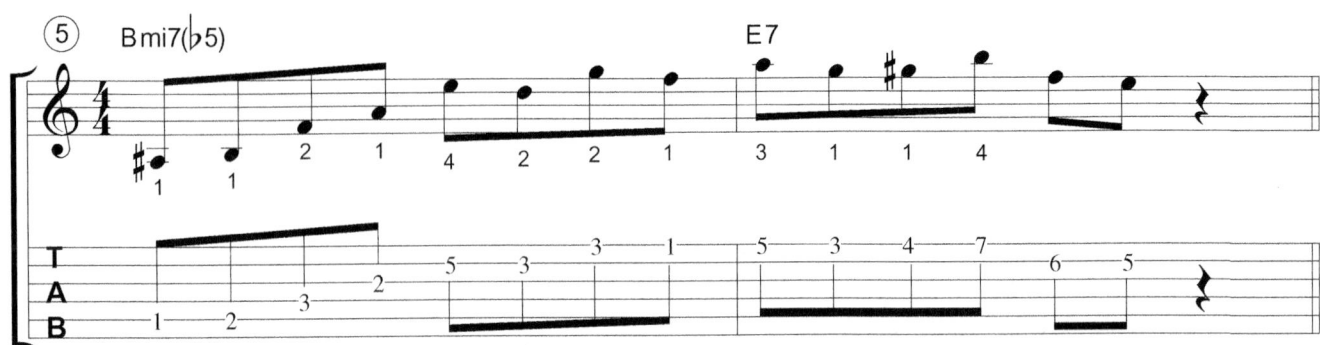
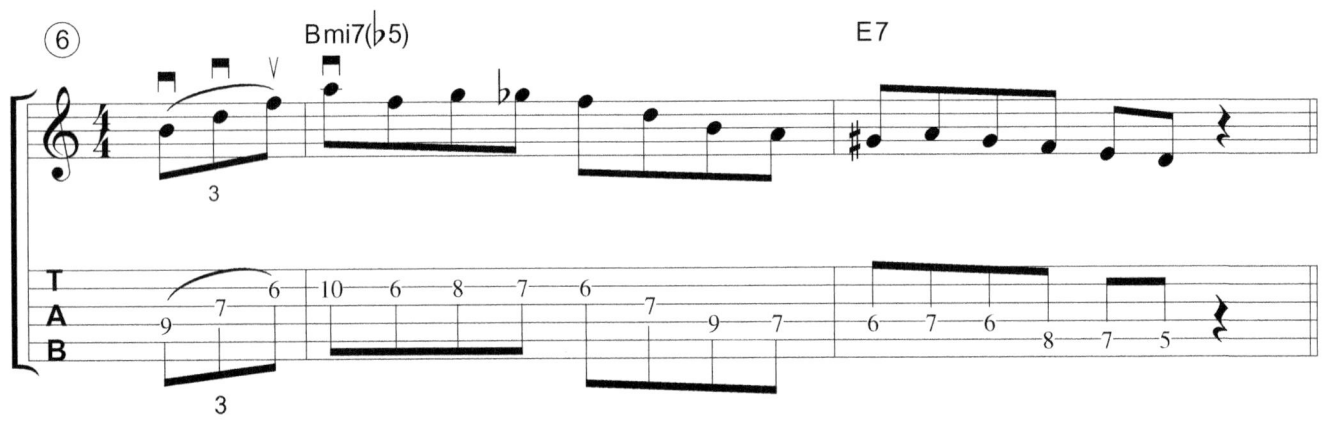
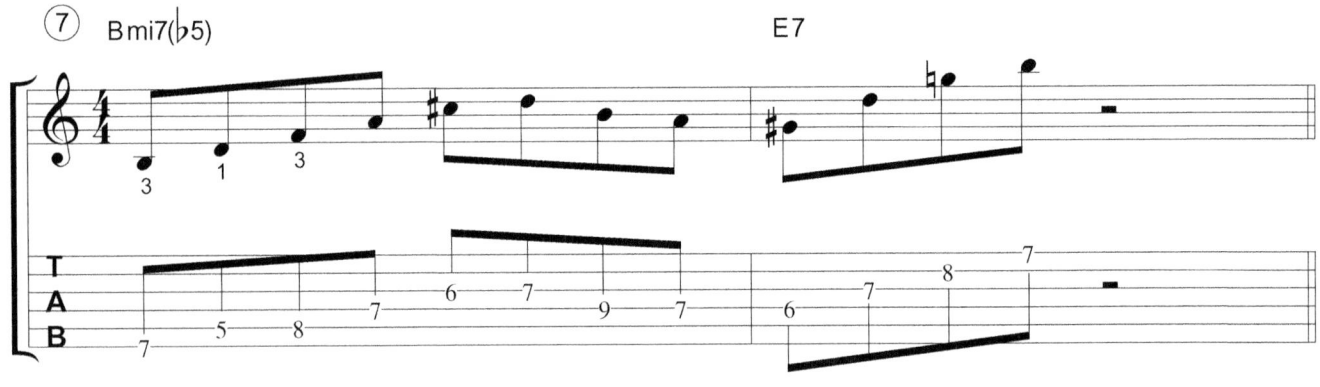
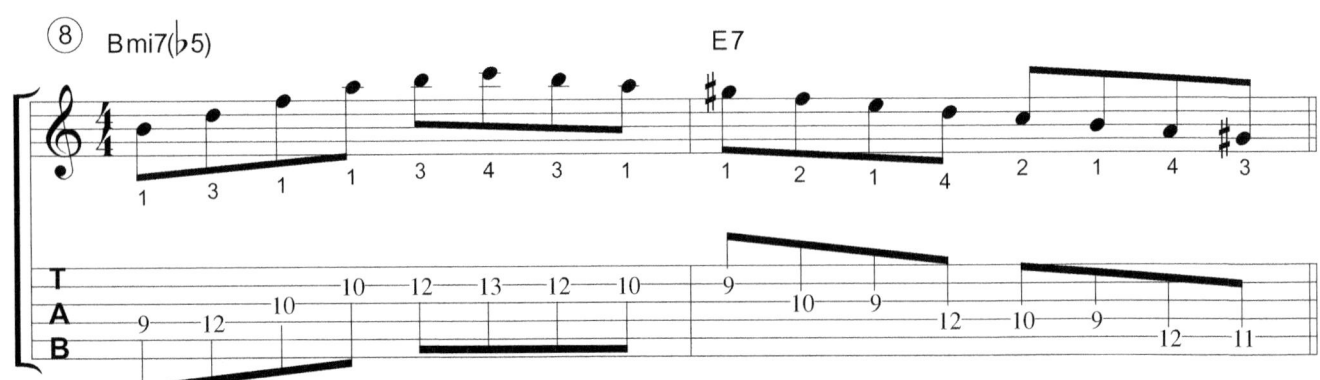

9
Concert

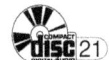

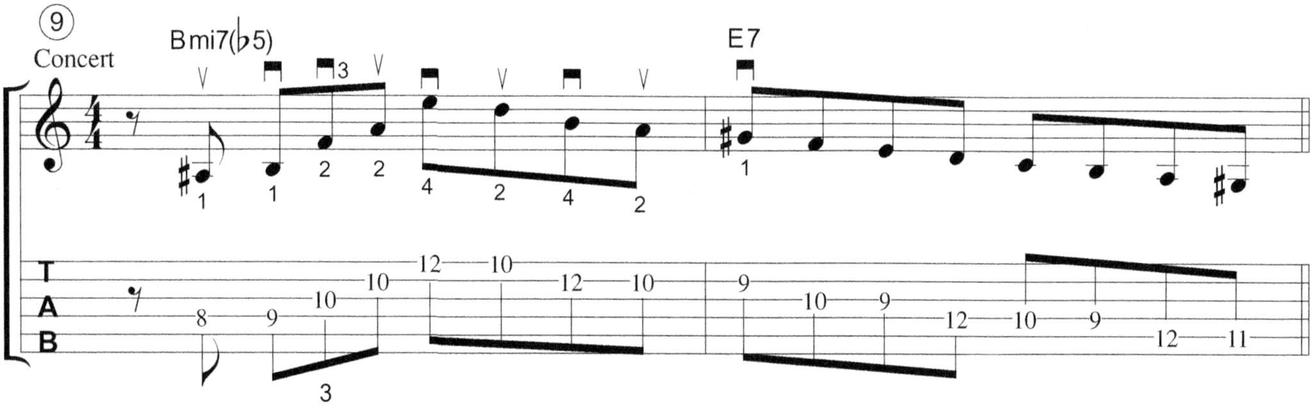

10
Concert

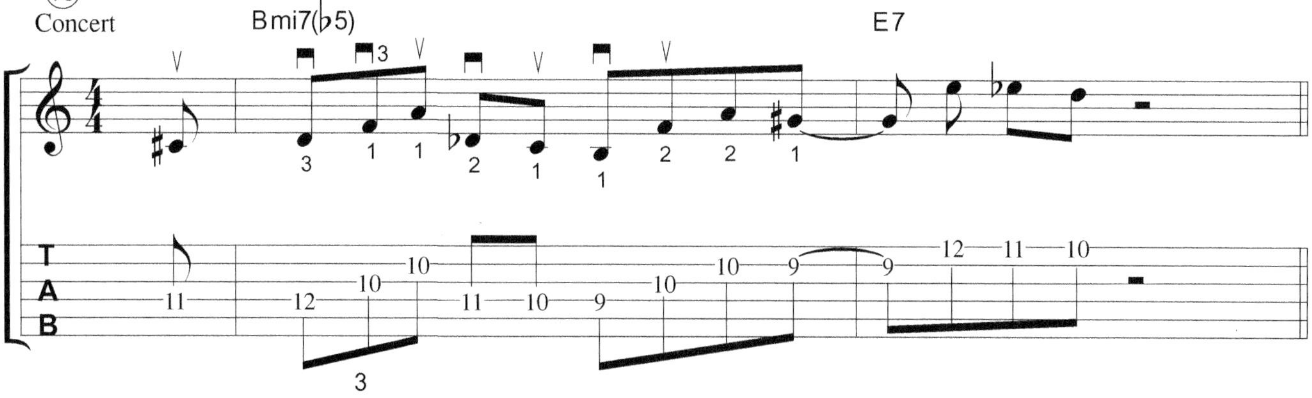

11
Concert

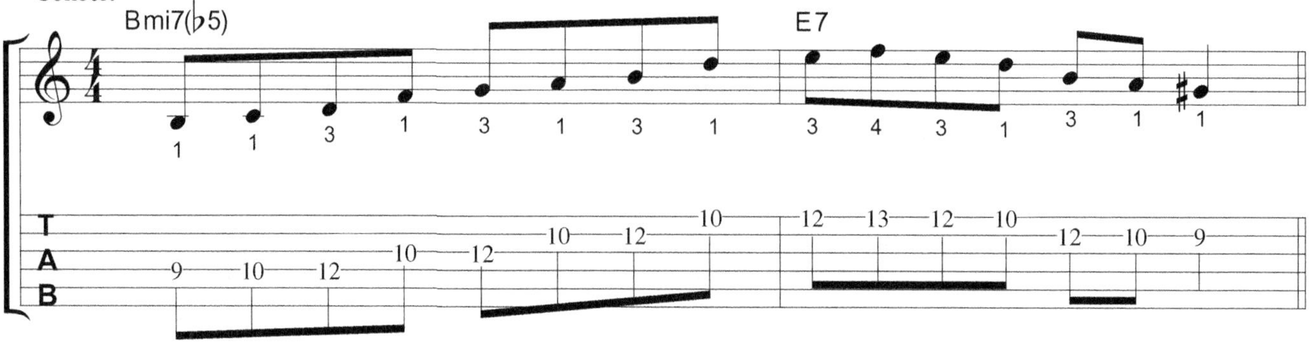

12
Concert

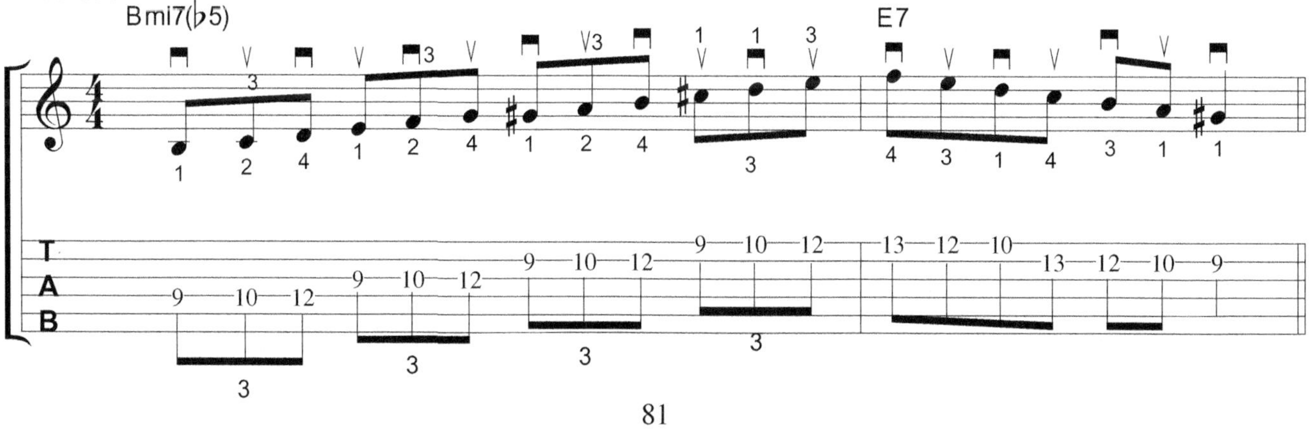

G Minor Patterns for Improvisation

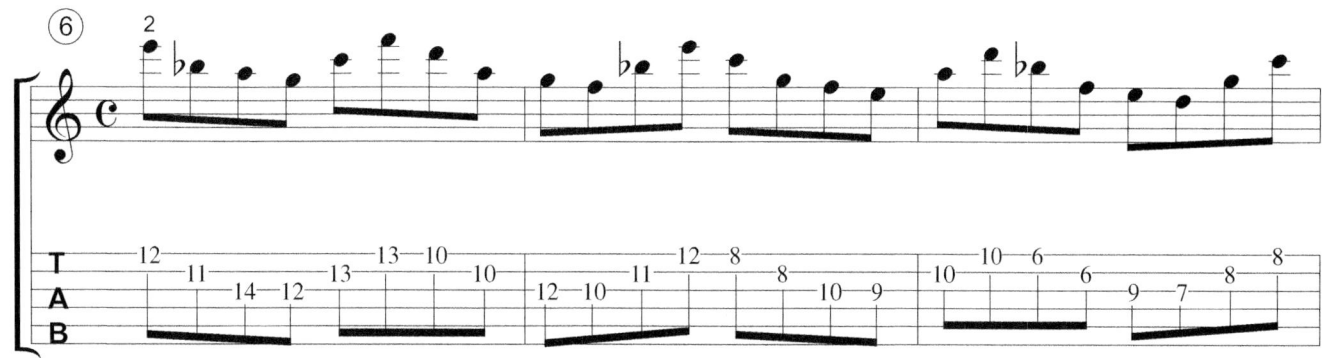
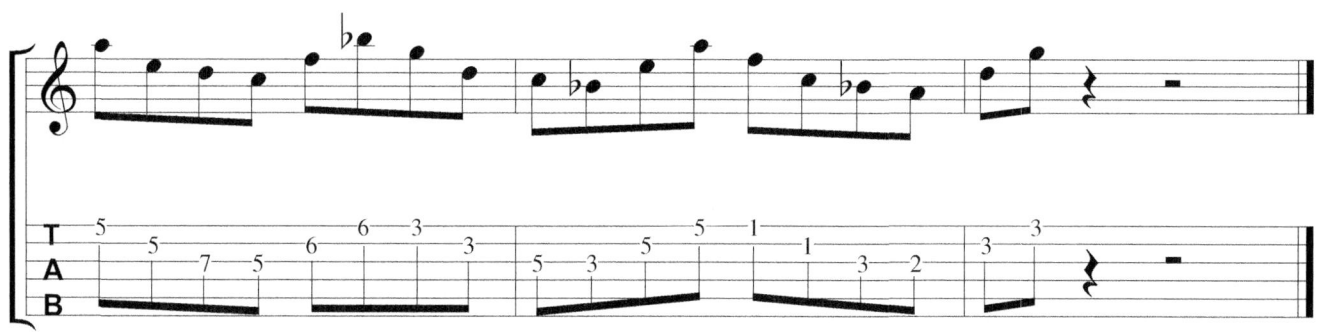
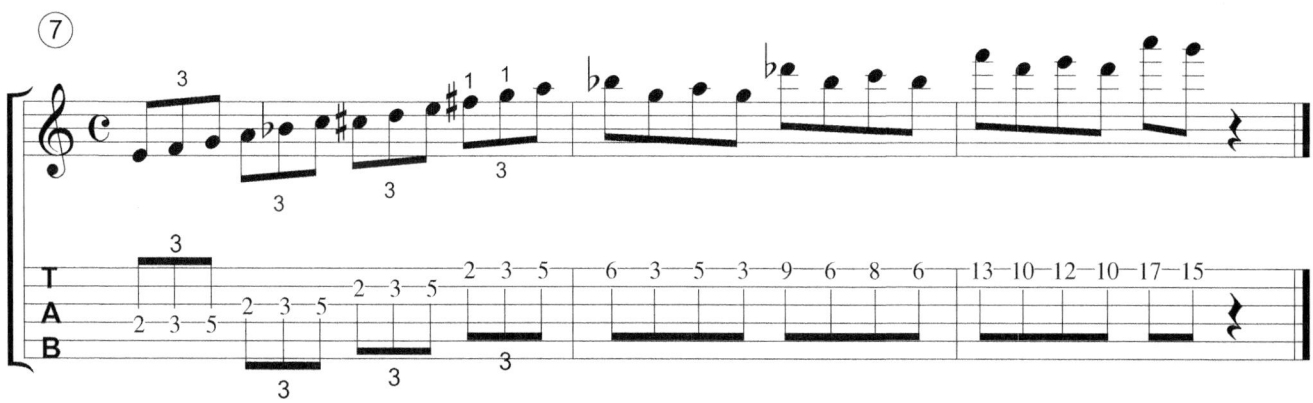
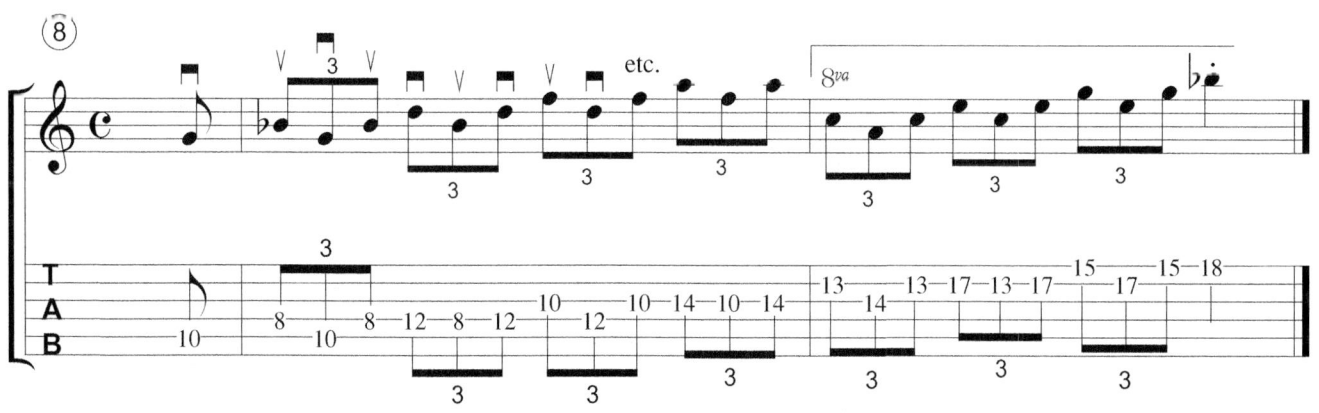

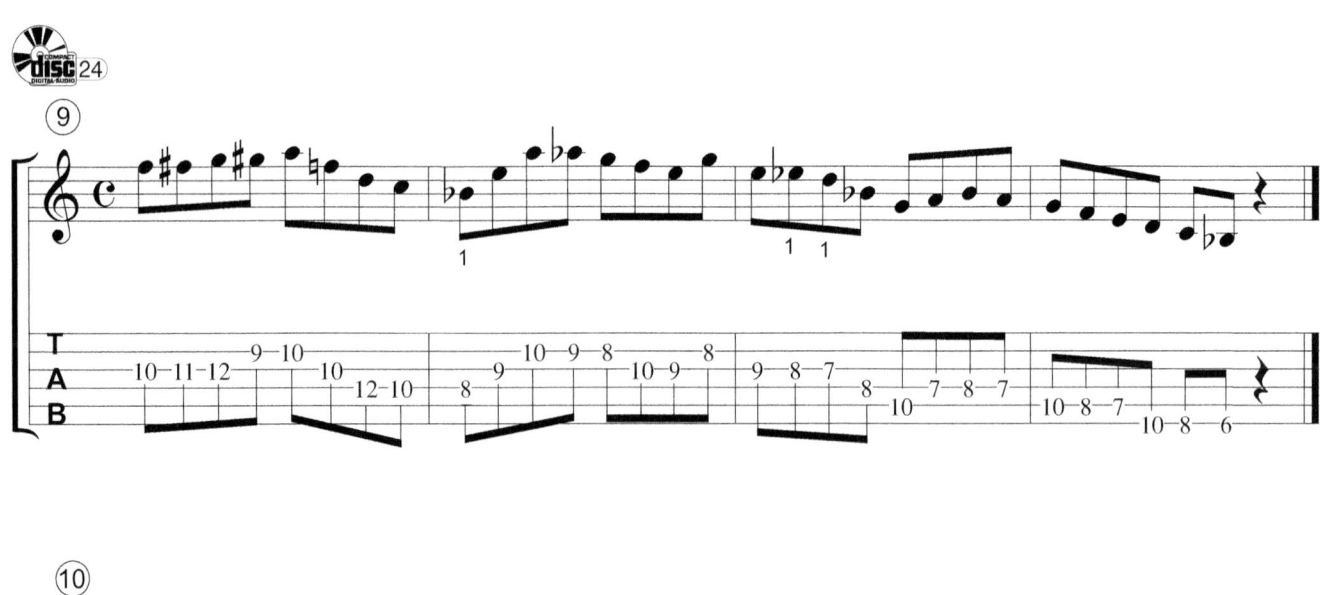
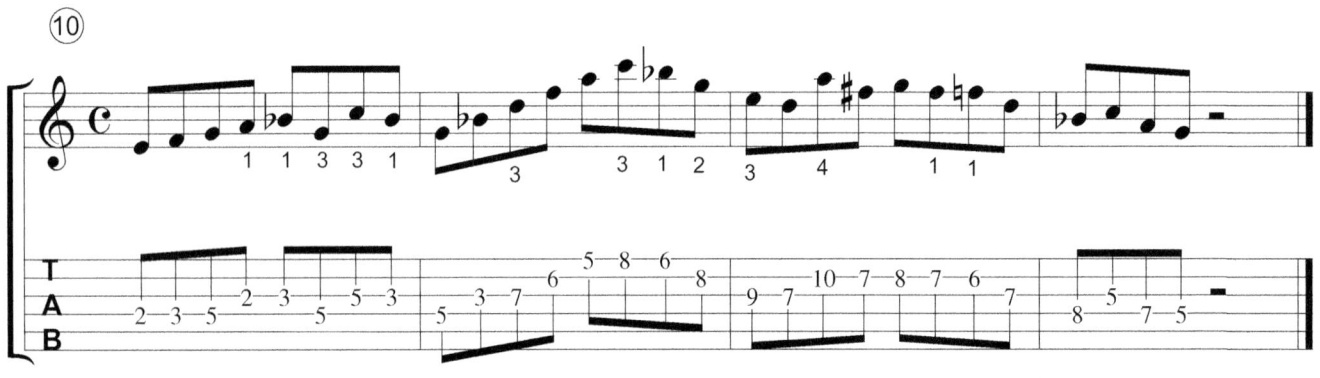

Polytonal Improvisation

Many guitarists have the need for scales and ideas to expand their melodic and harmonic conception of tonality and poly-tonality when improvising over a common dominant seventh chord.

The first scale, arpeggio and chord is based on a G7 chord. The G7 scale is a G major scale with a flatted seventh (F Natural). This scale, arpeggio and chord should be practiced first.

The second scale, arpeggio and chord is based on a G7b5b9 chord. The formula for this scale is half-step, whole-step, half-step, whole-step, etc. This scale can be related to an Ab diminished scale starting on G. Within this G half-whole diminished scale, you can find every major, minor, seventh and diminished chord related to the keys of G, Bb, Db, and E.

With this scale, the possibilities of poly-tonal improvisation are infinite. One rule to remember is "you can always go out if you come back." One aspect of improvisation musicians should be striving to develop, is employing larger skips in their playing in place of chromatic or diatonic lines. All of these runs are based on a G7 or G7b5b9 scale/chord.

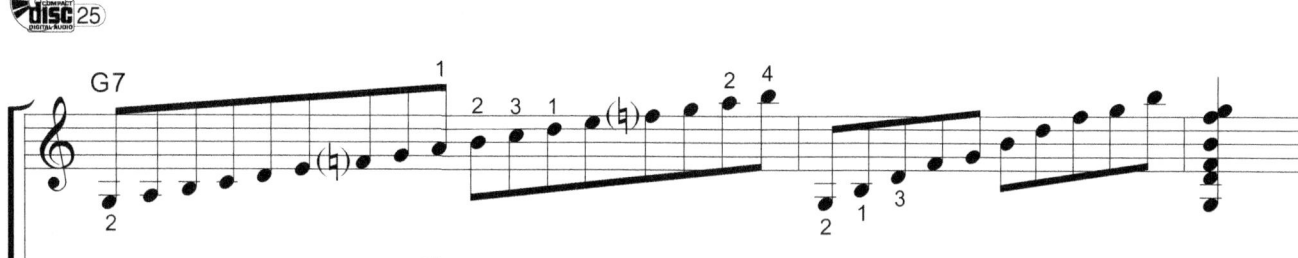

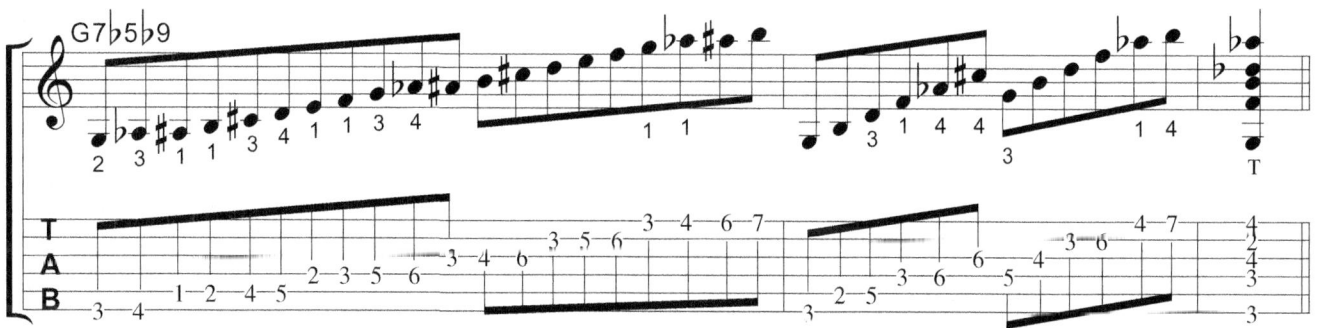

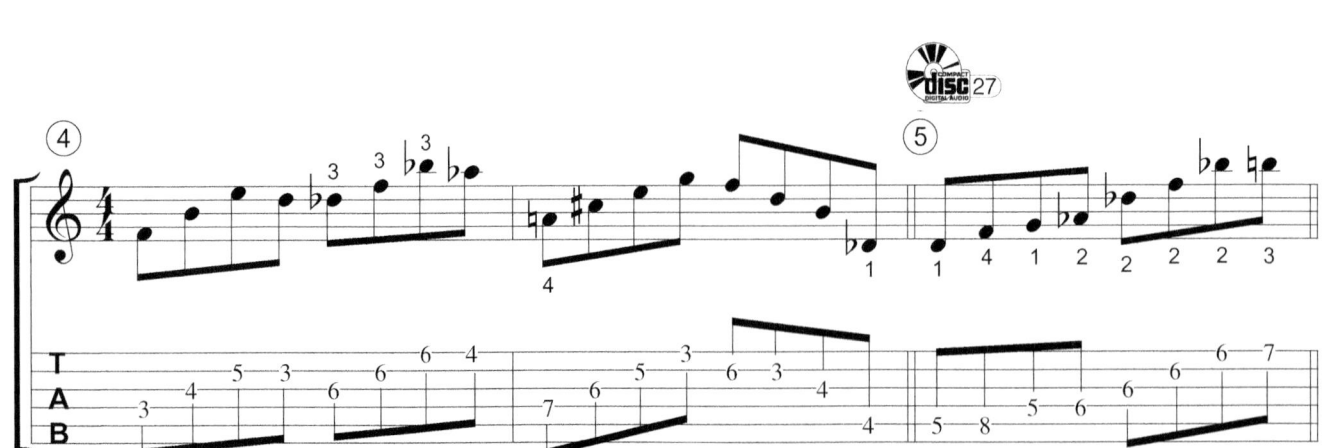

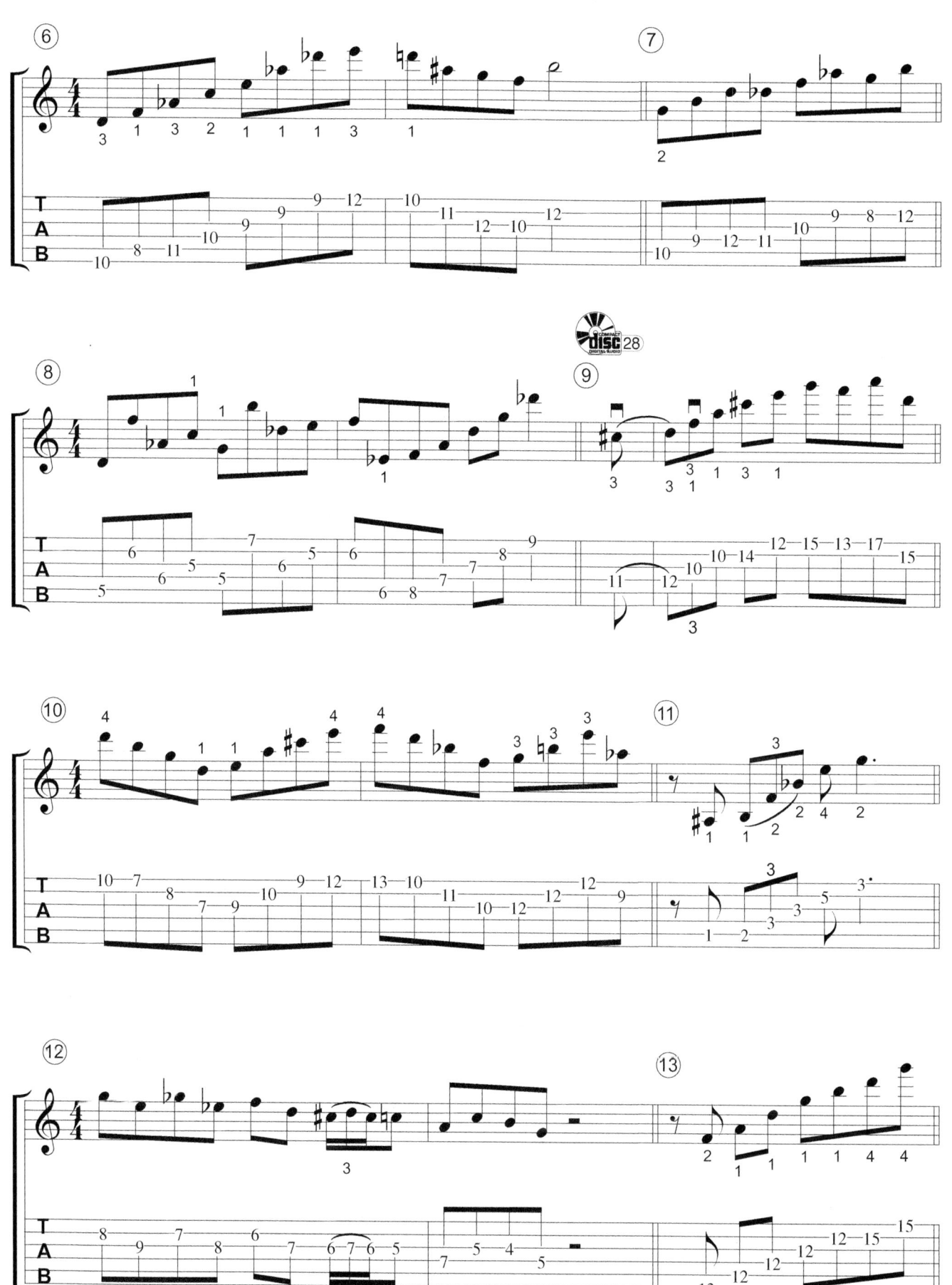

Polytonal Patterns

Here are two examples of how you can take a pattern with a small number of notes and move it all around; 1) while playing over a chord progression such as the first example which is a standard twelve bar blues; or 2) while playing over one chord such as the B♭7 chord of the second example. The first 5 bars of example 1 has the same four note pattern moving all around implying different harmonic extensions of the roots already established. The sixth measure has four minor second patterns. The seventh and eighth measure revert back to a four note arpeggio pattern which has the high notes of each chord (the first and last notes of each measure) moving up chromatically ending on the G♭ of the 9th measure. The 9th measure is a set up for the 10th measure to take it on home with an upward string of eighth notes ending on the B♭. The first half of measure ten is diatonic movement followed by chromatic movement which helps to tighten up the end of the line.

The four-bar line of example 2 is to be played over a B♭7 chord. The line consists of a similar four note pattern found in the first 5 measure of example 1. Here is an analysis of the harmonic implications which are indicated in parenthesis. The first half of measure 1 implies a B♭6 chord. The second half implies a B♭9 chord. The second measure implies a B♭13♭5♭9 chord. The first half of the third measure implies a B♭11 chord and the second half implies a B♭m7 chord which is resolved to a B♭7 chord by the D natural of the fourth measure. Notice that every four notes the direction of the line reverses.

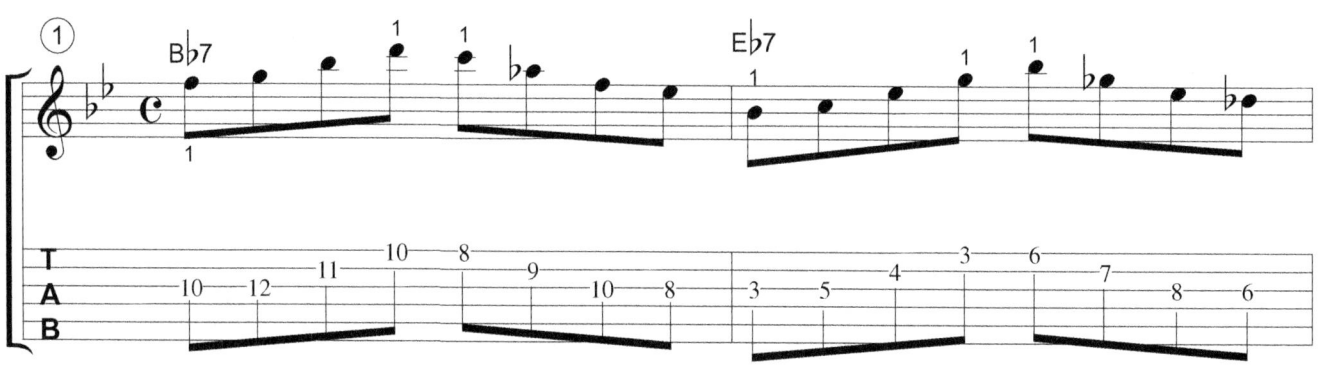
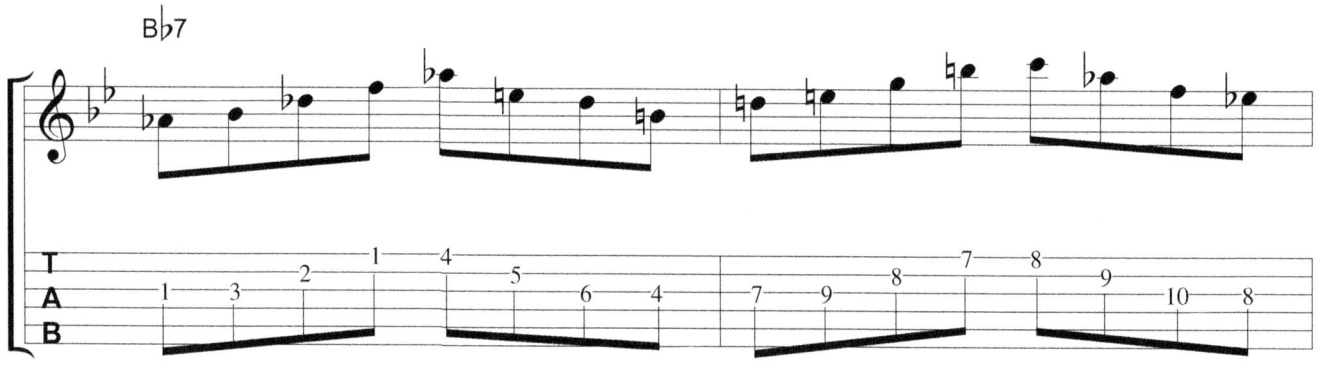
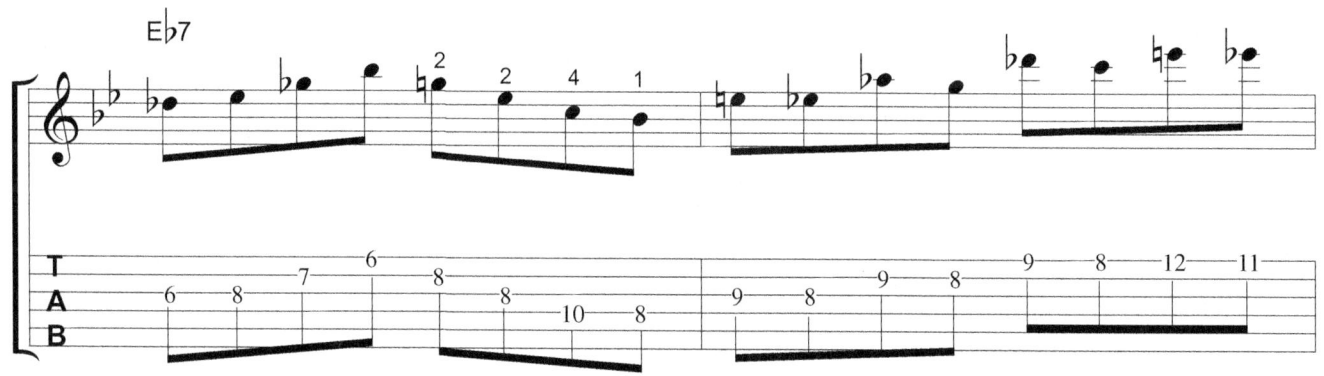
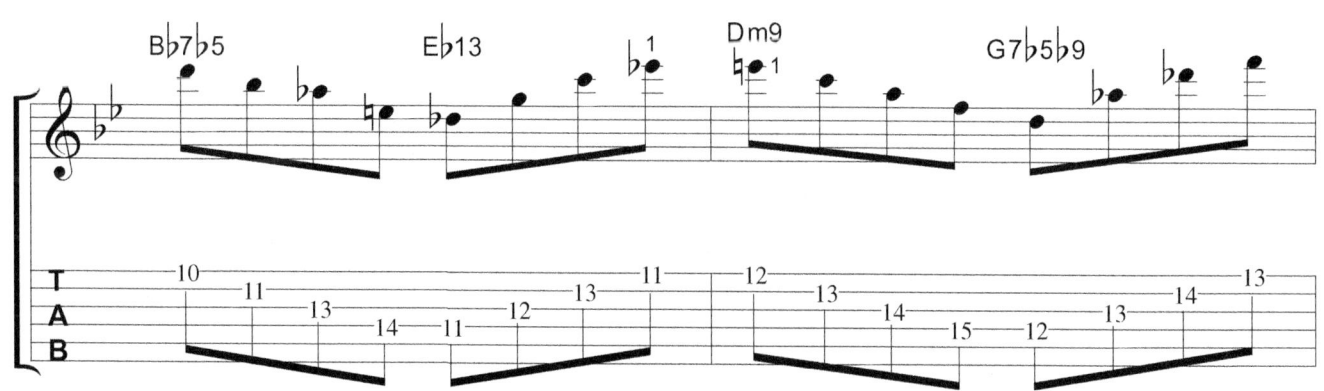

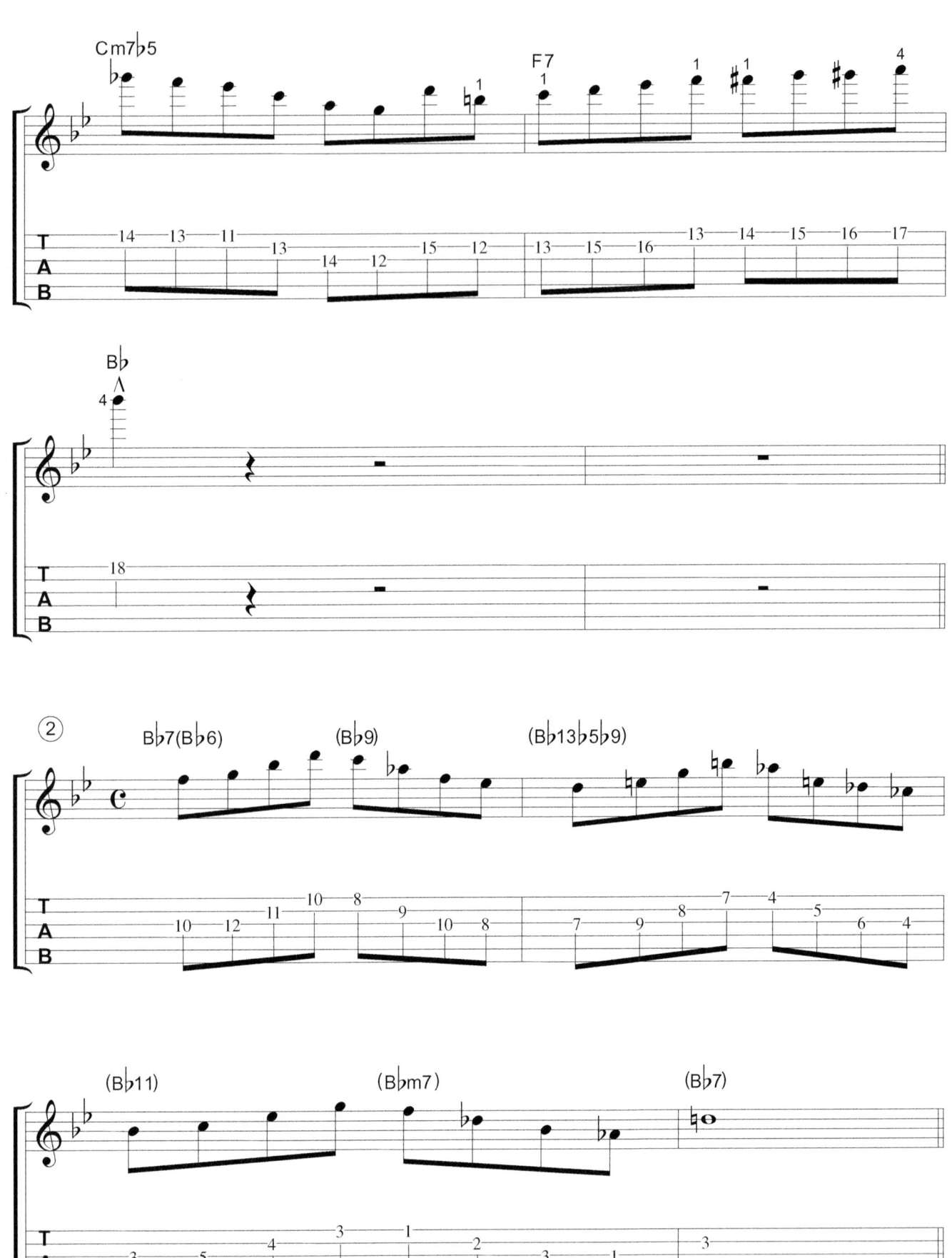

Pentatonics

The use pentatonic scales in jazz improvisation has become very popular in recent years.

The basic pentatonic scale is a five note scale which includes the 1st, 2nd, 3rd, 5th and 6th of major scale. The formula is whole-step, whole-step, m3, whole-step, m3. There are no half-steps. Much of pentatonic improvisation has an "open" sound due to the fact that if you skip any note of the pentatonic scale (with the exception of the 2nd degree), it creates a perfect fourth interval. Pentatonic scales can be particularly effective in modal playing and turnarounds. By creating patterns derived from pentatonic scales, an improviser is able to go "outside" while still retaining a logical basis.

This entire section should be played over a C7 chord. Example #1 is a basic C pentatonic scale. Examples 2 through 8 impose the first four notes of various pentatonic scales (indicated by the first note of each measure) over a C7 chord. Notice how they are resolved by one or two "inside" notes. Examples 9, 10 and 11 are patterns derived from various pentatonic scales. The 1st two measure of example #12 consists of four pentatonic patterns to be played over "Rhythm" changes. The entire section should be played with alternating picking.

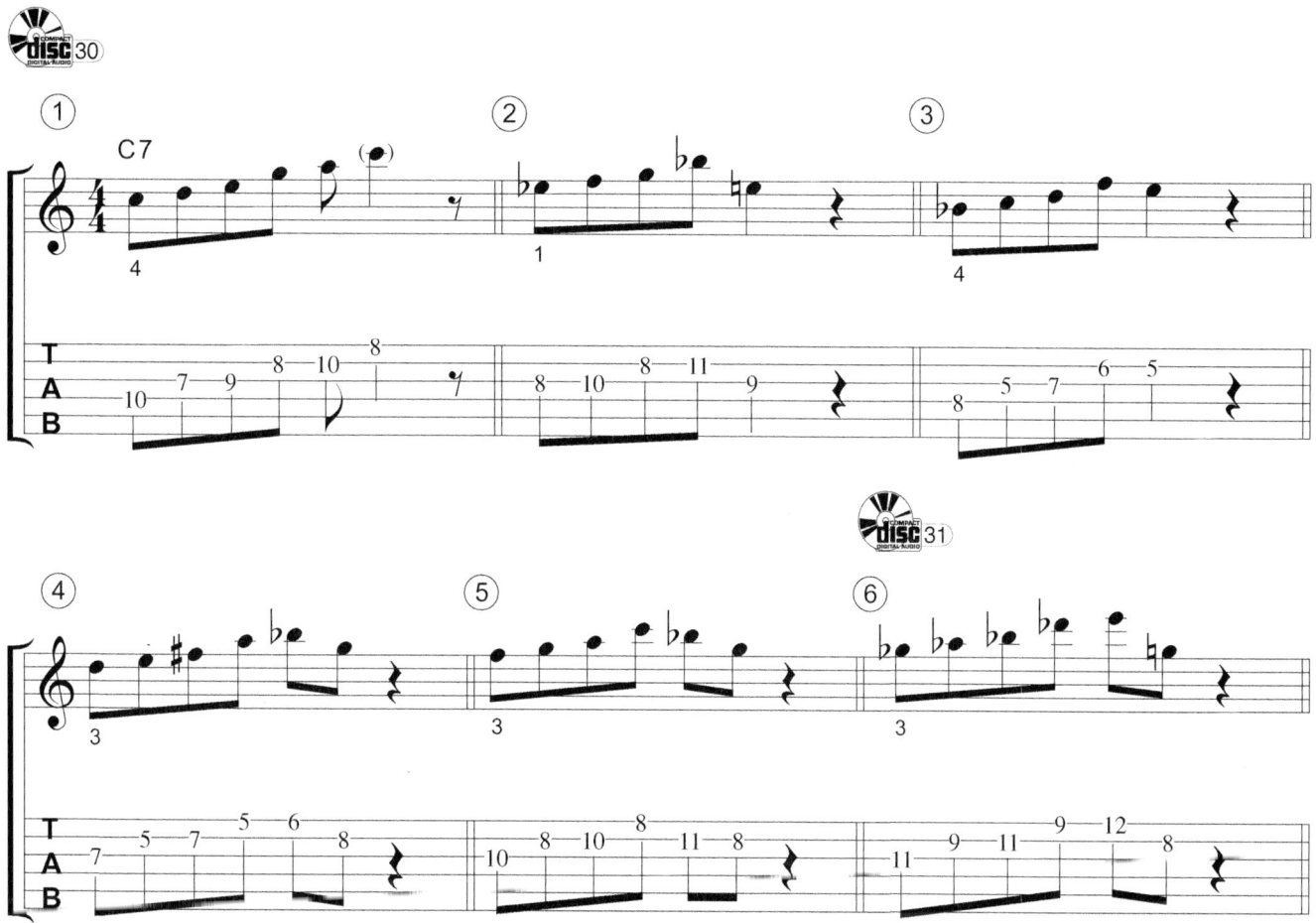

91

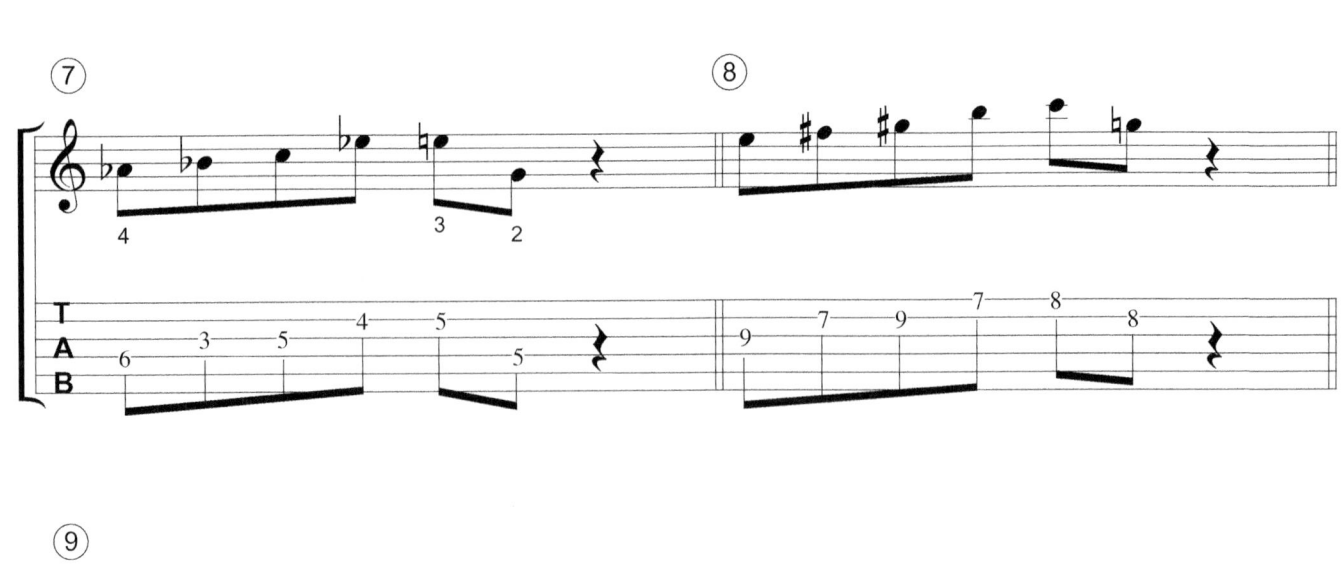
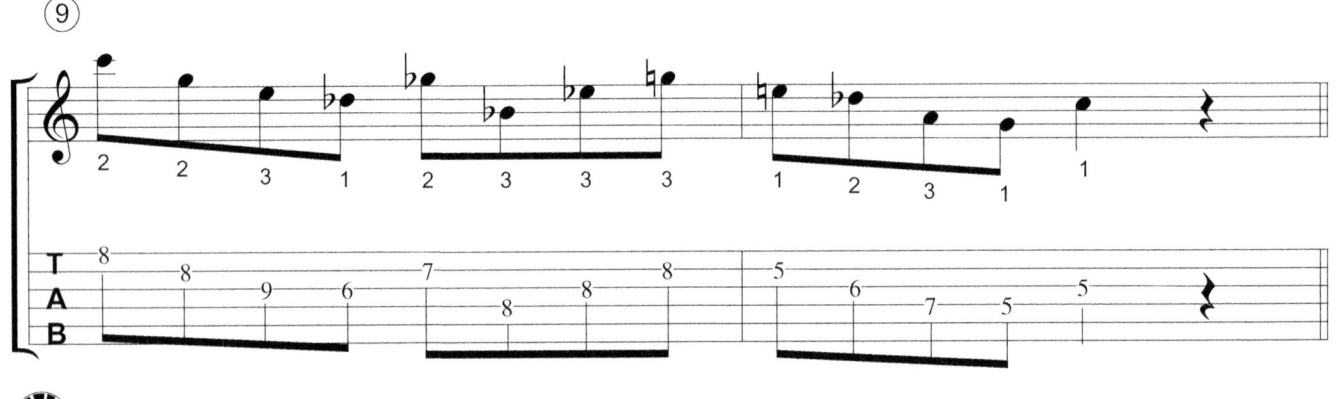
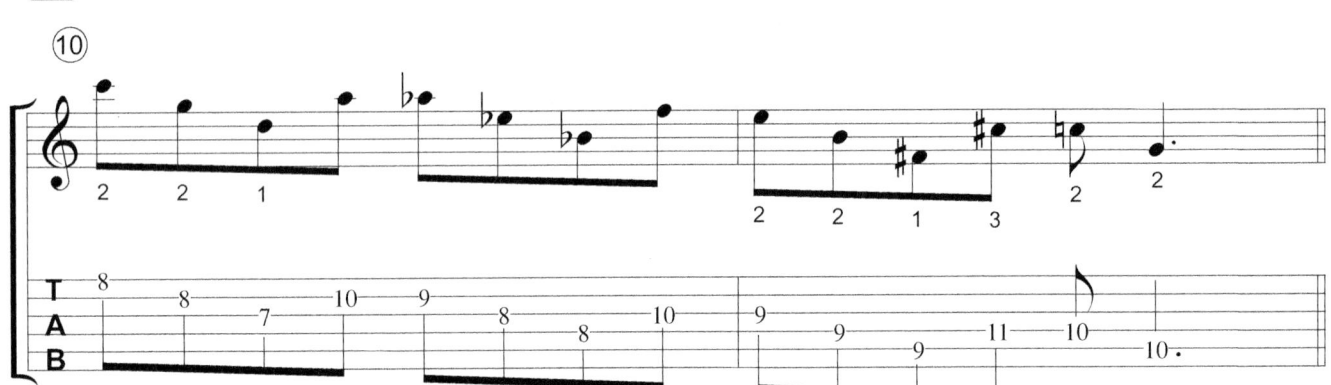
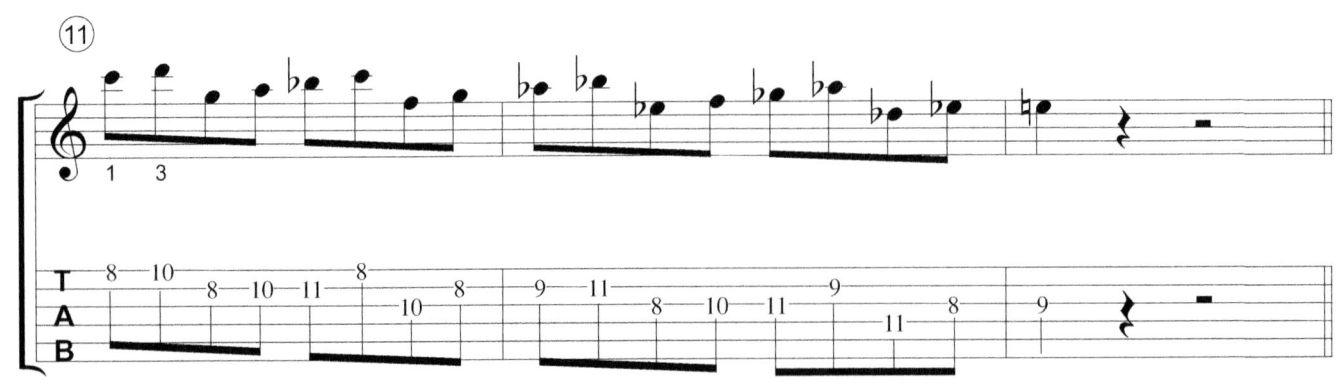

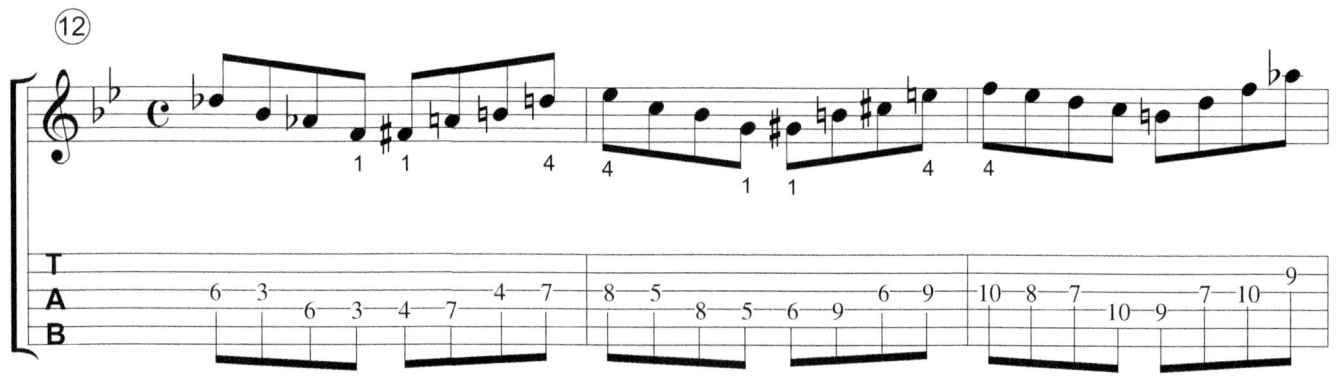
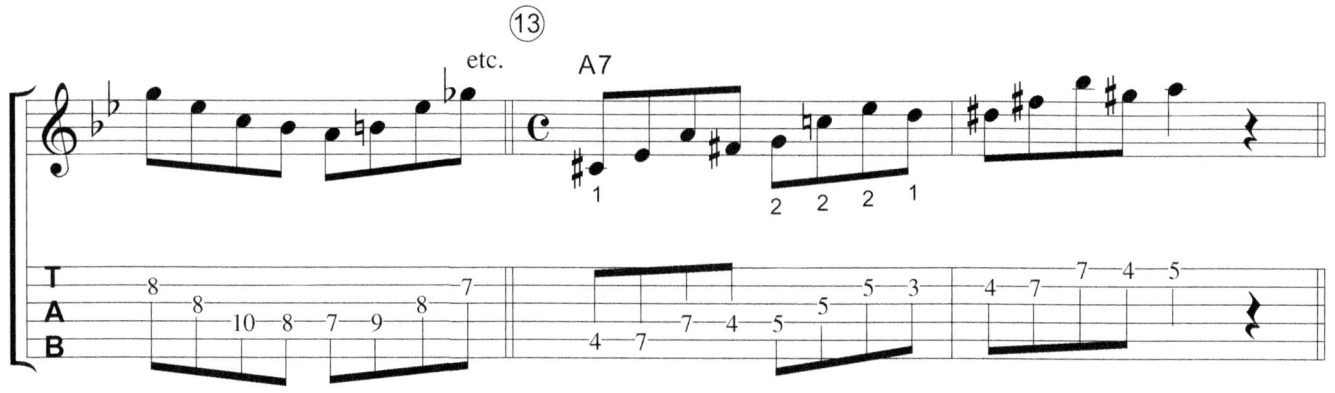
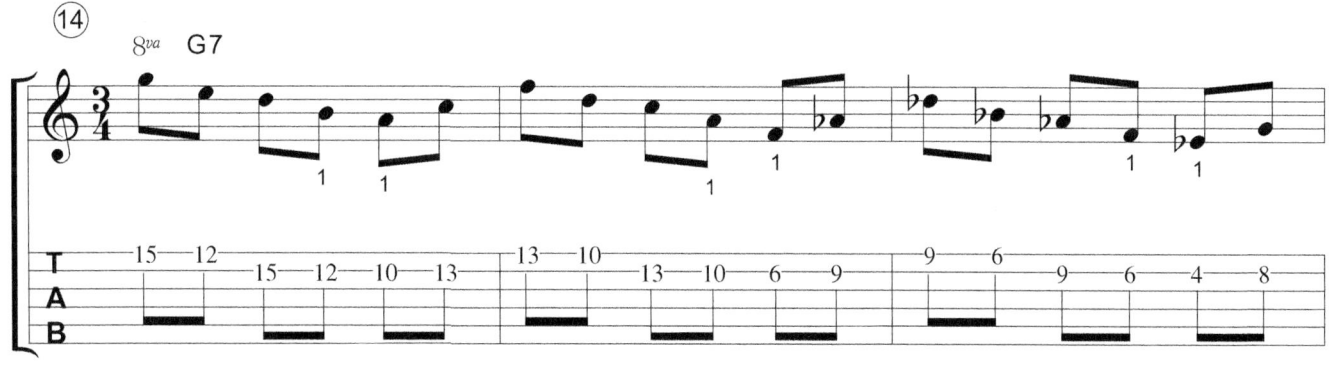
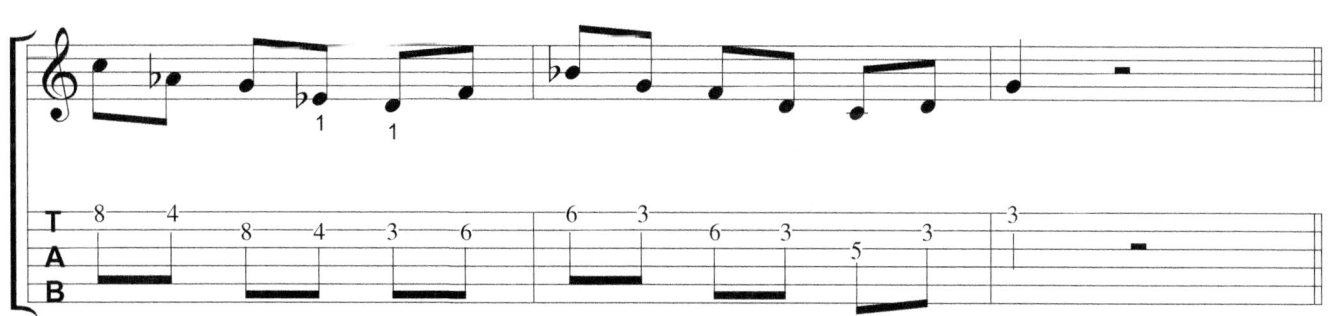

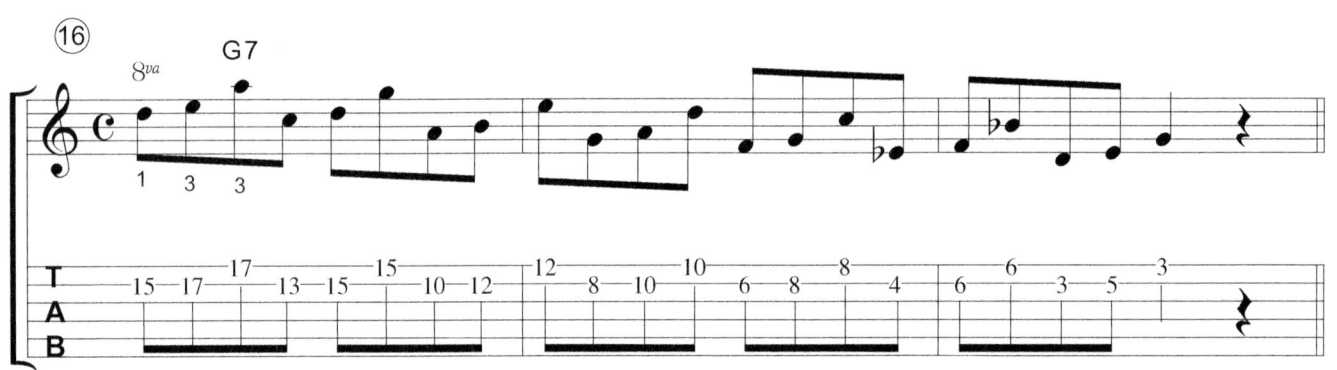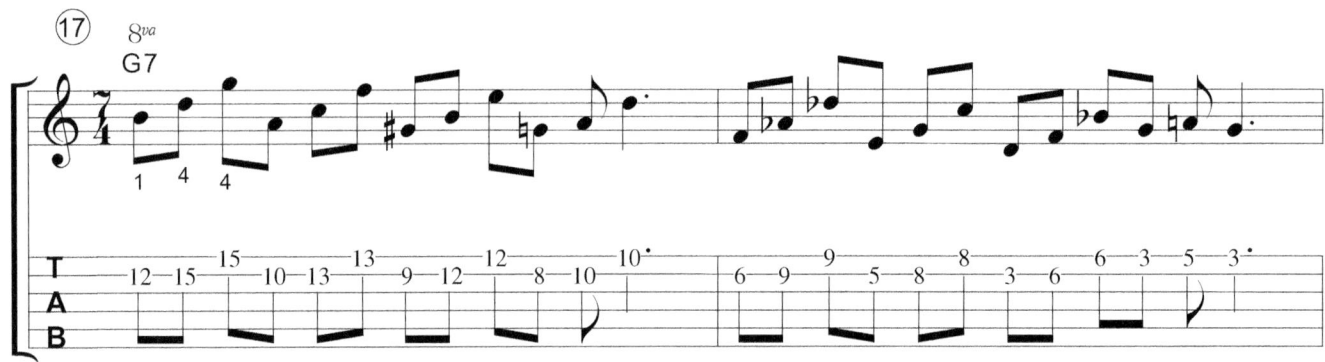

Modal Improvisation

Modal improvisation is characterized by the absence of frequent chord changes. Great examples of John Coltrane's modal improvisation contributions can be found on the albums "Live at Birdland" Impulse S-50, "My Favorite Things" Atlantic S-1361 and many others. The composition "Prime Time" on my album "Moses" Fantasy 9426 is an example of Jazz-Rock Modal Improvisation. Other modes frequently used would be the Lydian (starting and ending on the fourth tone of a major scale), the Ionian (a basic major scale) and the Mixolydian (starting and ending on the fifth tone of a major scale). The Lydian and the Ionian modes are used for major type chords. The Mixolydian mode is used for a dominant seventh type chord. The Dorian mode is used for a minor type of chord.

D Dorian

One of the most popular modes used in improvisation is the Dorian mode. The Dorian mode starts and ends on the second tone of a major scale. The structure of this mode may be examined by playing a C major scale from D to D (D - E - F - G - A - B - C - D). The Dorian mode is basically a minor scale to be played over a Dm7, Dm9, Dm11 or G11 chord.

One of the earliest and best examples of modal jazz improvisation is the recording of "So What" found on the Miles Davis album "Kind of Blue" Columbia CS-8163. "So What" and John Coltrane's "Impressions" have two sections of D Dorian (minor), one section of E♭ Dorian (minor) and then one more section of D Dorian (minor) which make up one complete chorus. This composition from is known as A - A - B - A. Each section is eight measures long.

Notice that within this solo the continuity is maintained through related melodic patterns. For example, the third measure starts with a four note pattern which reverses itself, goes slightly 'outside' in the fourth measure and then becomes the same pattern found in the first and second measure up an octave. I have purposely omitted rhythmic variation in the line so my students will not have to deal with that and can concentrate on the fingering and the line itself. Memorize this solo and practice it with a metronome.

D Dorian

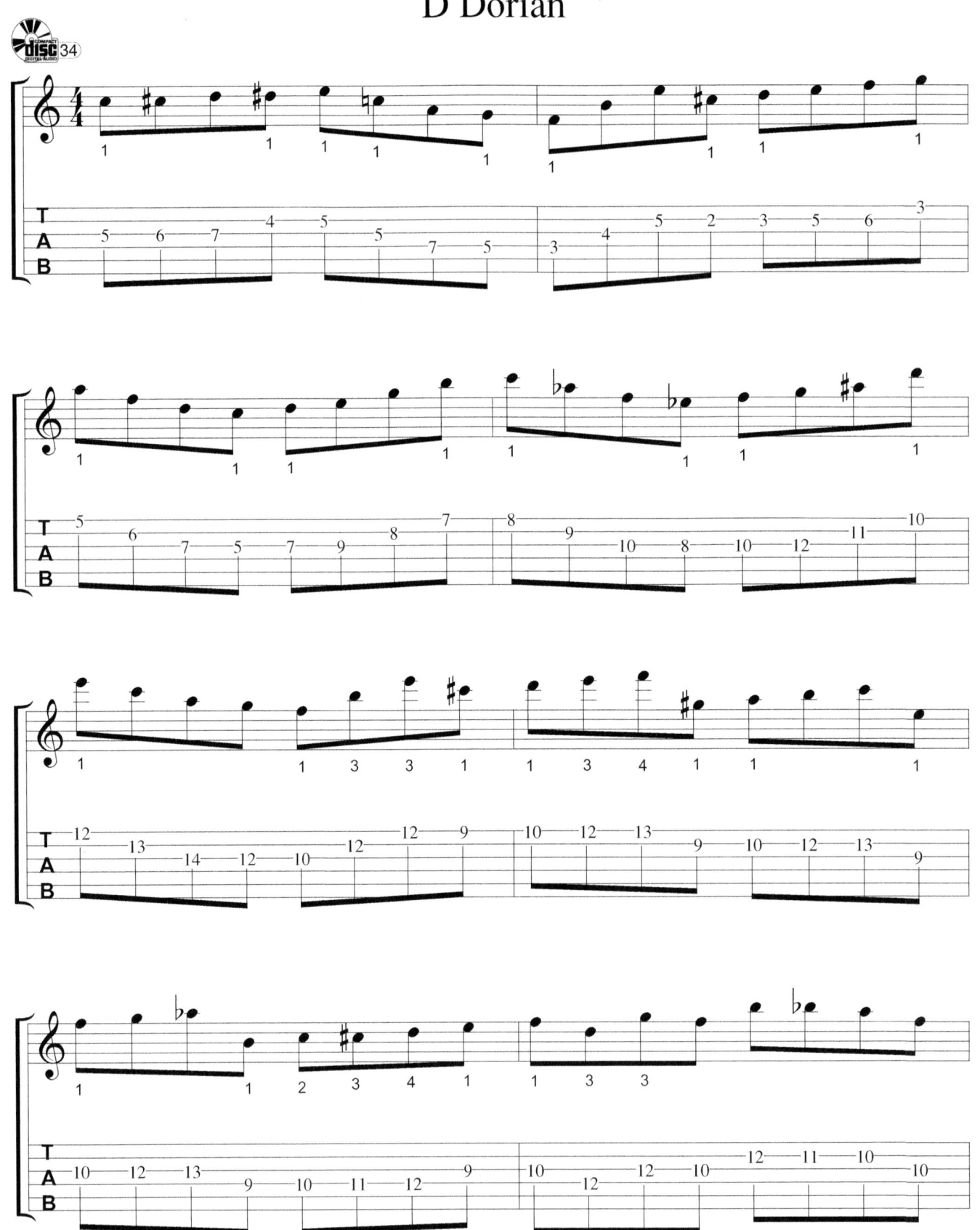

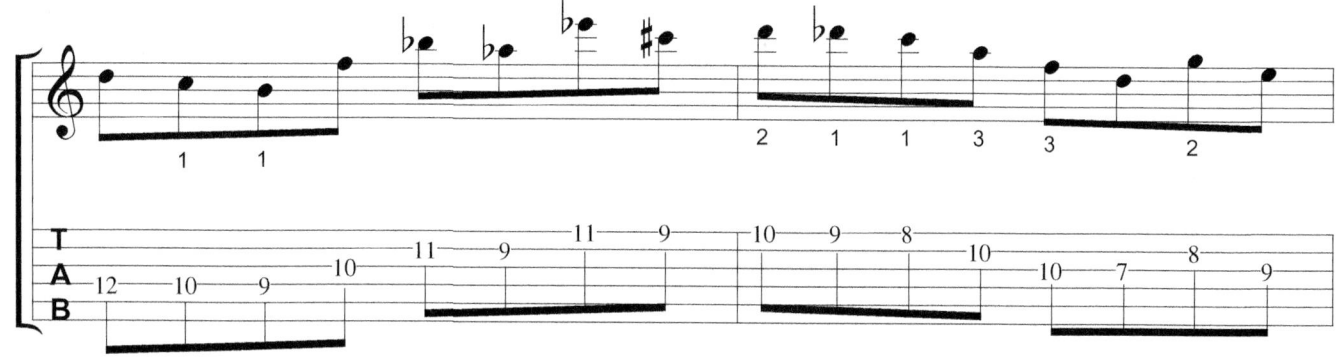
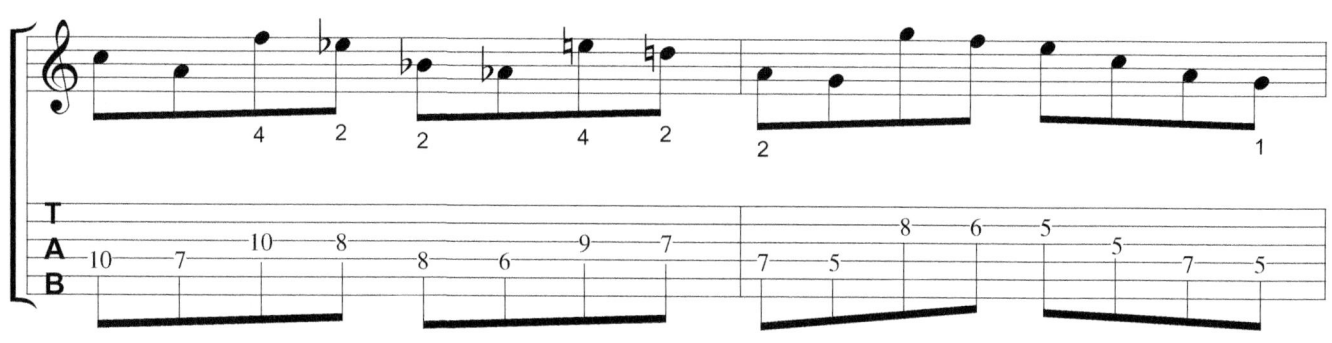
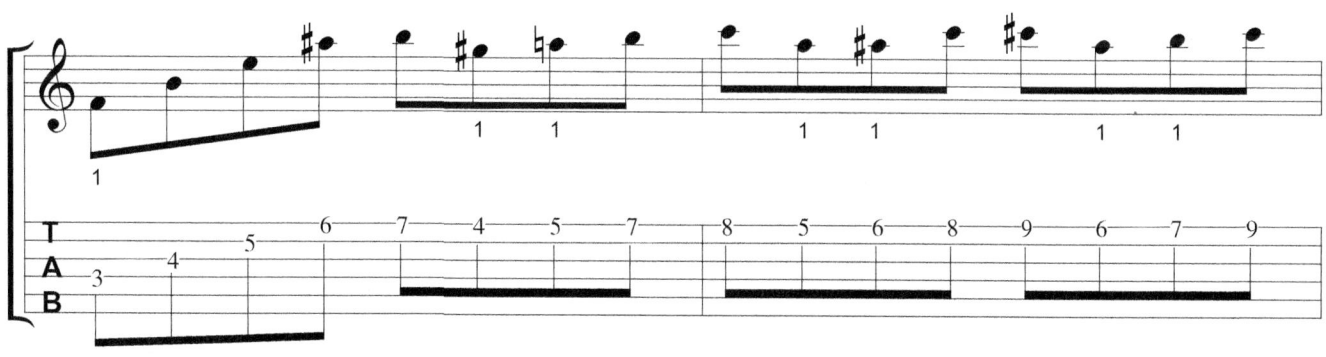
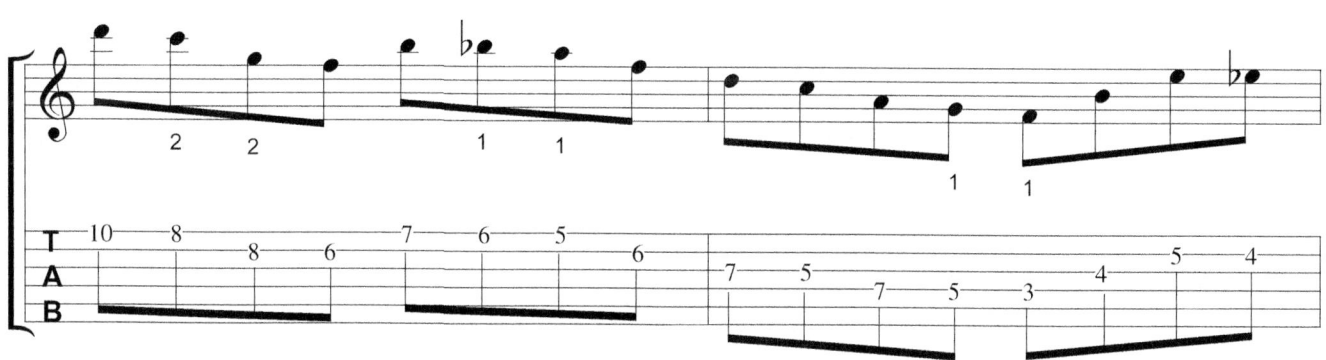

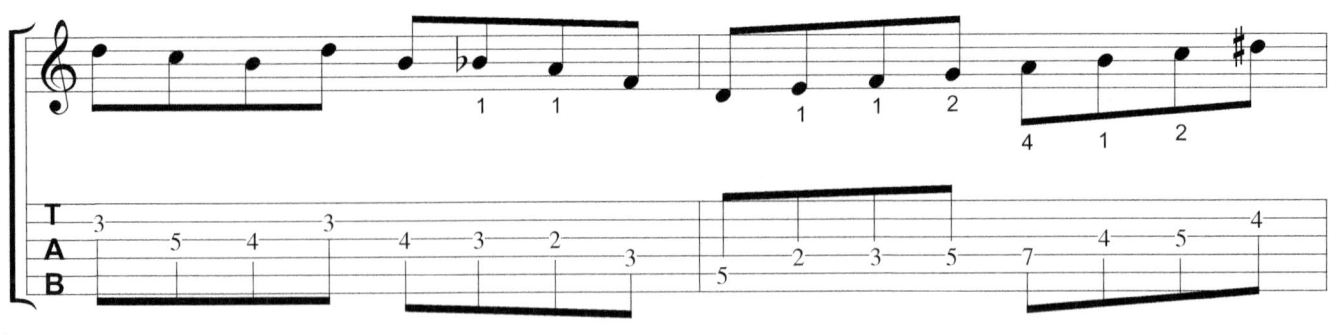
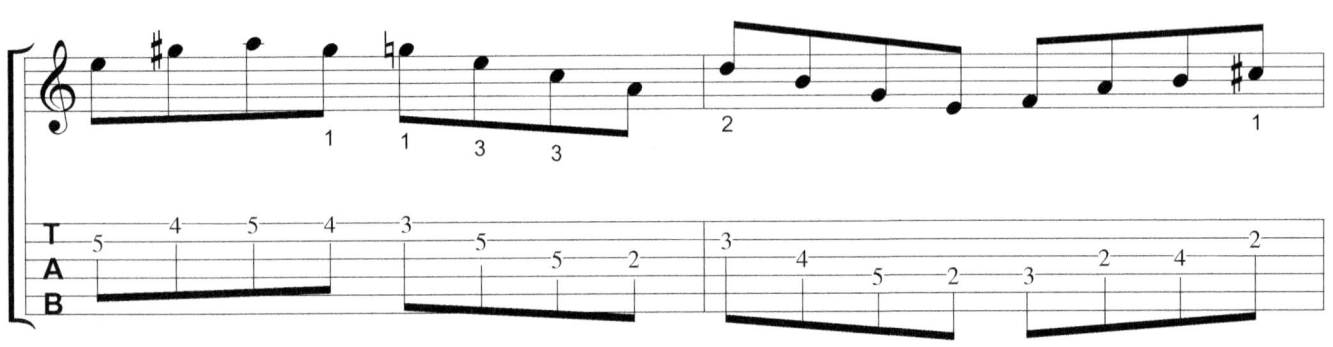
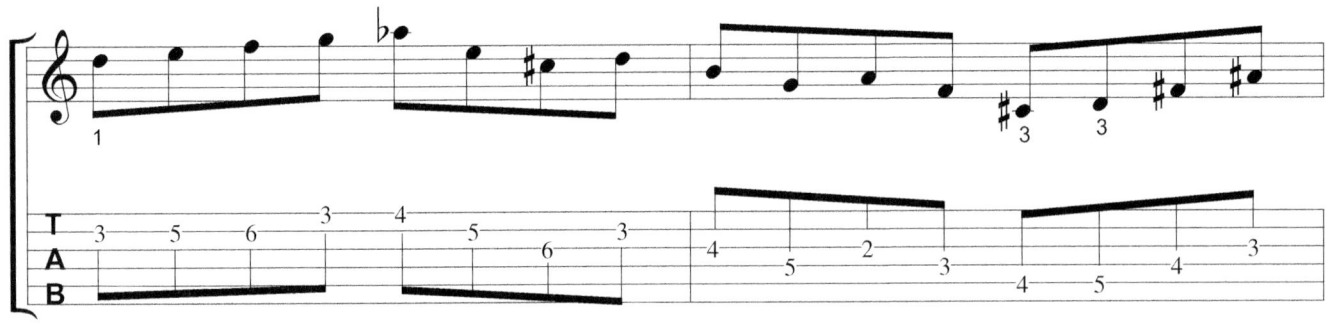
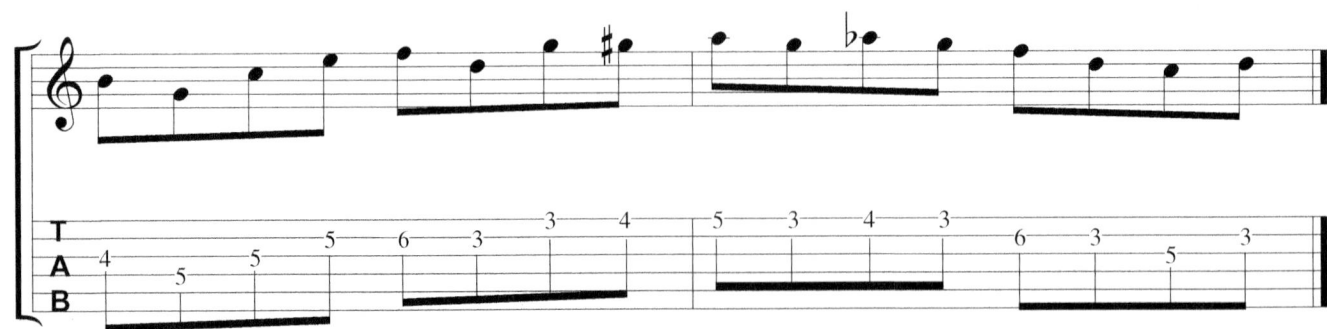

E♭ Dorian

This solo based on the E♭ Dorian mode to be played over the B section of "So What" or "Impressions". The key signature is five flats because the E♭ Dorian mode is D♭ major scale from E♭ to E♭ (E♭ - F - G♭ - A♭ - B♭ - C - D♭ - E♭). The third measure starts "outside" but comes back in by the fourth measure. In the fifth measure there is an "outside" linear line which is quickly resolved by moving it up a half-step. The important notes of melodic development in the sixth and seventh measures are the D♮, D♭, C, C♭ and B♭. The eighth measure includes a triplet which becomes a motif developer of the tenth and eleventh measure. Starting with the second "G" of the fourteenth measure, two separate lines develop in opposite directions, each containing chromatic movement. The last five measures are written in "concert" (actual pitch).

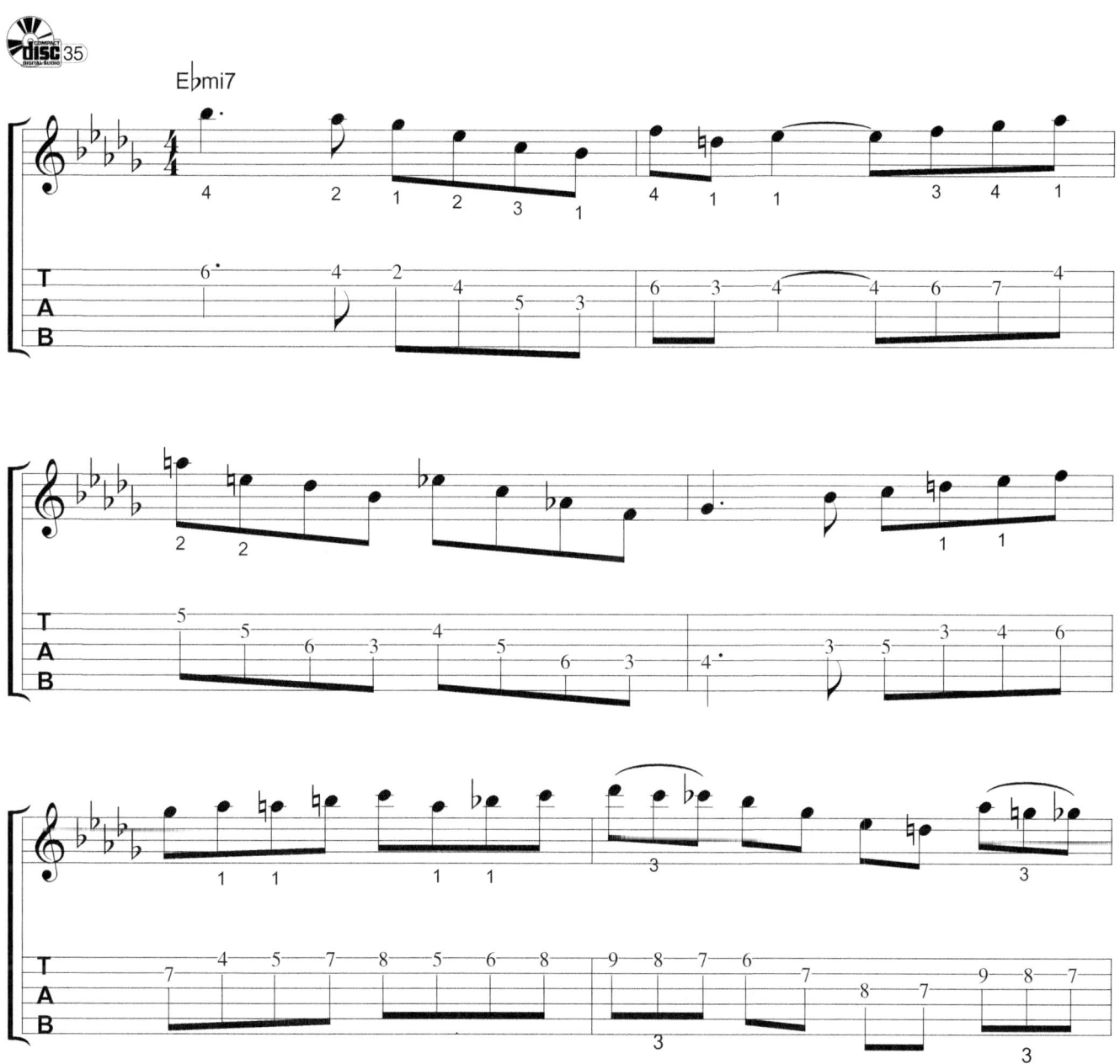

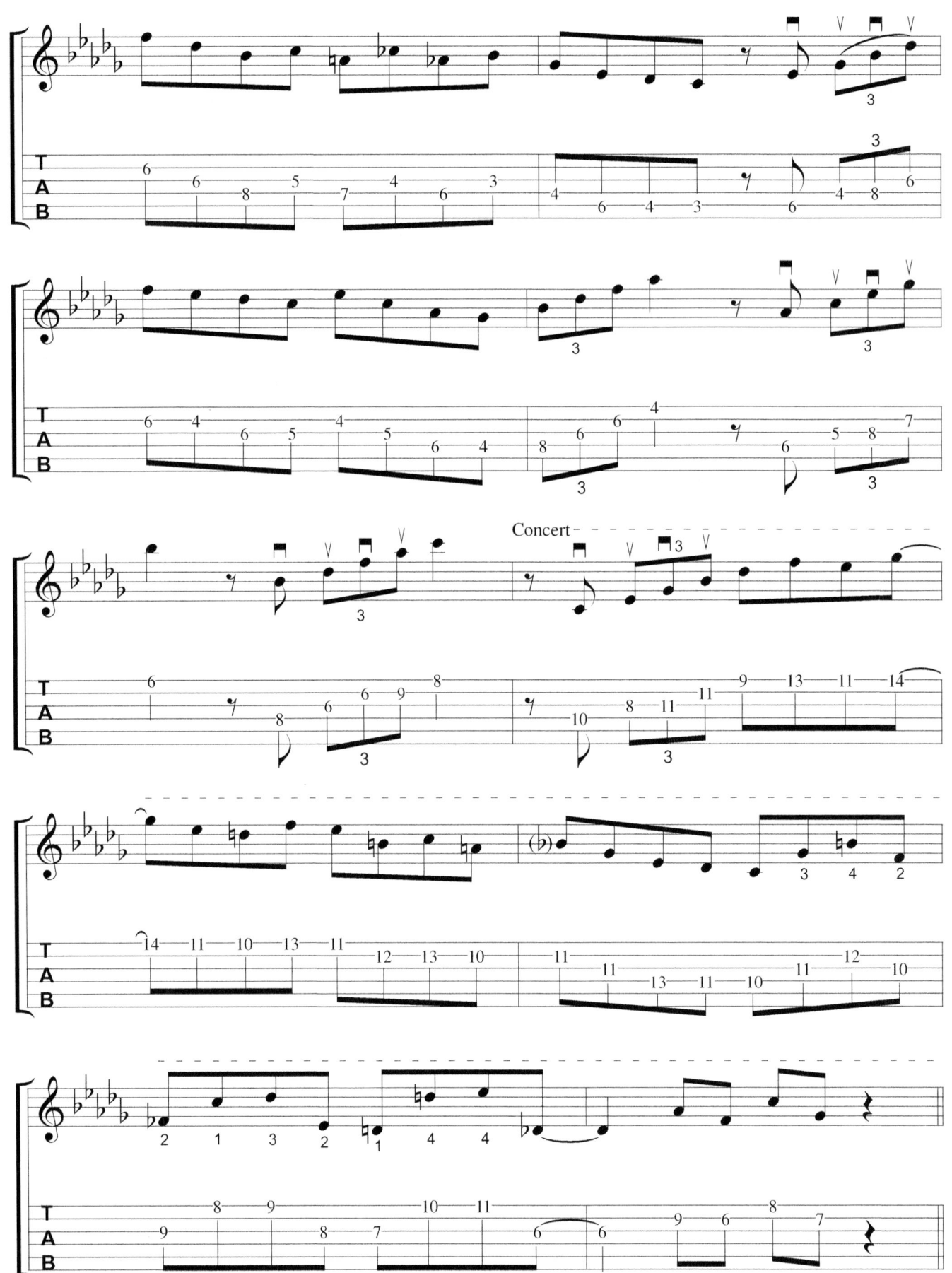

The Language of Jazz

Complex jazz improvisation is a mystery to many of the students that come to me who are primarily into rock and blues. When they hear and see me play, they have questions such as, "Do you think about every note that you play?" I usually reply with, "When you ask that question, do you think about every letter and syllable in that question?" The answer is always no. When learning a foreign language, you usually start with simple phrases such as "How are you?", and "My name is - -." As your vocabulary increases, you find ways to connect your phrases together so that you can make simple conversation. As you practice and study, eventually you are able to converse with your new language on a variety of subjects. After years of experience, you are able to talk about anything. So it is with jazz improvisation. You might pick up a short pattern (phrase) over a certain chord from a record, book or you might figure out one of your own. Collect these patterns in a notebook. Write them down. If you can not transcribe or read very well, use tablature. By memorizing patterns and solos, you increases your "jazz" conversation, providing the subject matter is not too complex, (i.e. the chord progression and tempo). The jazz language can be as complex as a verbal language. Communication through jazz takes a lot of practice, time, dedication and experience. If a group of people are talking to each other on different subjects at the same time, there is not going to be much understanding. Similarly, if a group of musicians are playing together but not listening to each other, the communication with the audience is going to suffer. If you memorize a pattern a day, in one year you will have memorized 365 patterns. START TODAY. Memorize this 12 bar blues in B♭.

Jazz Language

Changing Positions

My students often ask me to teach them a long connecting guitar line which will cover a large part of the fingerboard. Beginning players are frequently limited to improvising in one position on the neck and are unable to move up and down the fingerboard with much fluidity. I have written out a solo over a twelve-bar blues progression in the key of G that encompasses three octaves on the guitar. In the first four bars I have written in the implied passing chords but decided not to do the same on the remaining eight bars because I would like the solo to be interpreted in a melodic sense rather than a harmonic sense. Using the same finger for two different notes on the same string is often the solution to changing your hand position on the fingerboard. This solo should be practiced with and without the slurs.

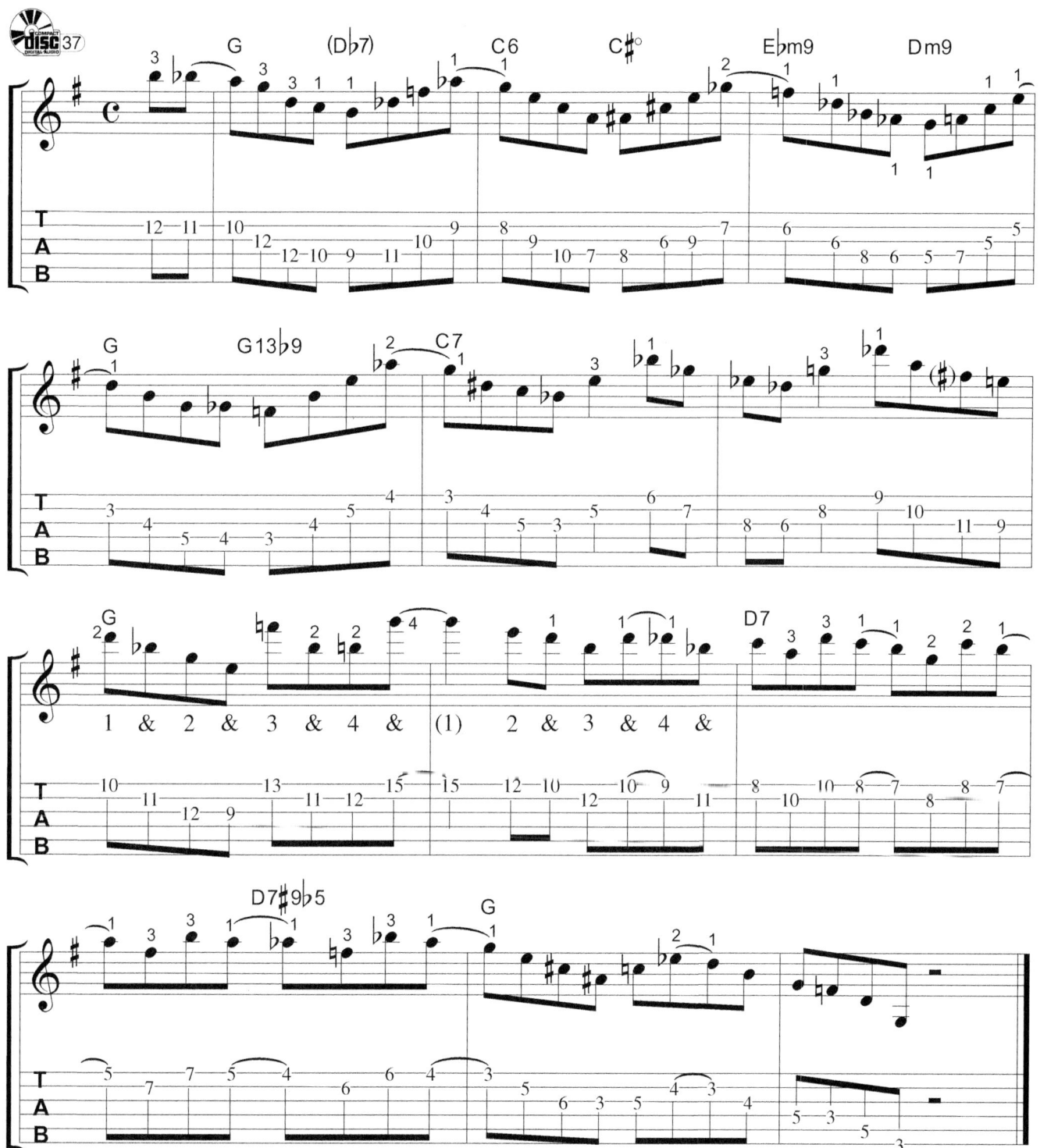

Complete Fingerboard Knowledge

Many guitar players are limited to position playing; they have two or three positions to play out of when improvising over a specific chord. Complete fingerboard knowledge is essential when viewing the fretboard as a whole, instead of isolated positions on the neck. This requires one to be familiar with all of the scale-arpeggio-chord relationships in at least five different positions for every chord. You should also be able to identify every note in any chord as to its interval relationship to the tonic.

This 12-bar jazz/blues is in the key of E♭ and covers a range of more than three octaves.

"Malachi"

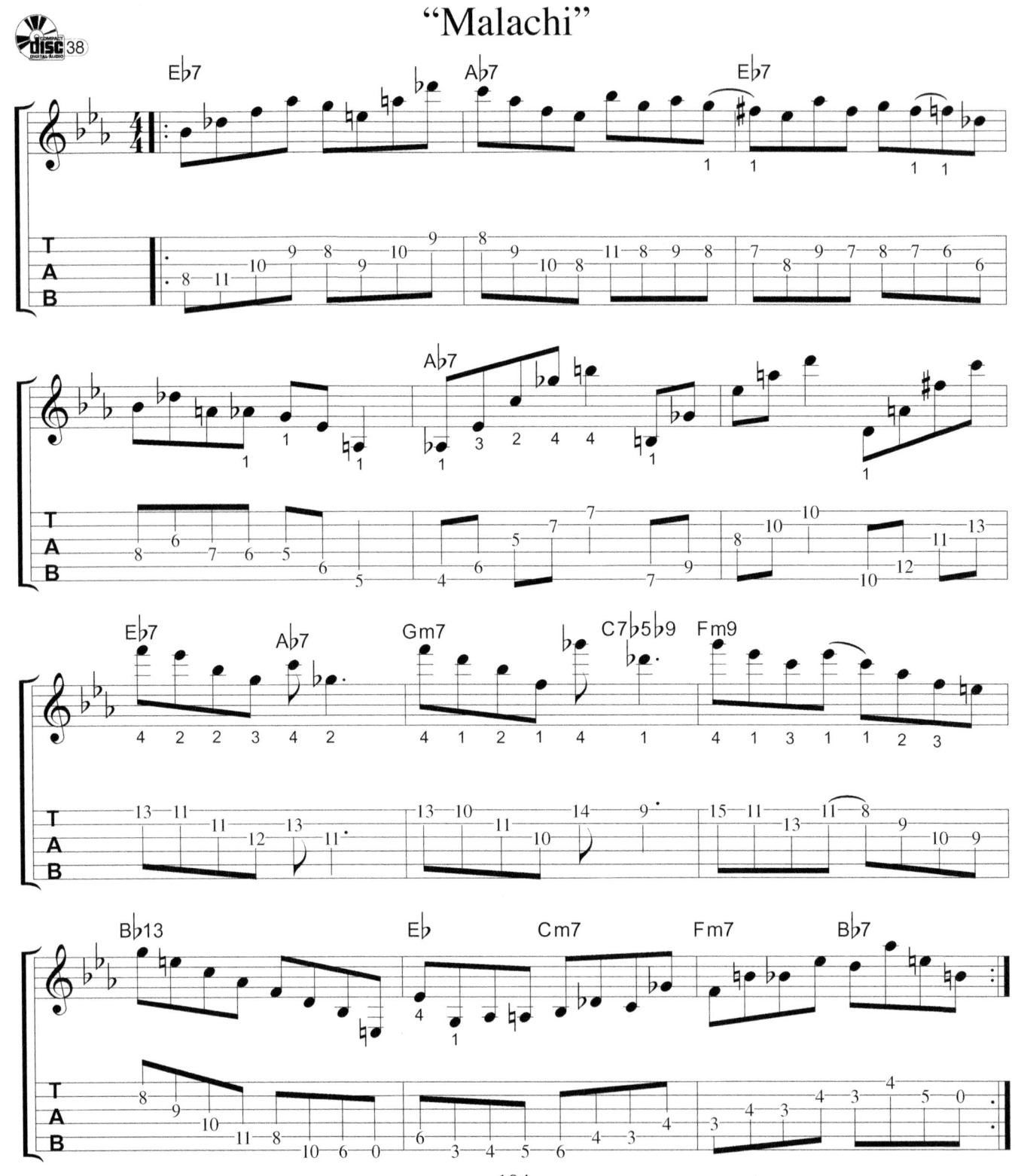

Jazz Blues Solo

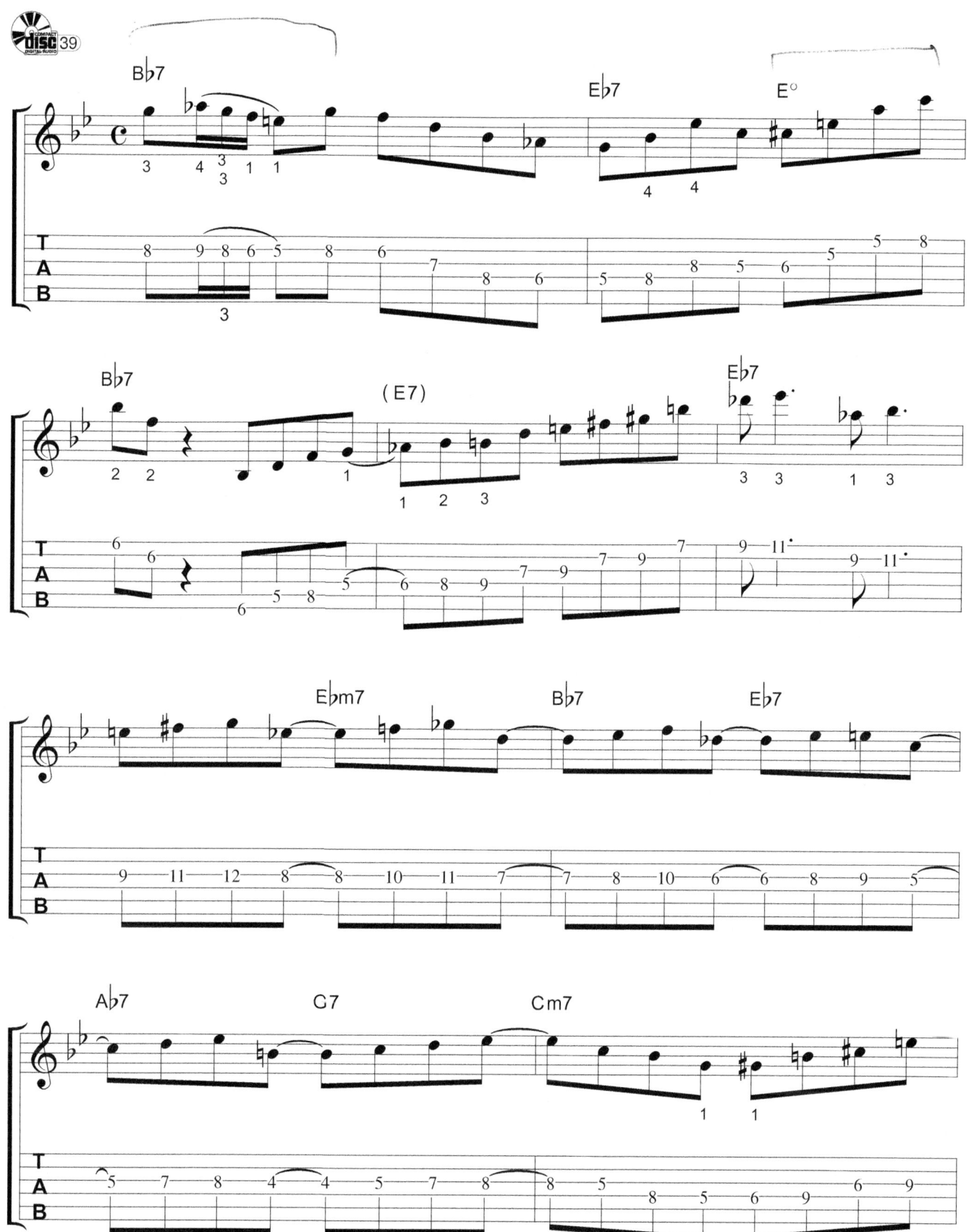

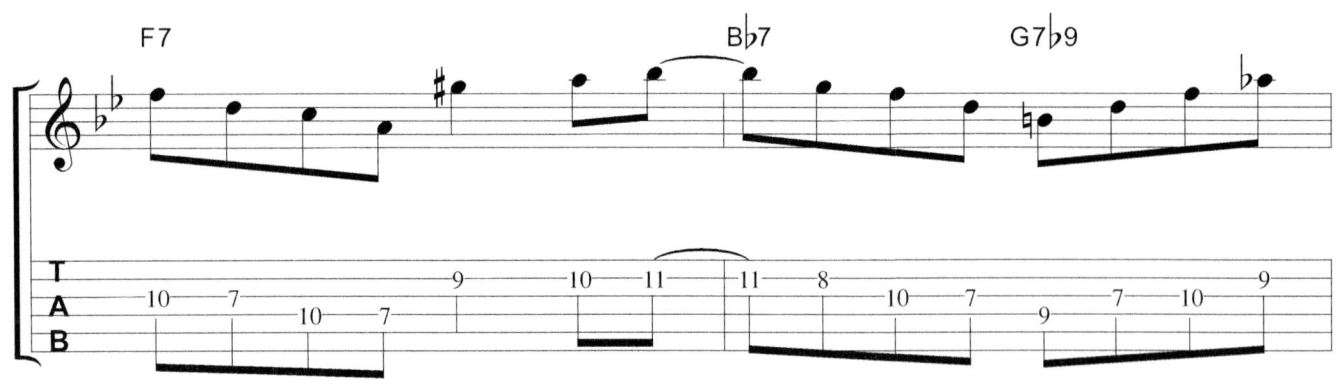
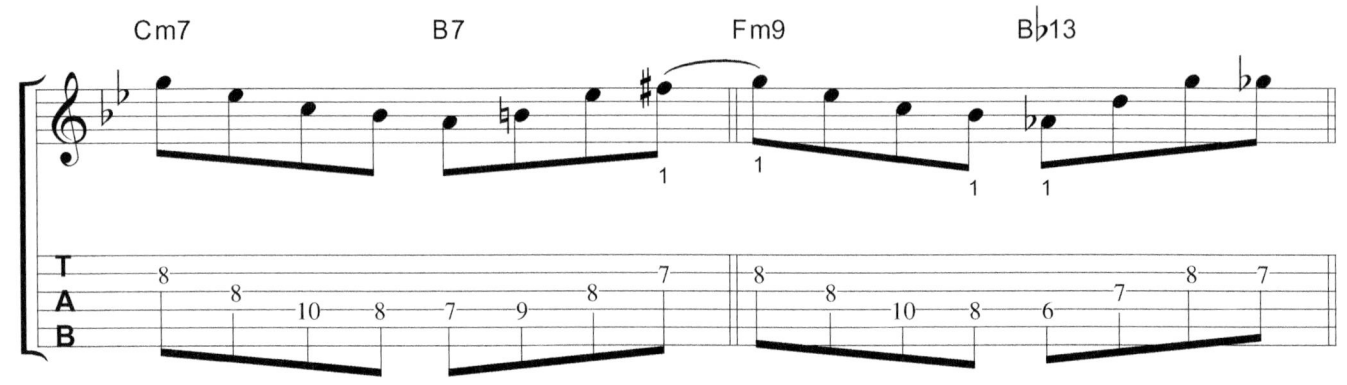
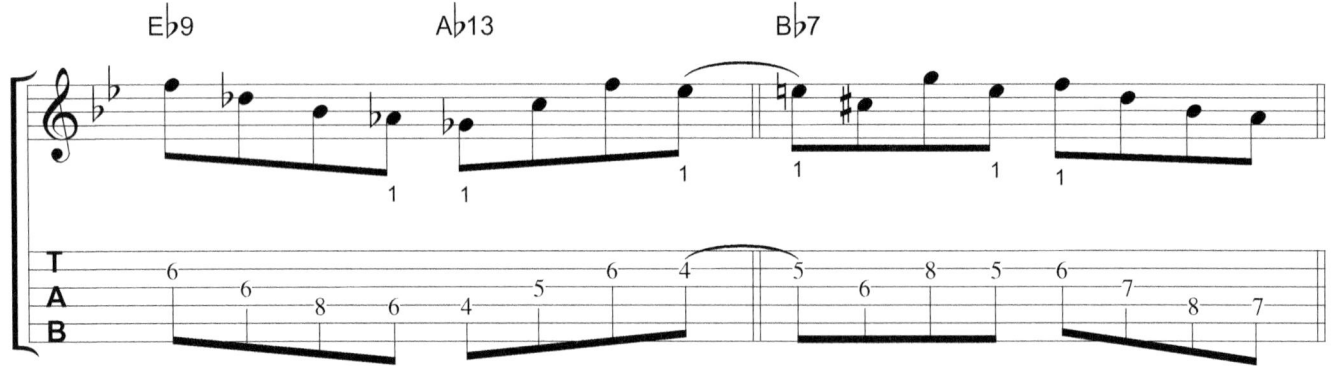
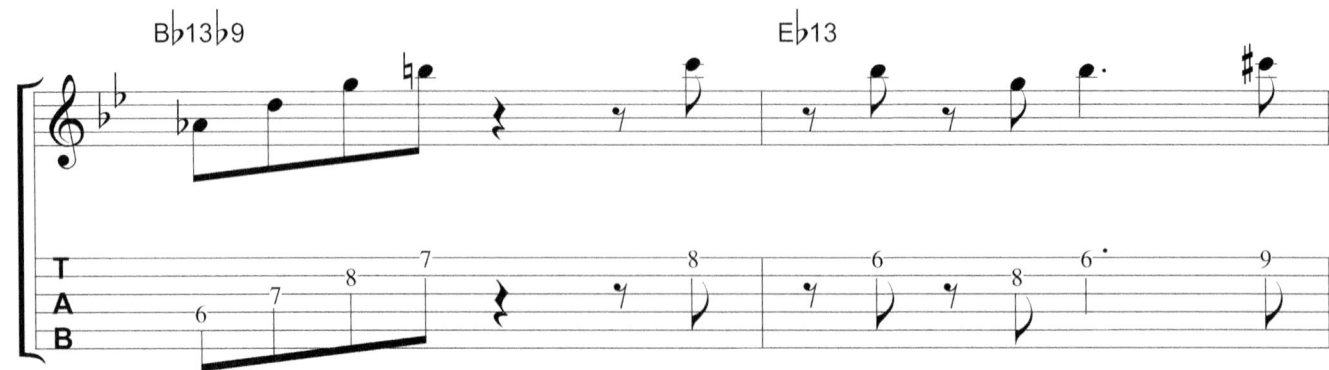

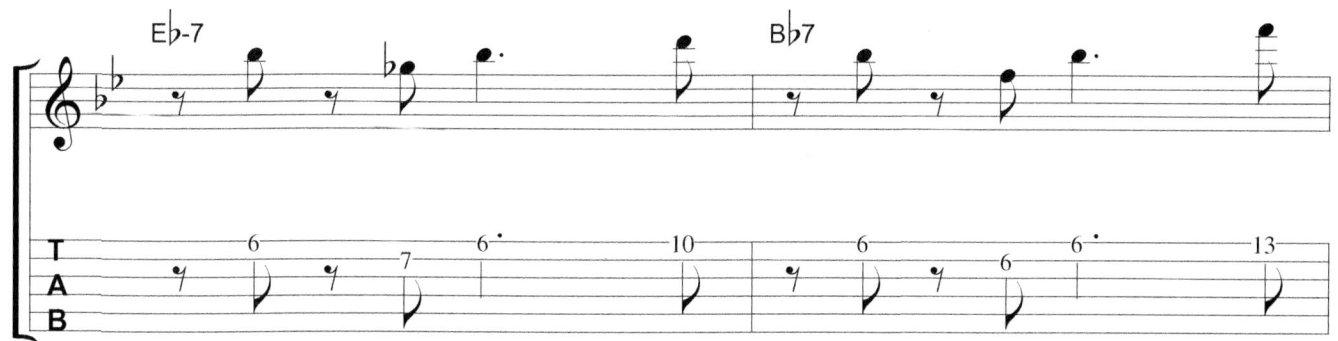
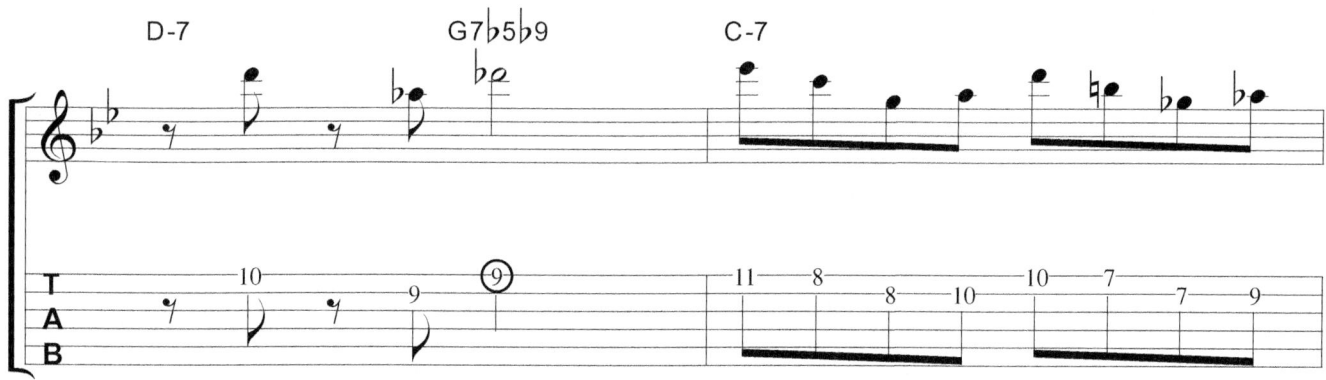
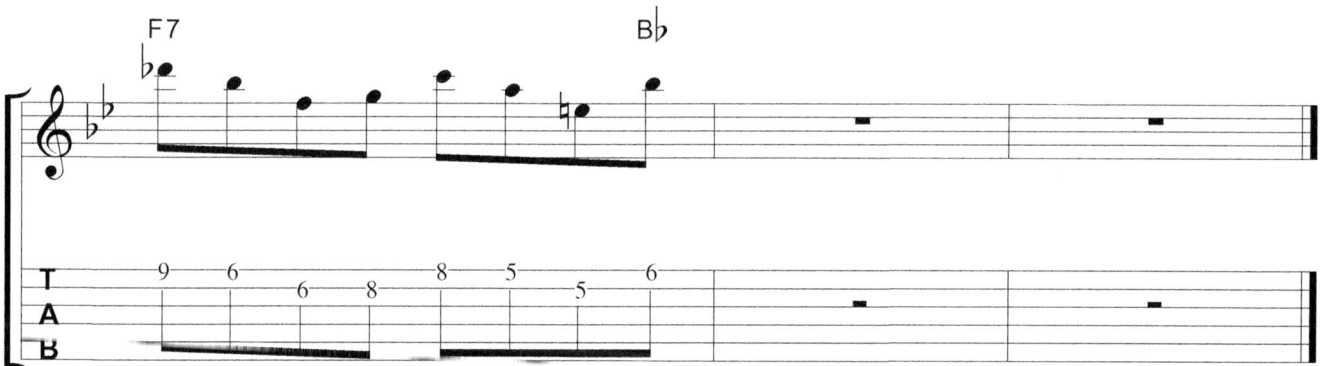

107

II-V7-I Cycle

This is a twenty-four measure solo to a series of II-V7-I progressions. This type of progression is one of the most common in jazz. If you were to move the first sixteen measures down a half-step, this could be a solo to the bridge of "Cherokee." The abbreviation (alt.) which appears after the G7 chord symbol in the second measure indicates that the G7 chord will have an altered fifth and/or ninth present in the chord. The parent scale for this chord is an altered dominant (diminished-whole tone) scale. A major seventh, sixth or ninth may be added to any of the major chords. A ninth may be added to any of the dominant seventh chords. You should practice the chords first. Memorize and practice this solo with a metronome, always being aware of the chord progression.

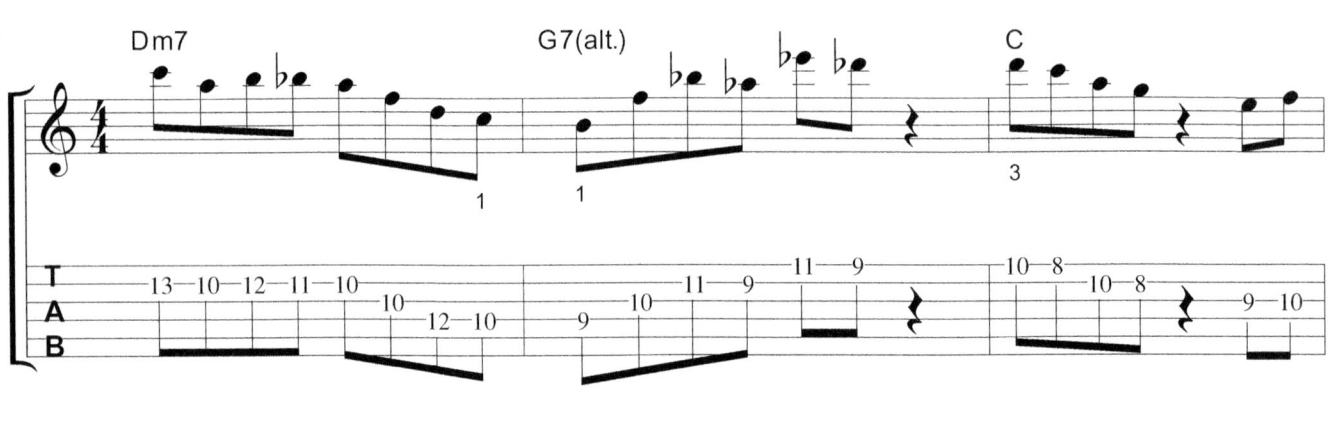

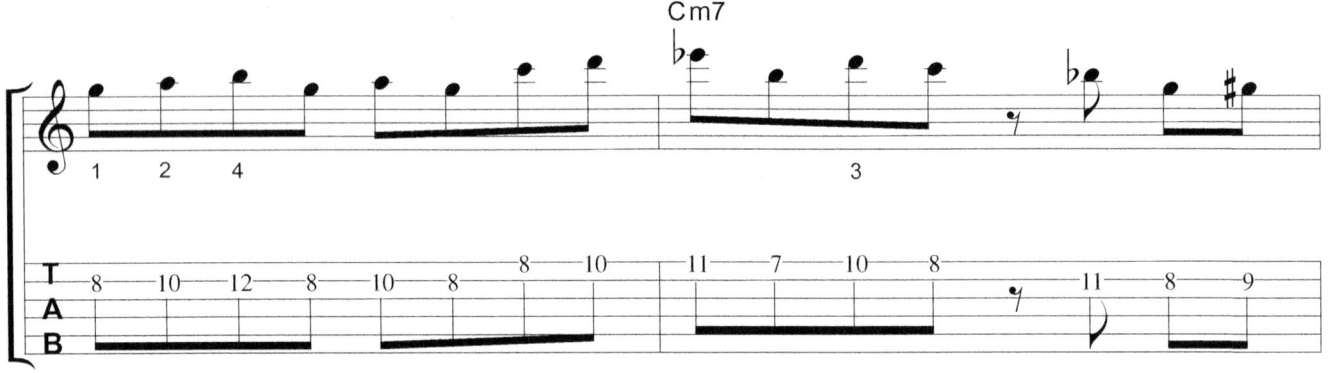

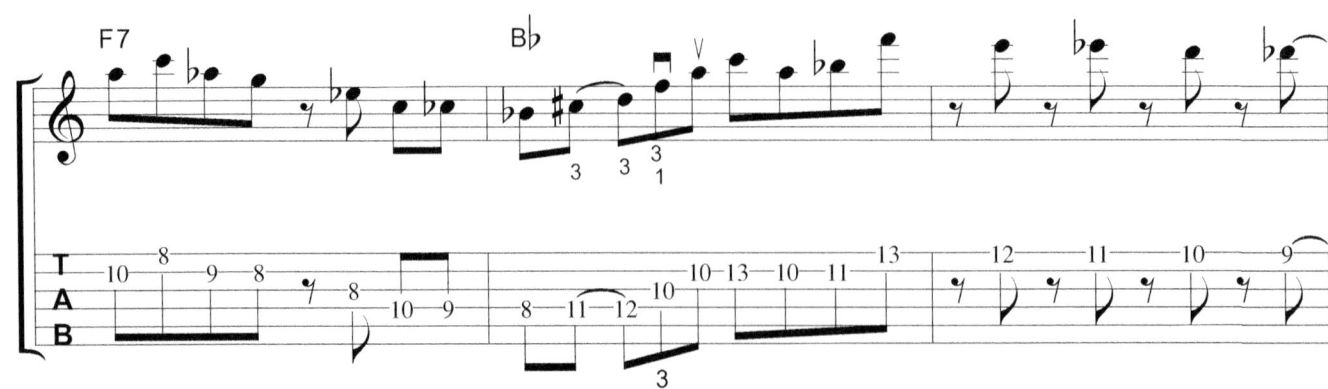

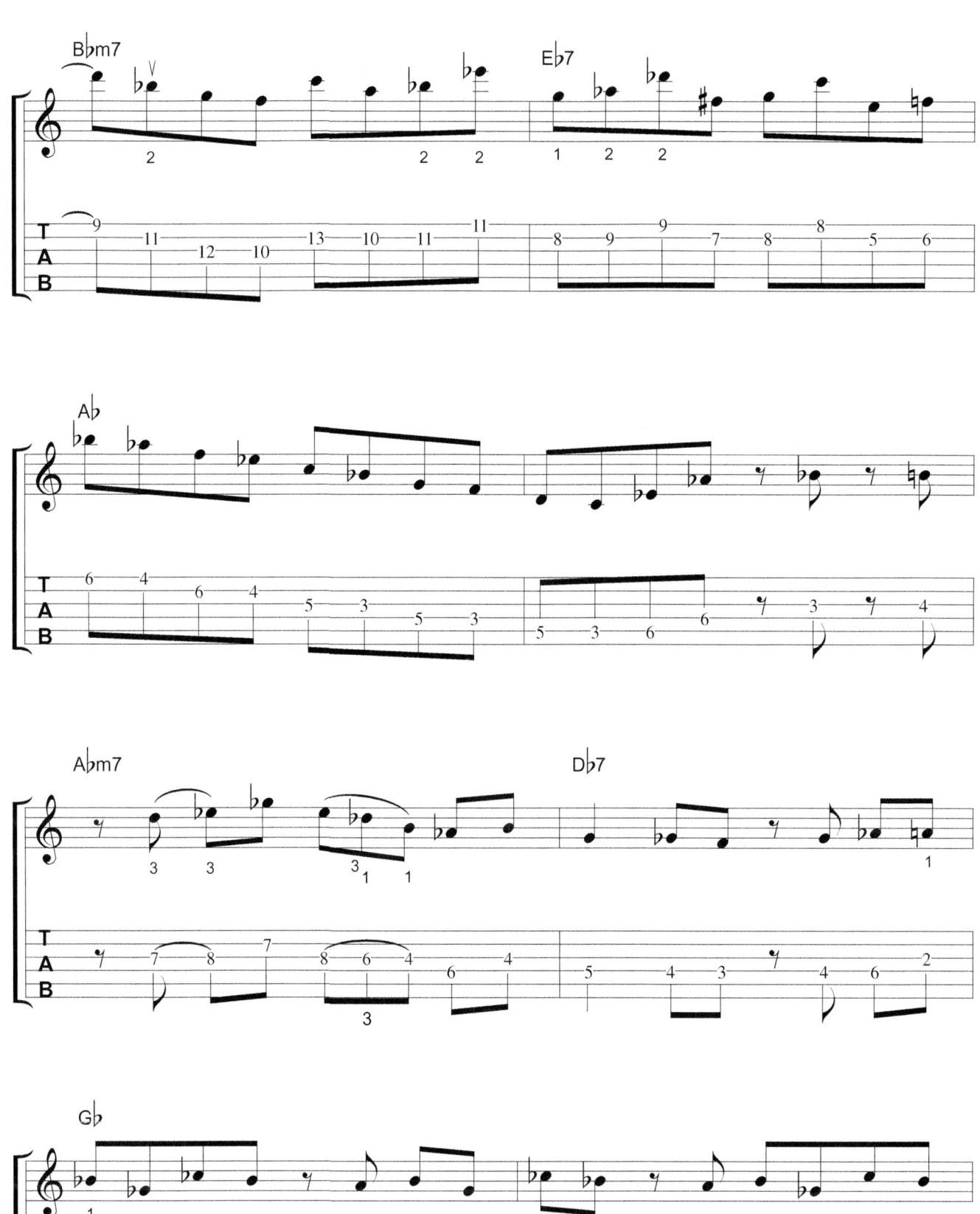

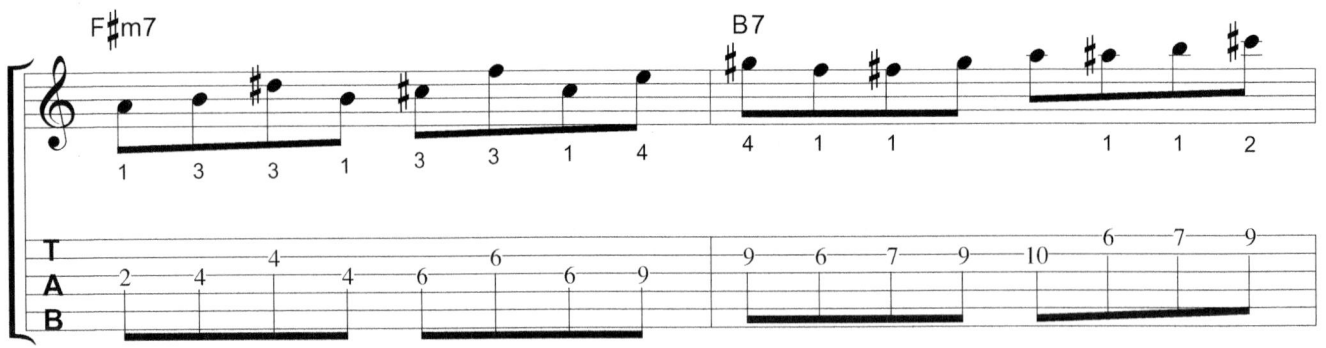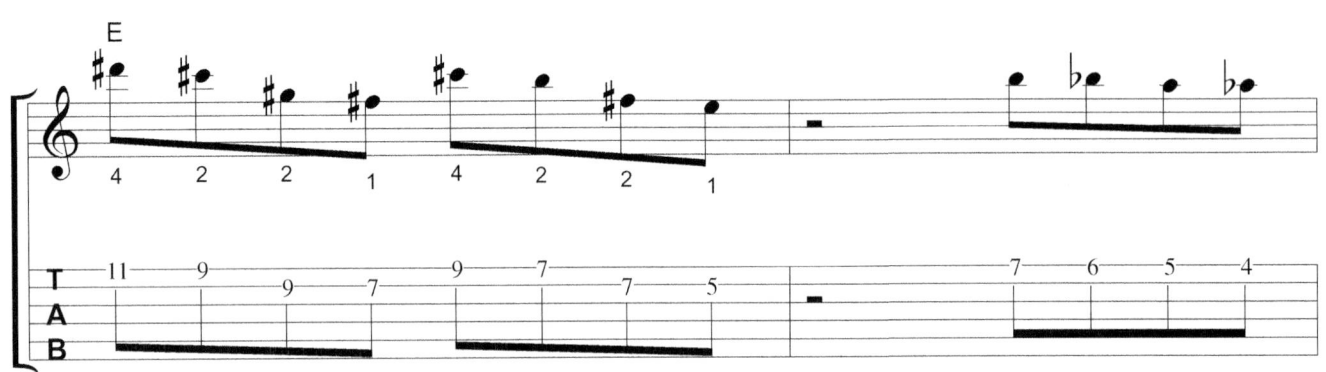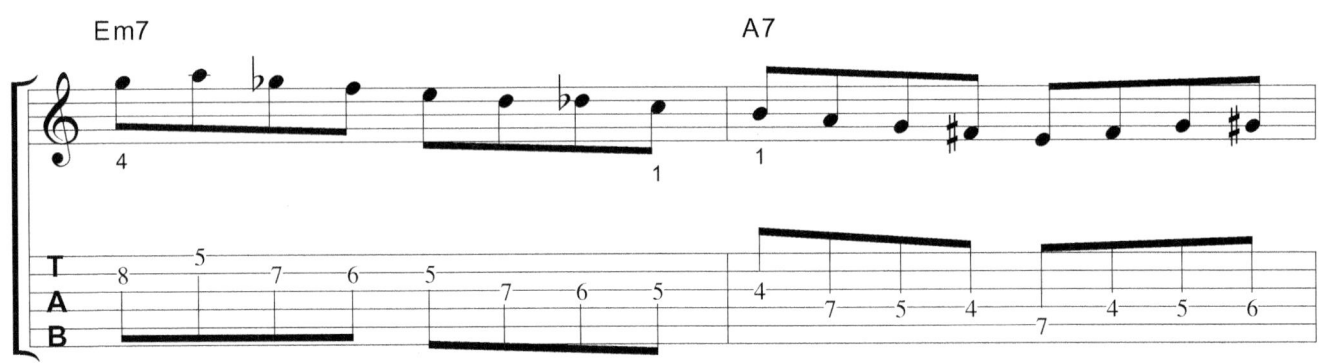

Here is a solo written to a chord progression similar to the chord changes of "Giant Steps."

Giant Steps Ahead

By Jerry Hahn

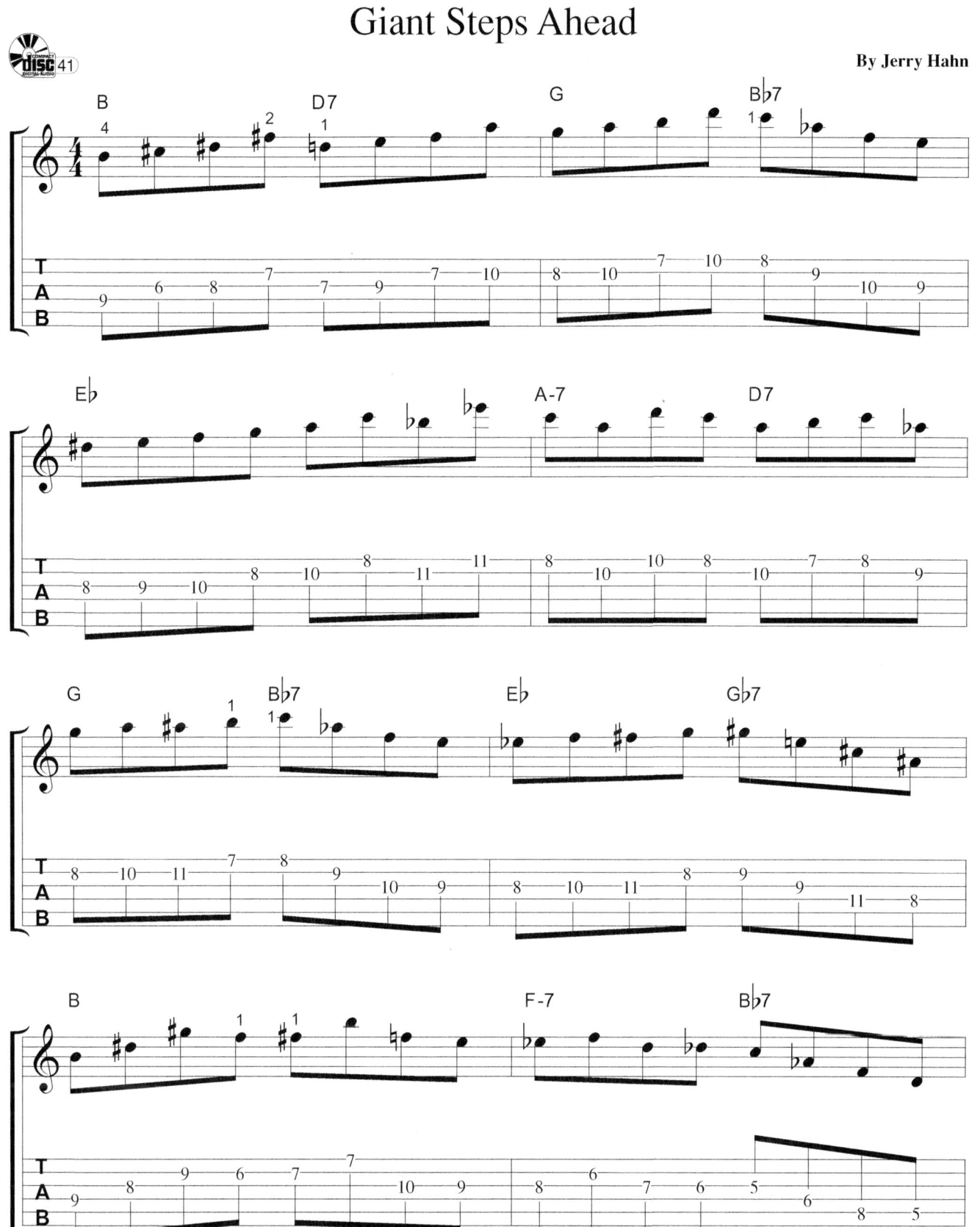

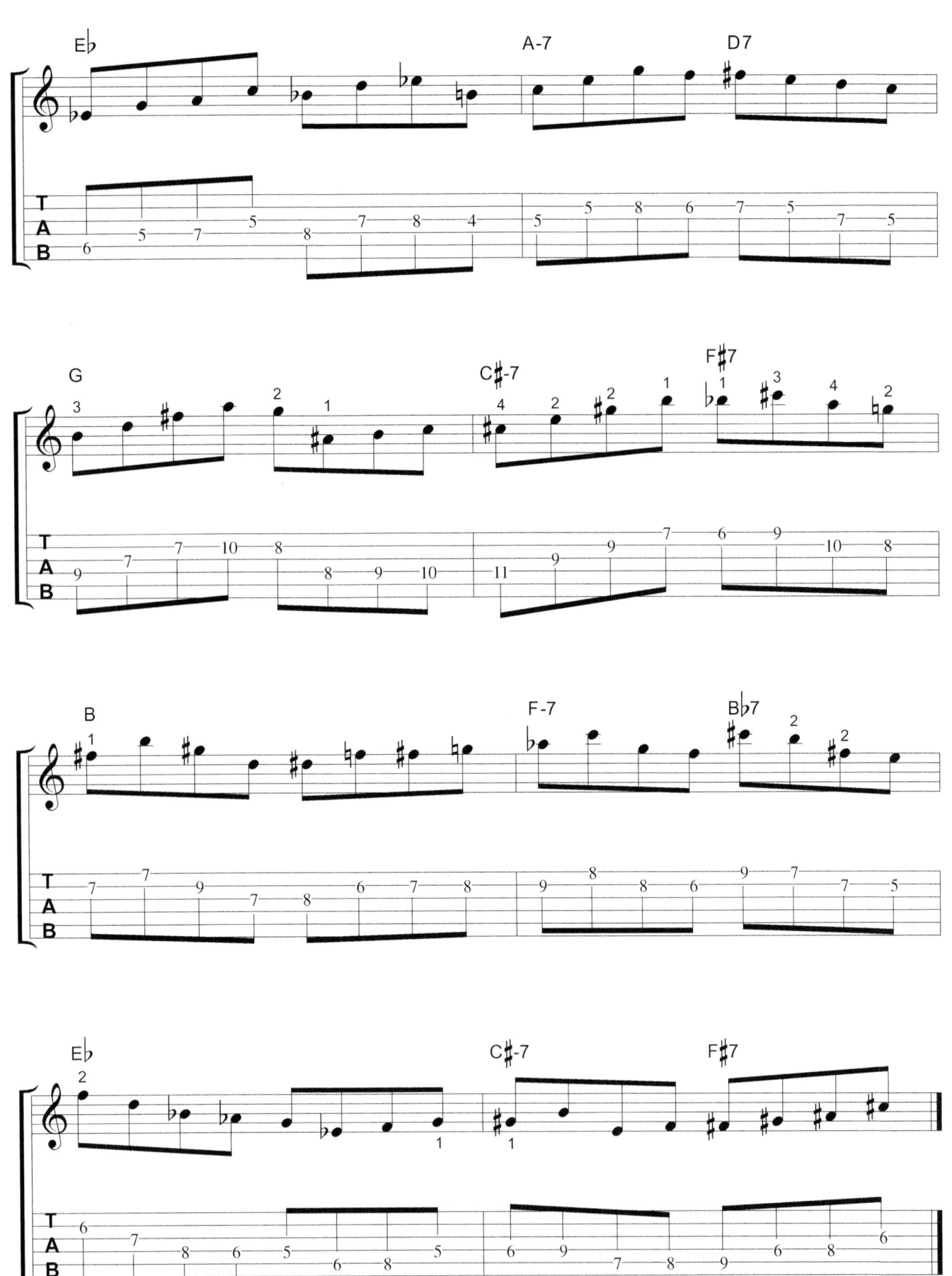

The first six measures of "Giant Steps Ahead" is very difficult to improvise on at a fast tempo, particularly the 1st and 2nd measure (B - D7 - G - Bb7) and the 5th and 6th measure (G - Bb7 - Eb - Gb7). Here is a solo to be played over the first six measures of "Giant Steps Ahead".

"Concert"

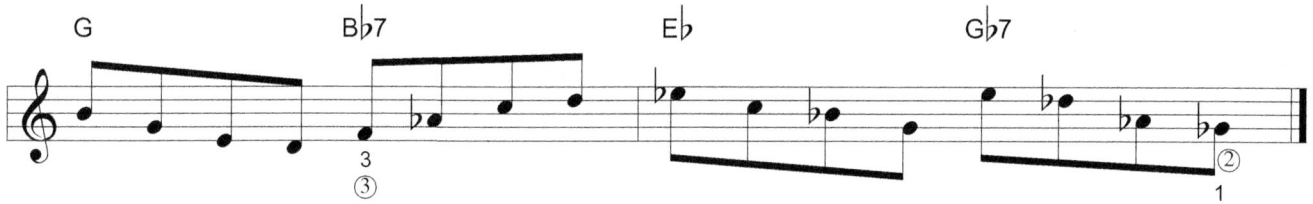

Here are some melodic ideas to be played over the 1st and 2nd measures of "Giant Steps Ahead."

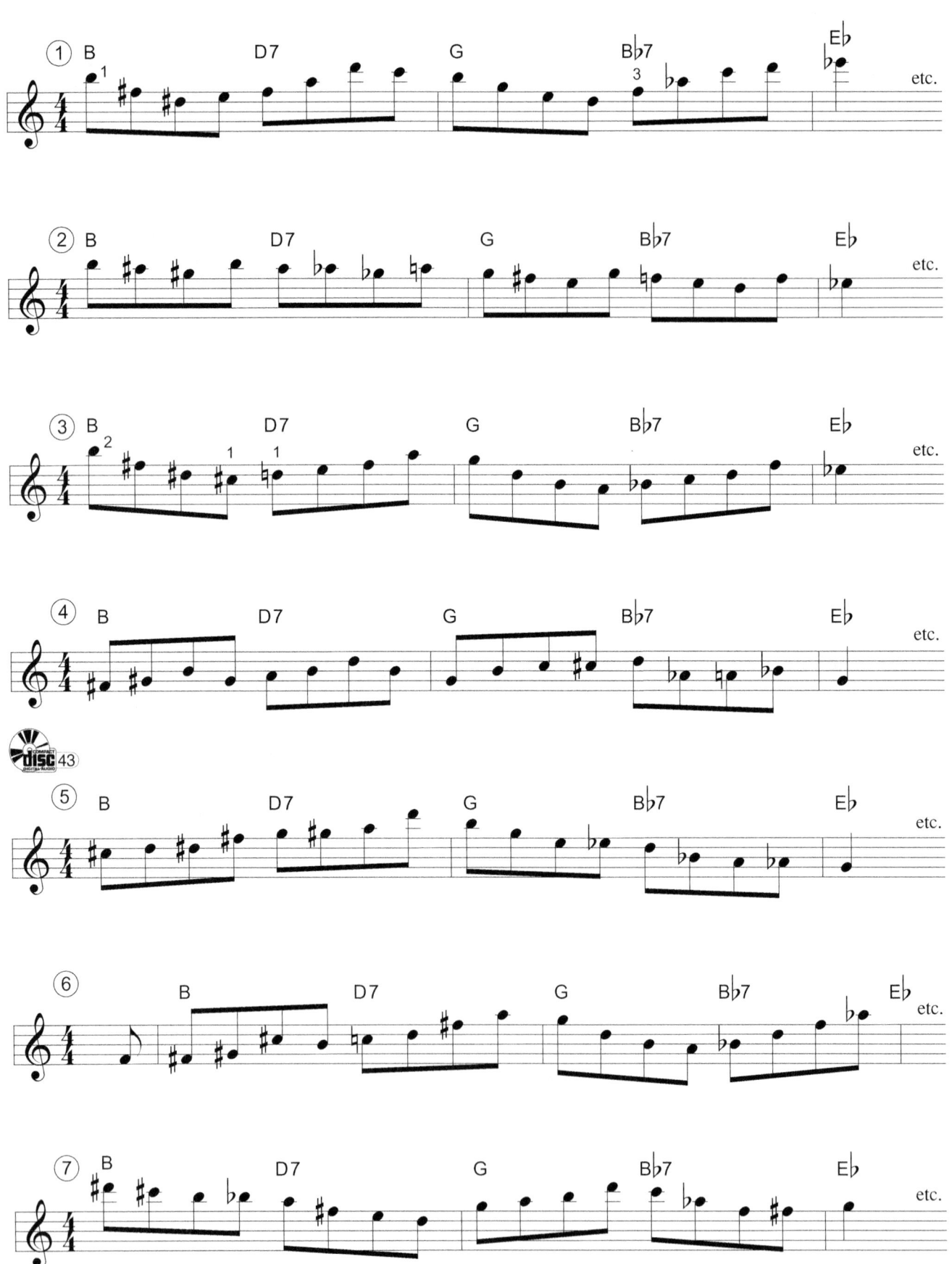

Here are some melodic ideas to be played over the 5th and 6th measure of "Giant Steps Ahead."

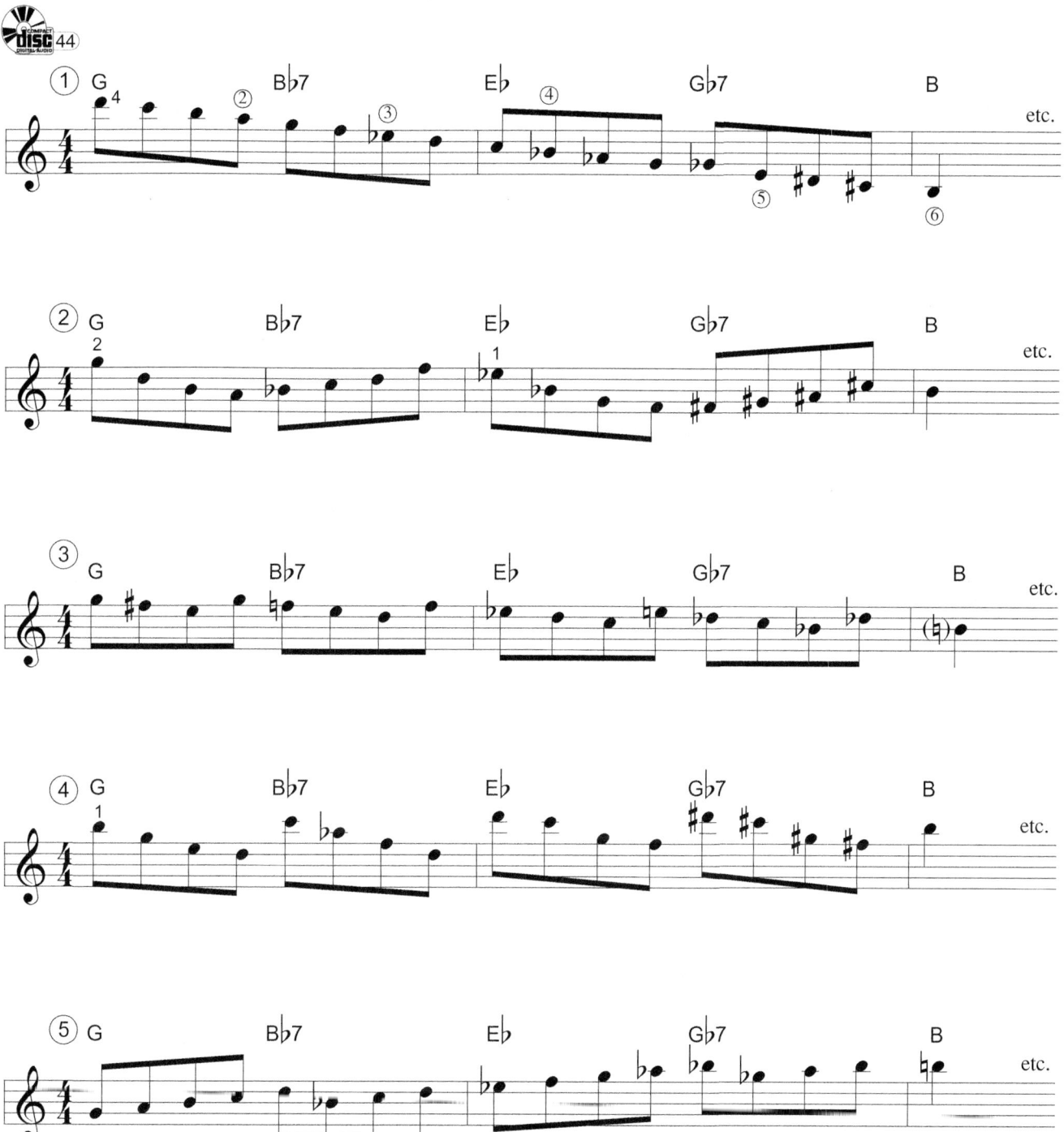

All the Things You're Not

Slow version

Fast version

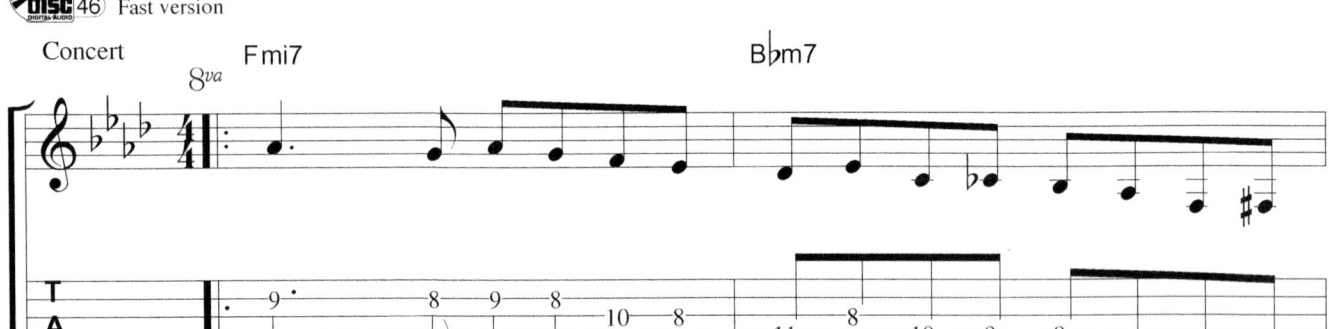

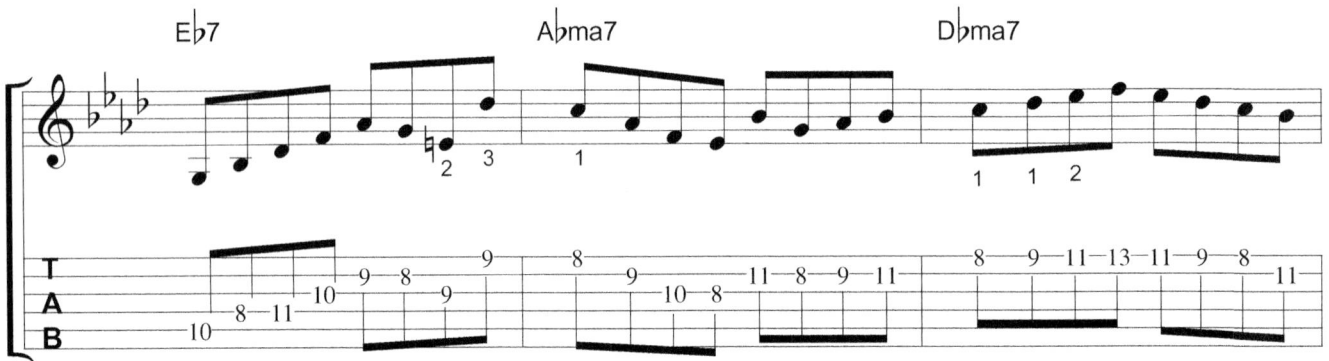

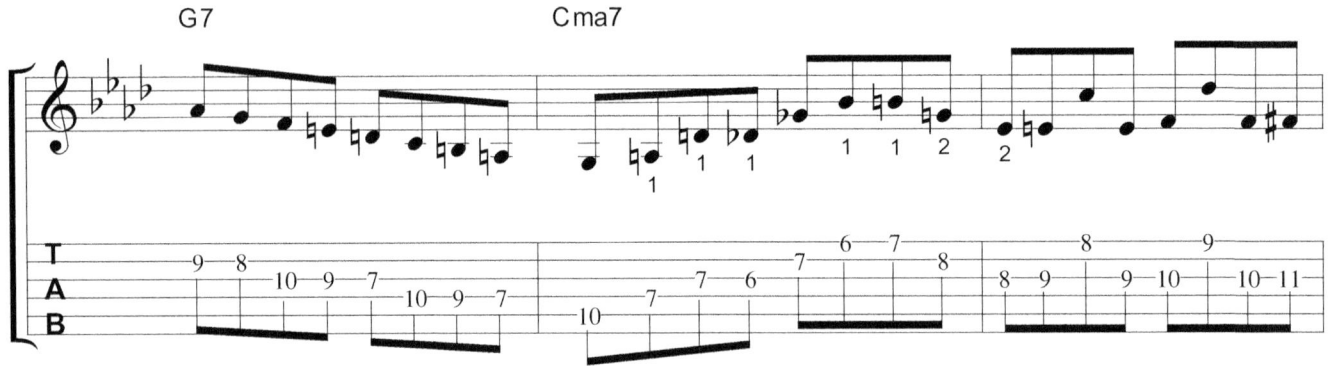

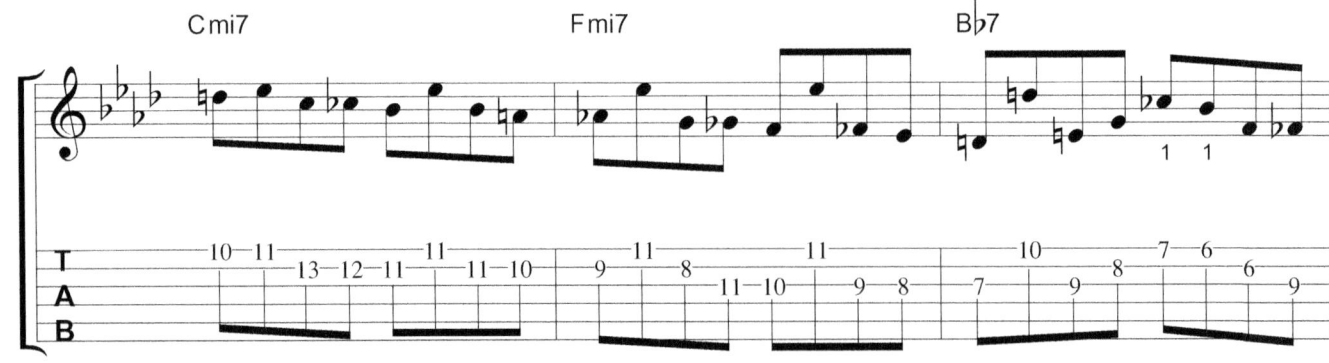

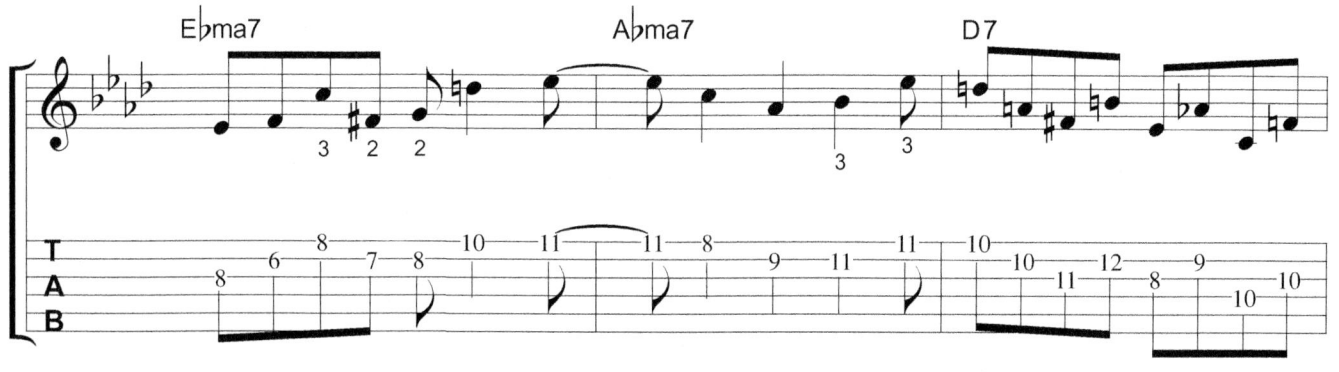
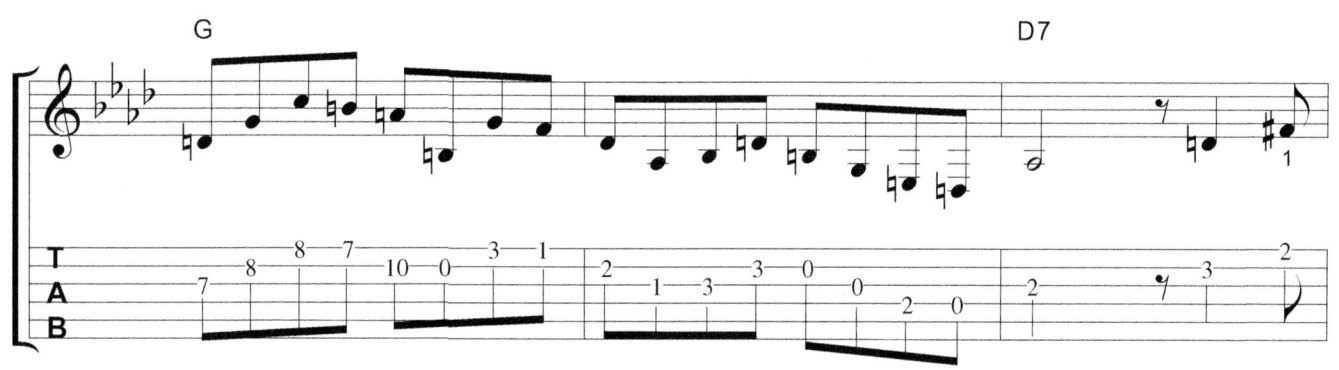

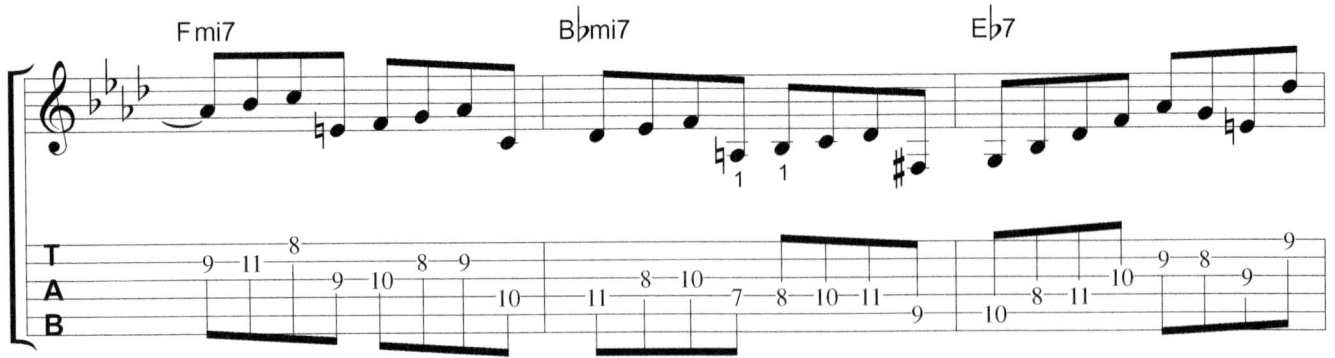
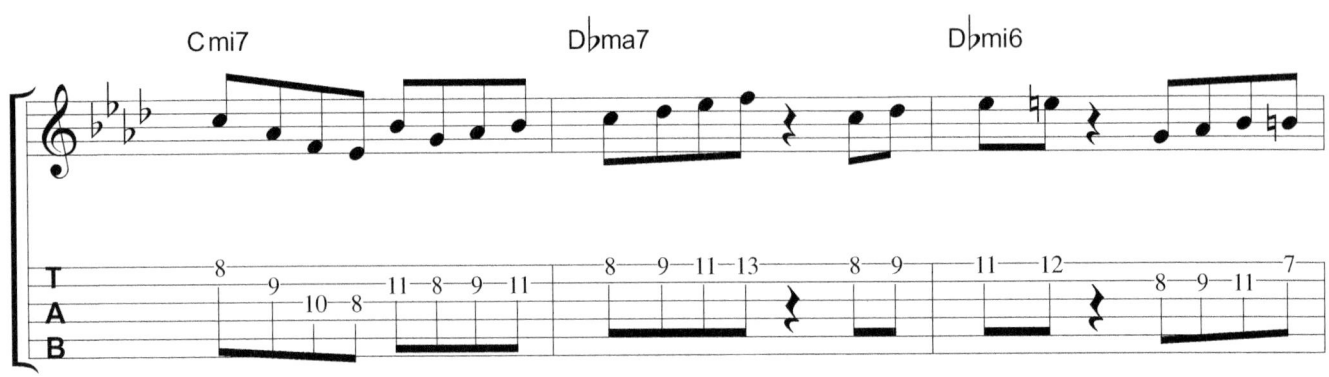
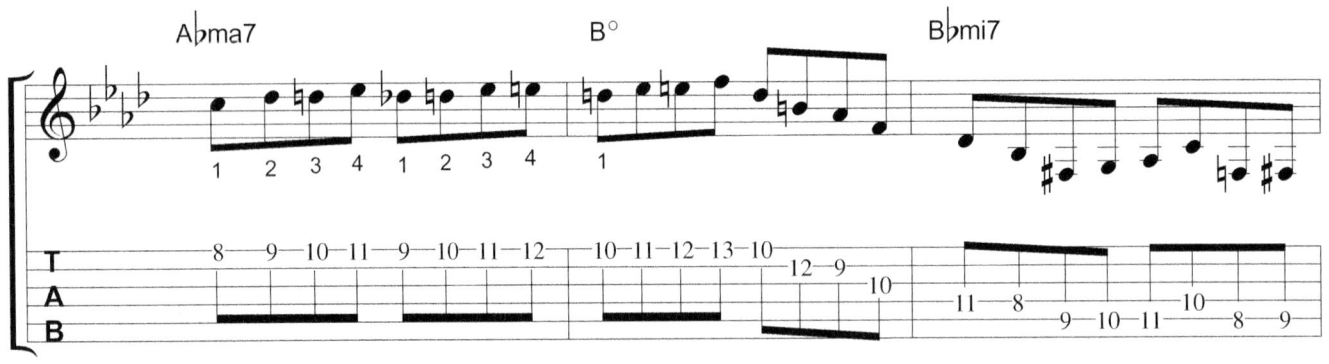
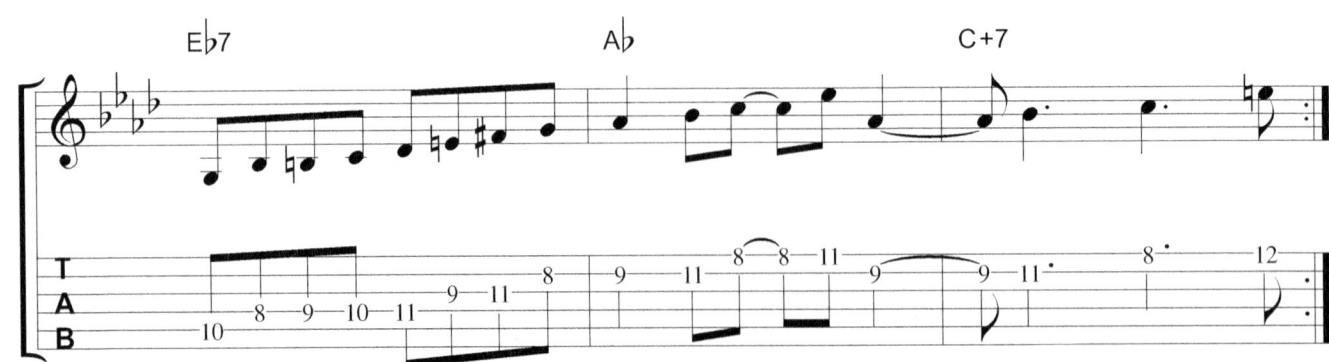

Joy Springtime

By Jerry Hahn

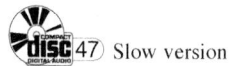 Slow version

 Fast version

 Original version

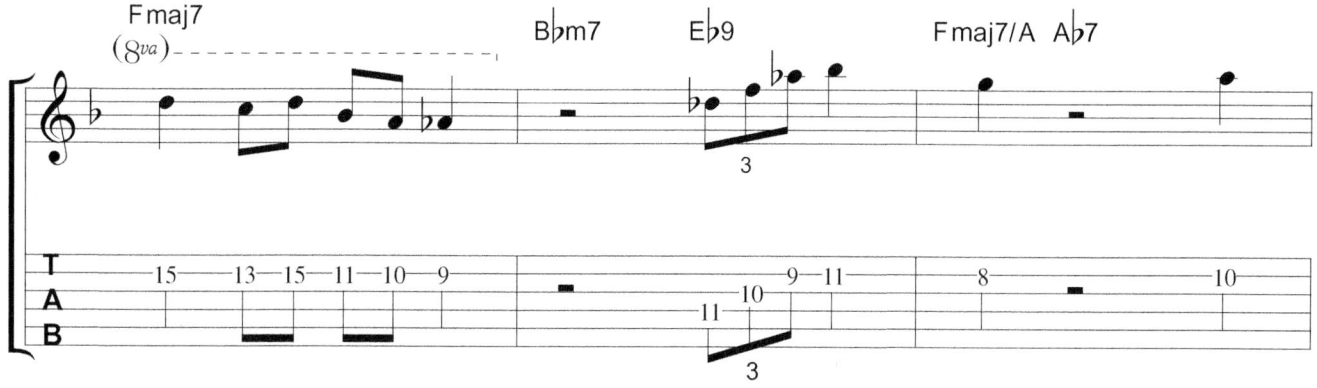
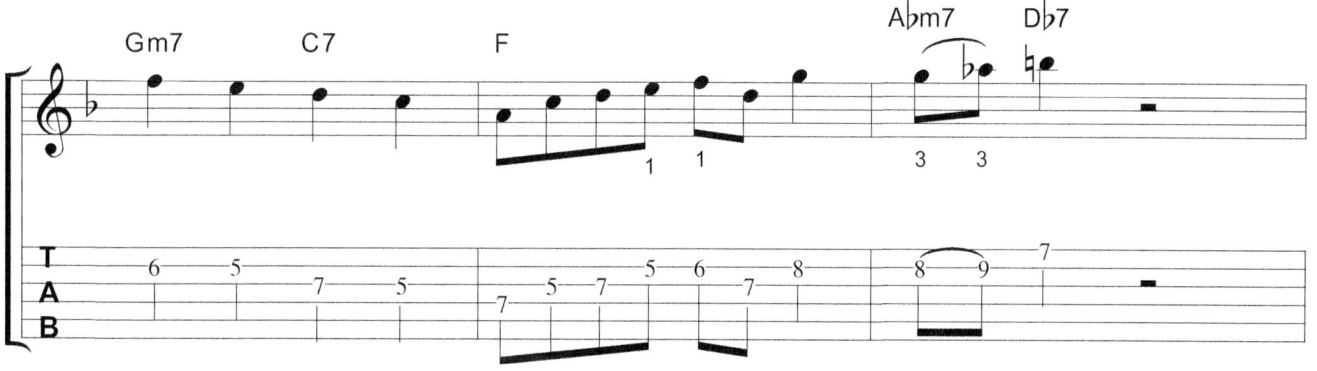
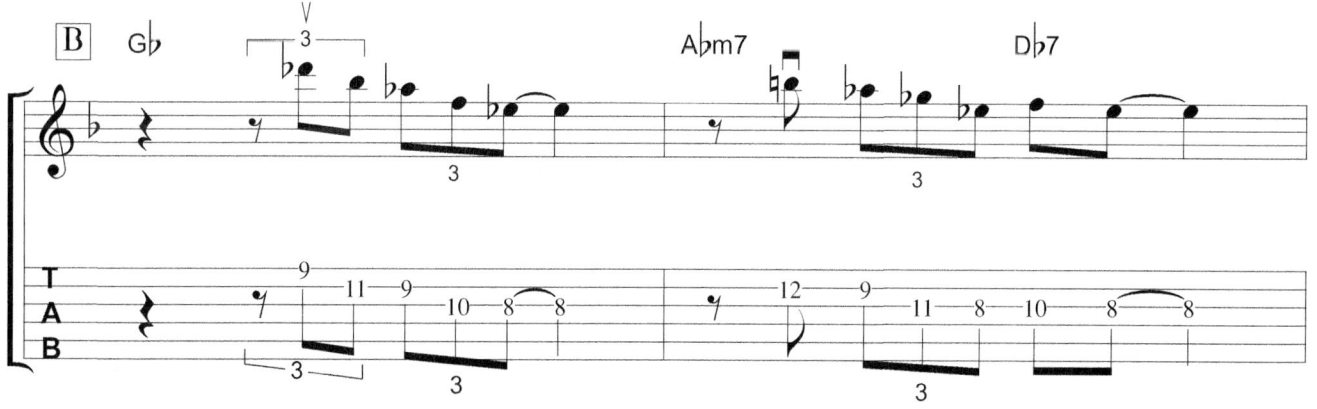

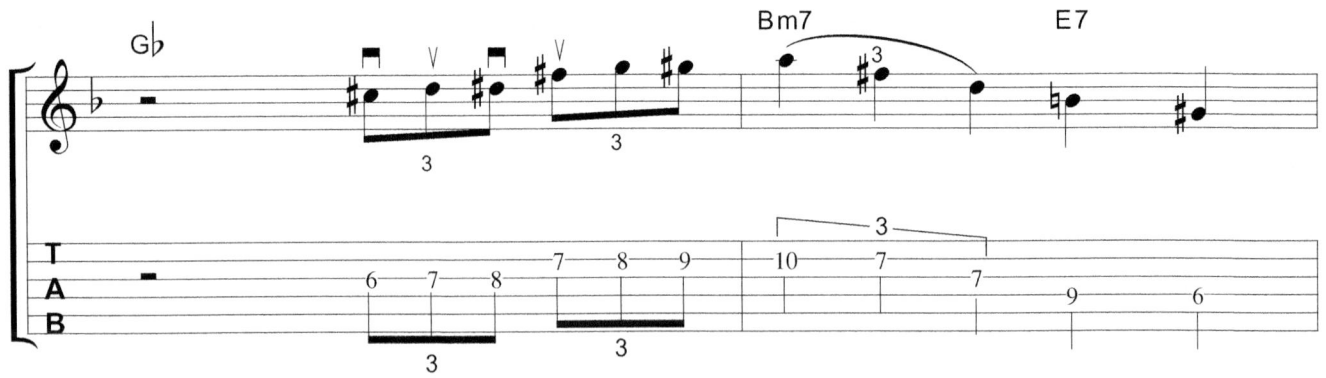
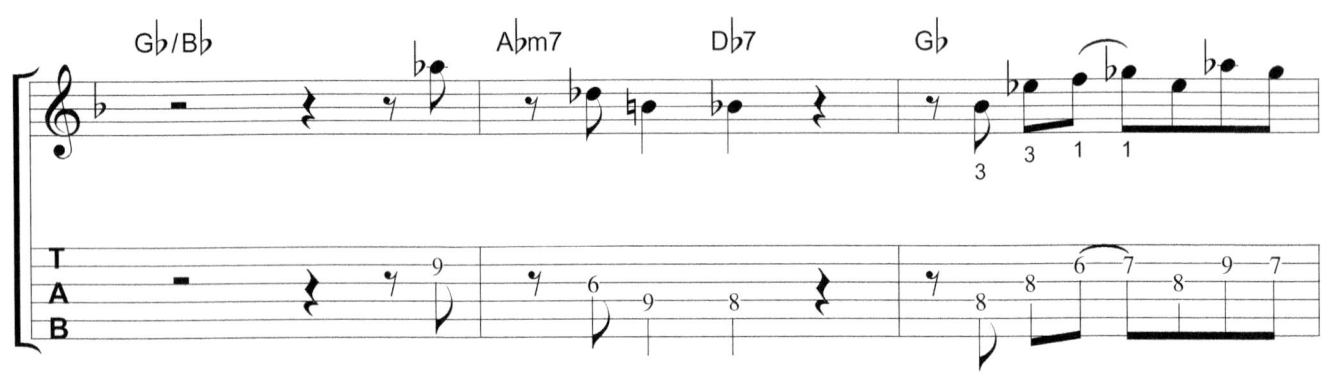
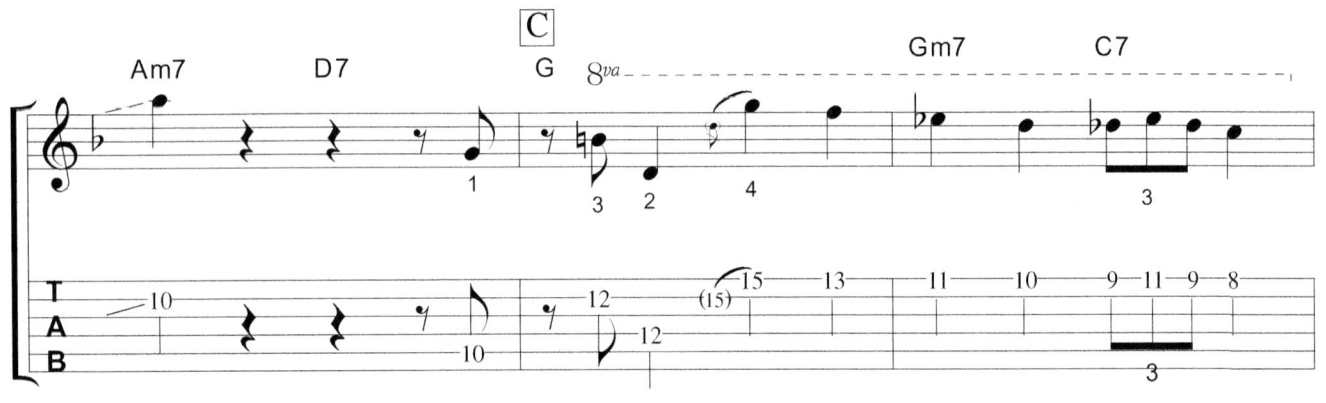
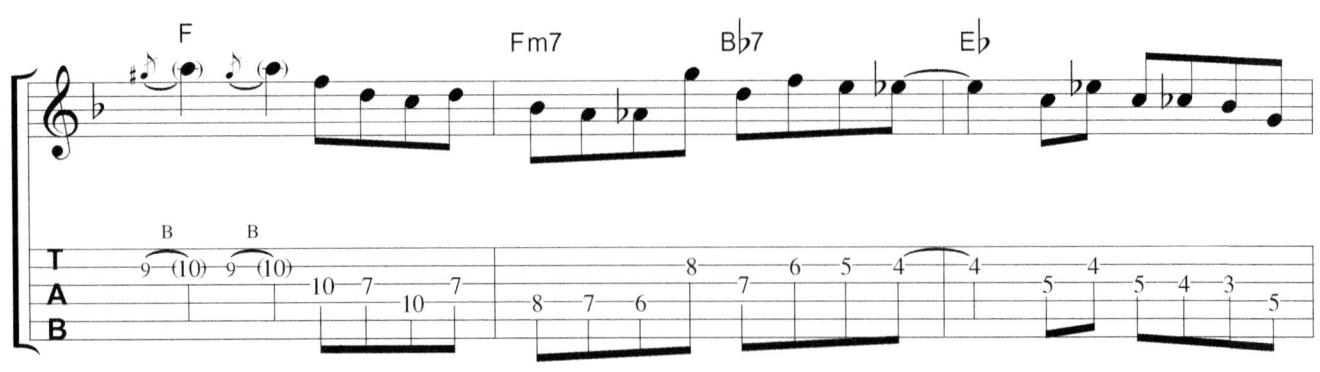

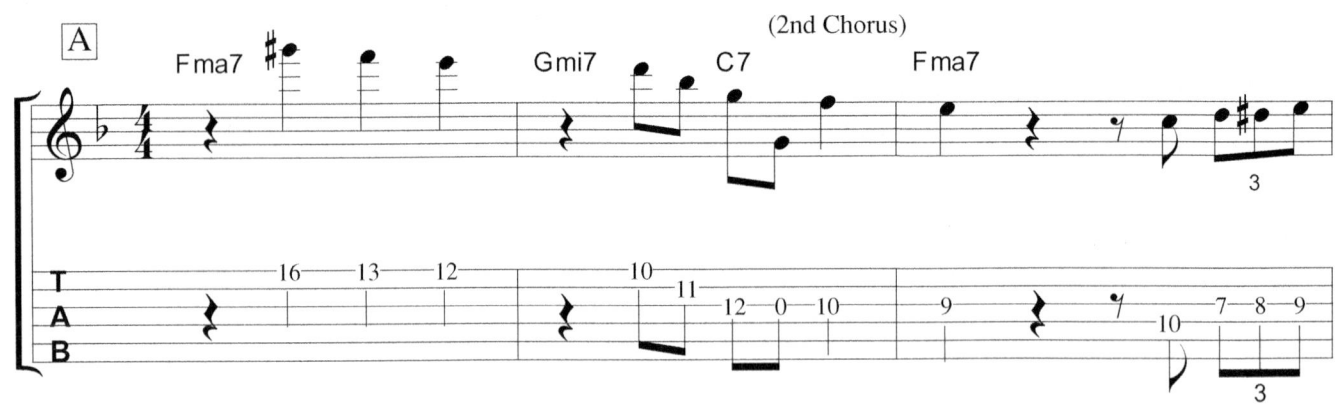
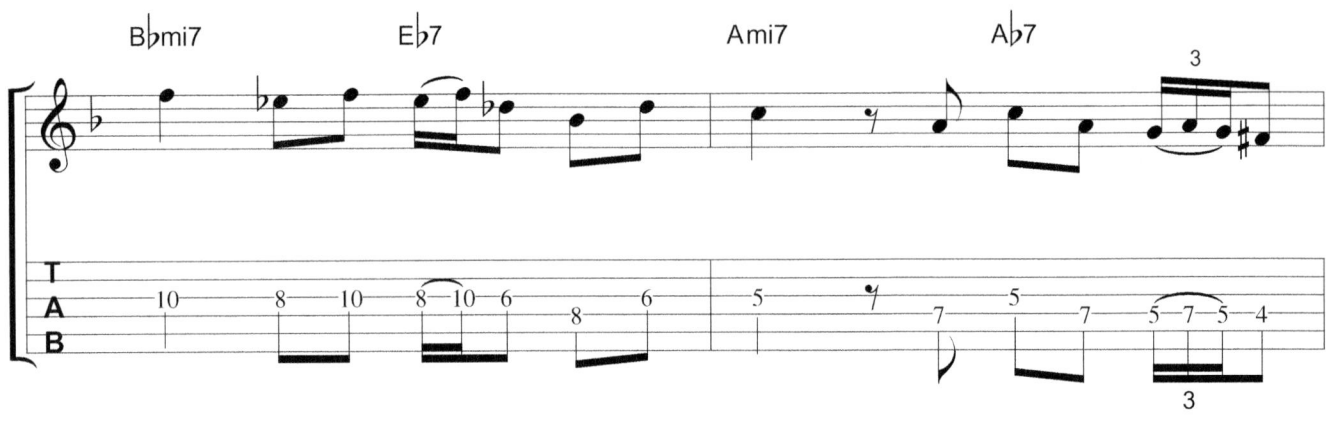
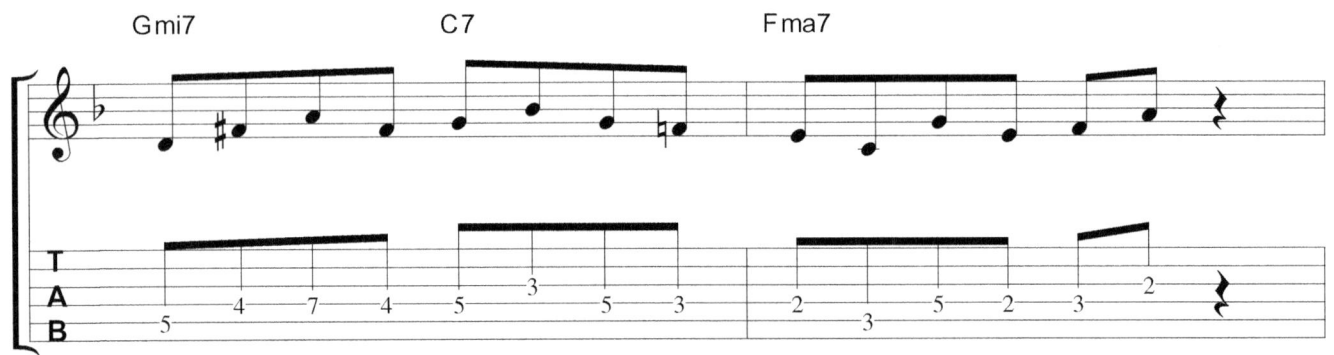
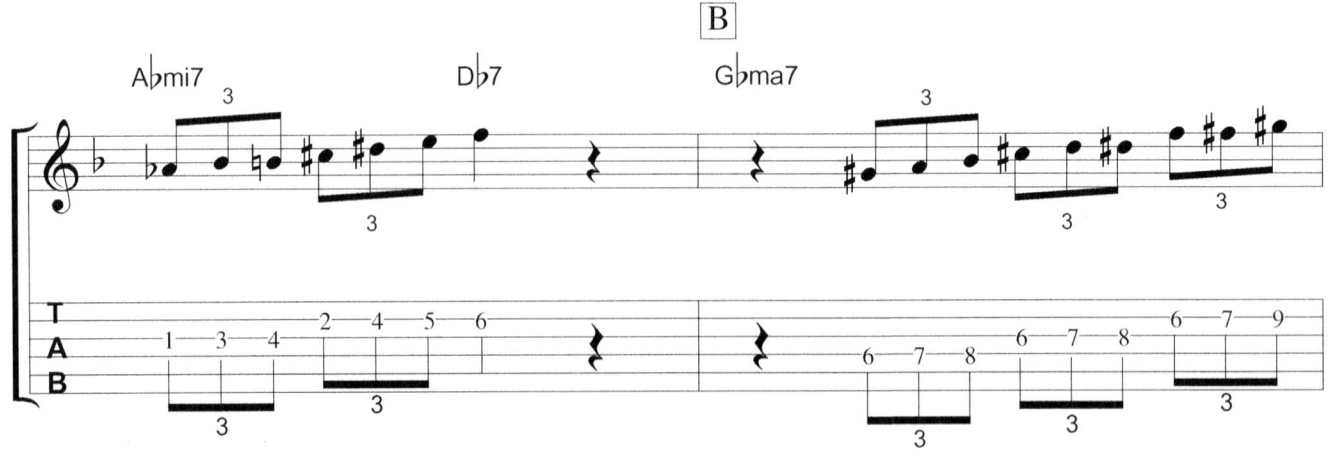

Rhythm Changes

Many of the bebop tunes that emerged out of the 40's and 50's via Charlie Parker, Dizzy Gillispie, Bud Powell and others were based on chord progressions from popular tunes of the day. It has been written that the record companies encouraged the jazz musicians to write their own melodies over the original progressions so that there would not be any royalties paid to the original composers. With the exception of the twelve bar blues, the most popular chord progression used was based on the tune "I Got Rhythm" by George Gershwin. Jazz tunes based on rhythm changes (jazz shorthand for the chord progression derived from "I Got Rhythm") are standard literature for the jazz musician. "Oleo" by Sonny Rollins, "Thriving On A Riff," and "Dexterity" by Charlie Parker are three tunes based on rhythm changes. Every aspiring jazz musician should learn to improvise over this progression which is one of the most difficult styles of jazz to master. The form of this progression is A - A - B - A. Many times the B section consisted of a chord progression without a melody. There are many chord voicings and substitutions possible within this progression. For instance, the second half of the first and third measure could be D♭7♭9, D♭7♯9, D♭7♭5, D♭7♯5, D♭m7, B°, G7♭9, G7♯9, G7♭5, G7♯5, Gm7 or any combination of these (ex. G7♯5♭9). If you were to add a G to the bottom of the B° chord it would then become a G7♭9 chord.

Study #1 contains two different styles of comping on rhythm changes. The chords of the first two A sections of Study #1 and all of the A sections of Study #2 are written in half-notes, but you should try to vary the rhythmic concept after becoming familiar with the progression. Harmonized bass lines dominate the B section as well as the last A section of Study #1. There are more examples of this type of rhythm playing in the "Harmonized Bass Lines" section.

Comping Rhythm Changes

Study #1

Comping Rhythm Changes

Part II

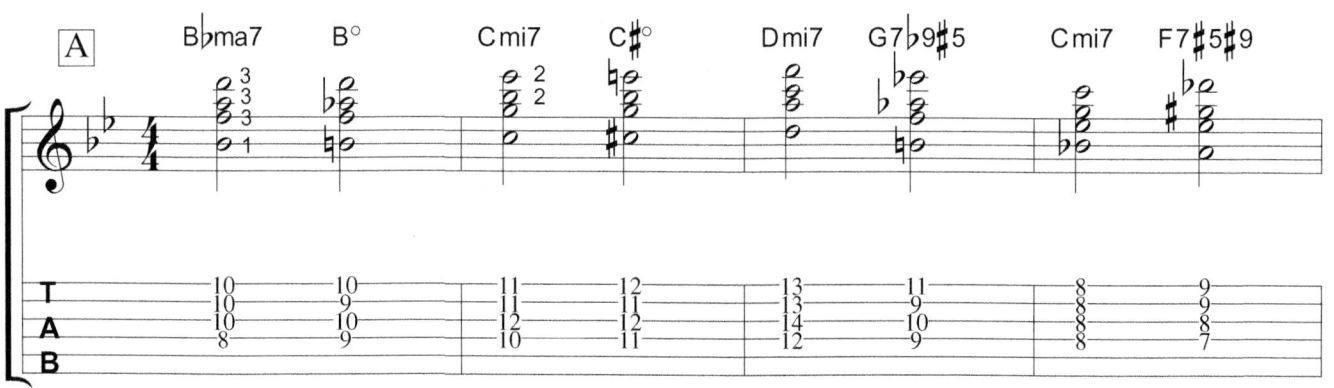
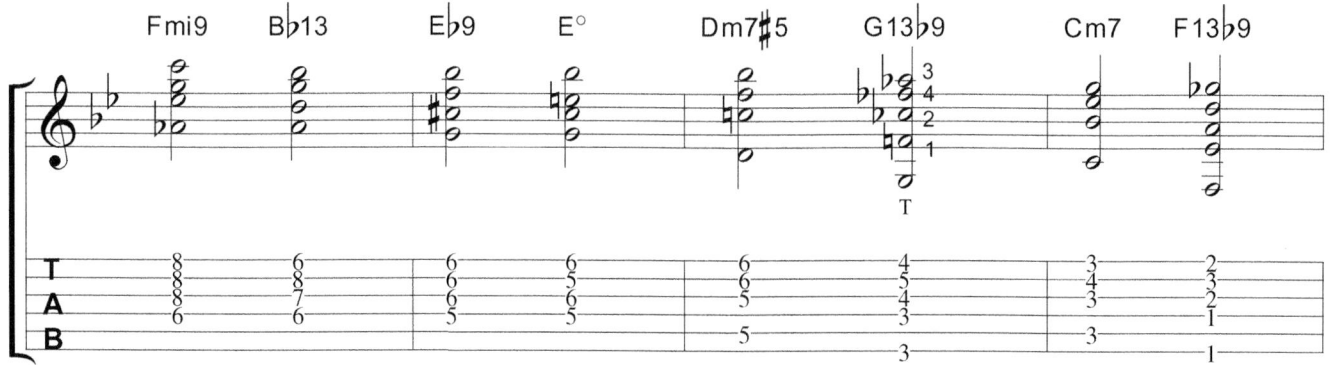
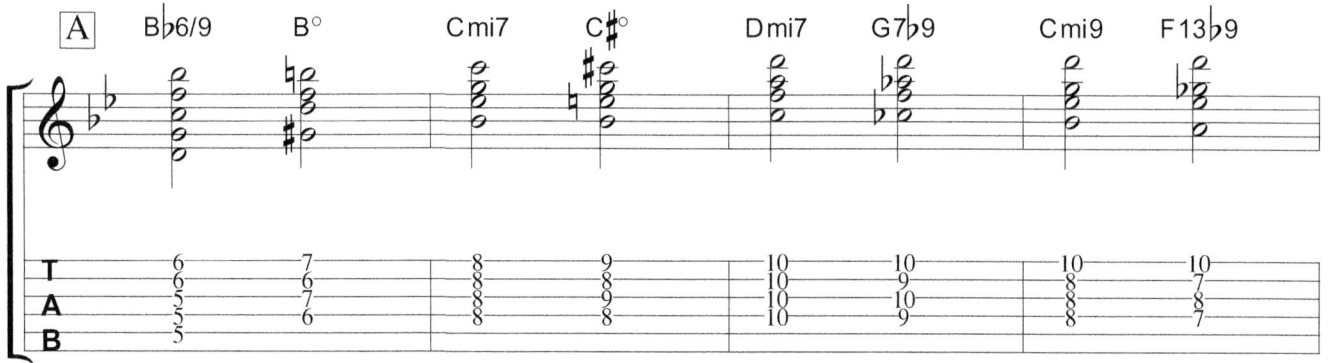
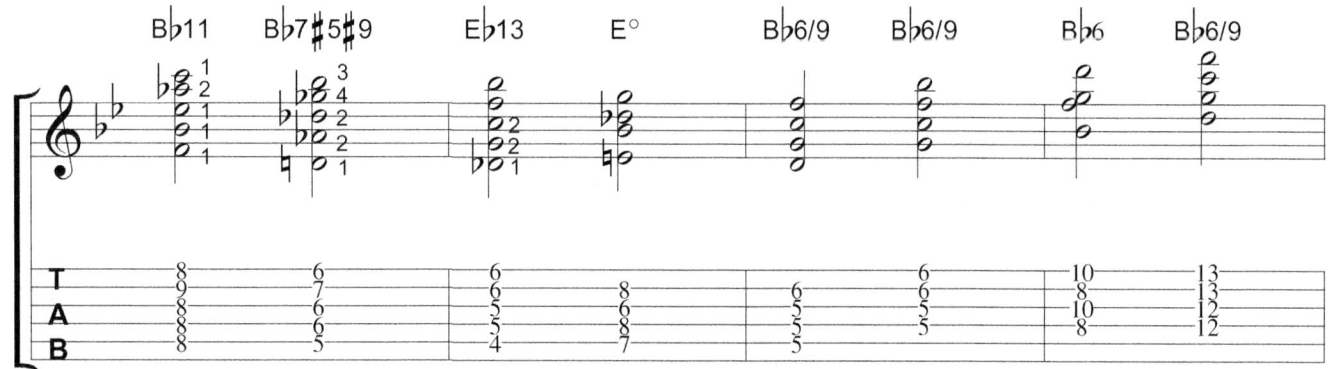

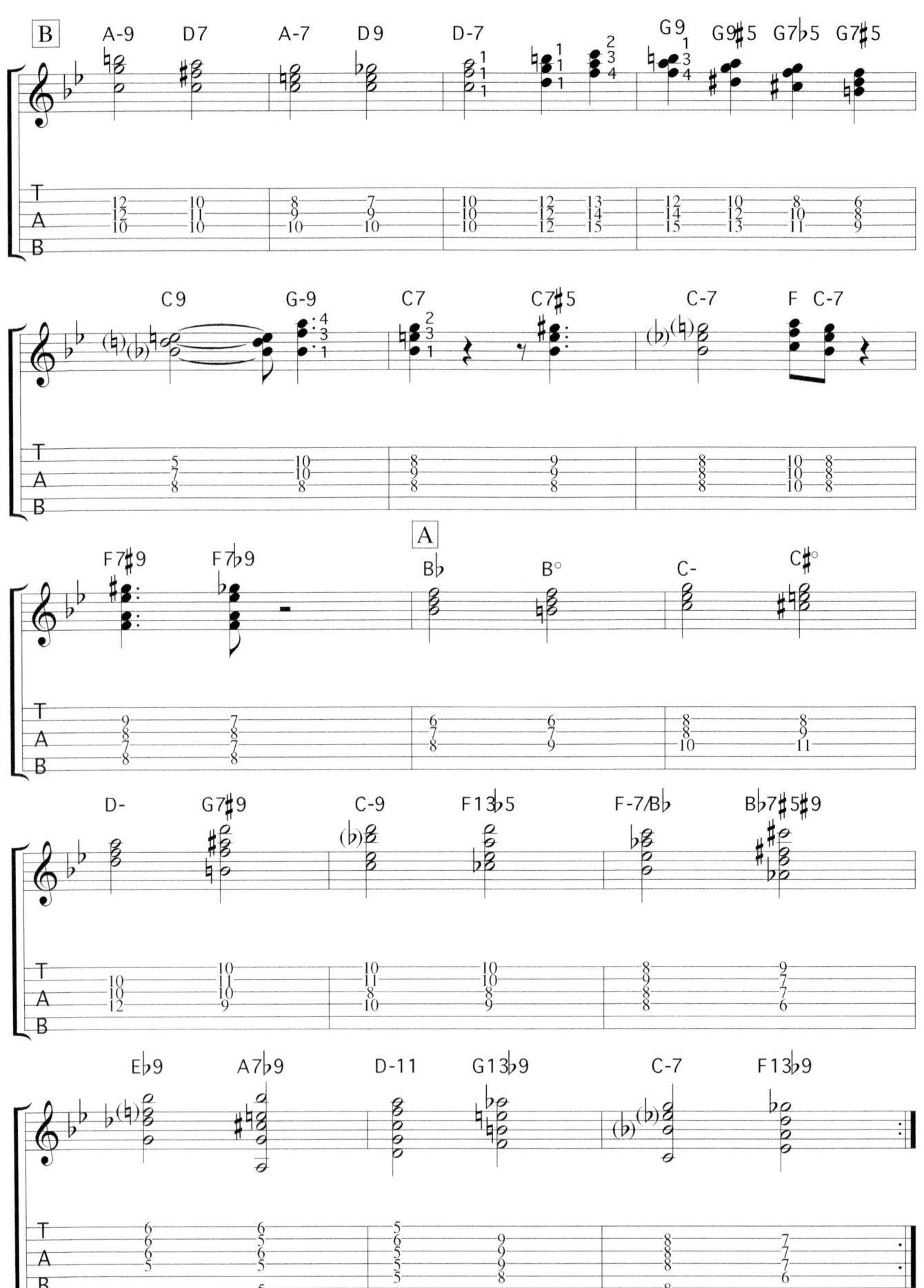

"Titus" is a rhythm changes tune in which I have included some substitute changes along with the basic changes. The melody for the "B" section is to be improvised.

Titus

By Jerry Hahn

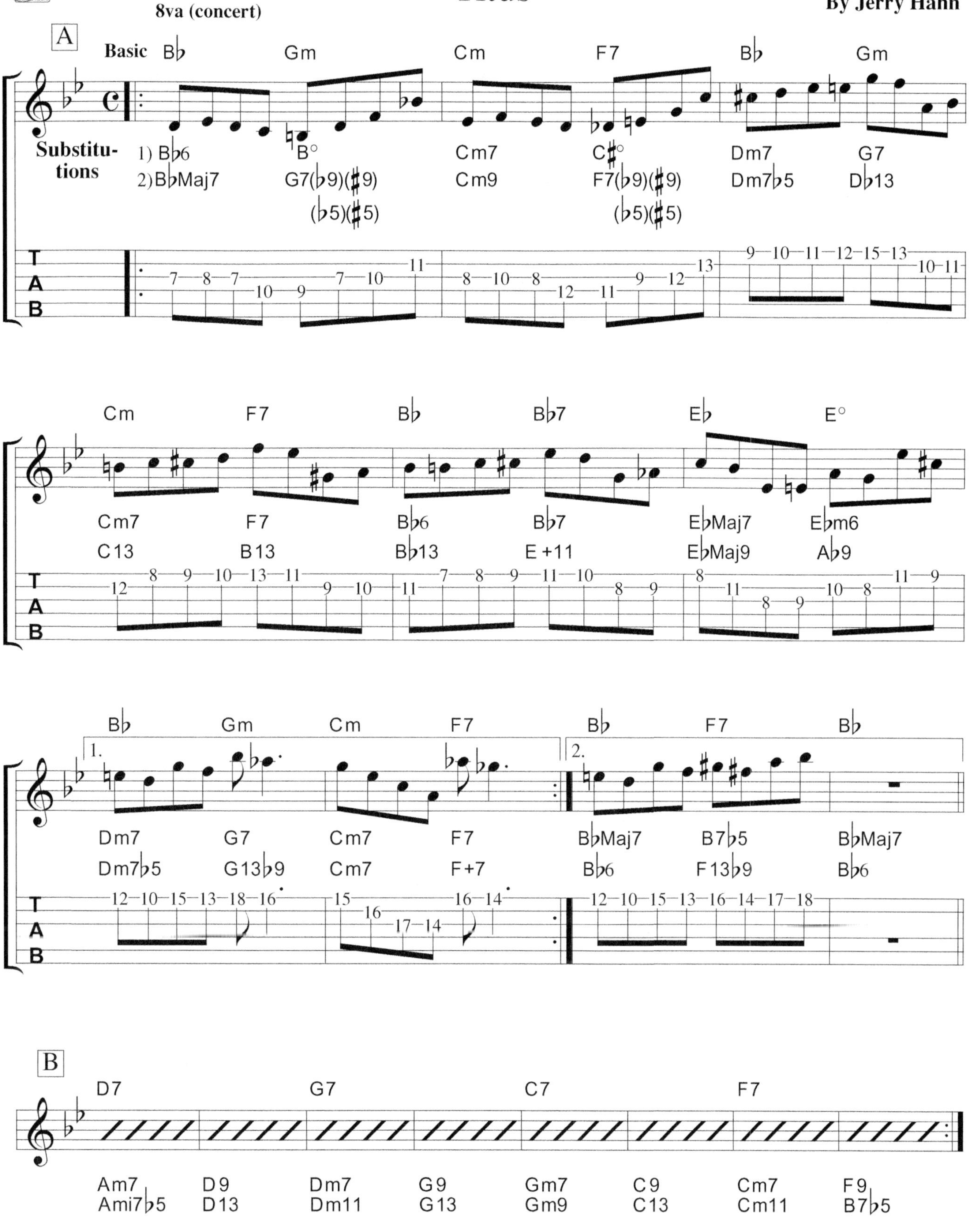

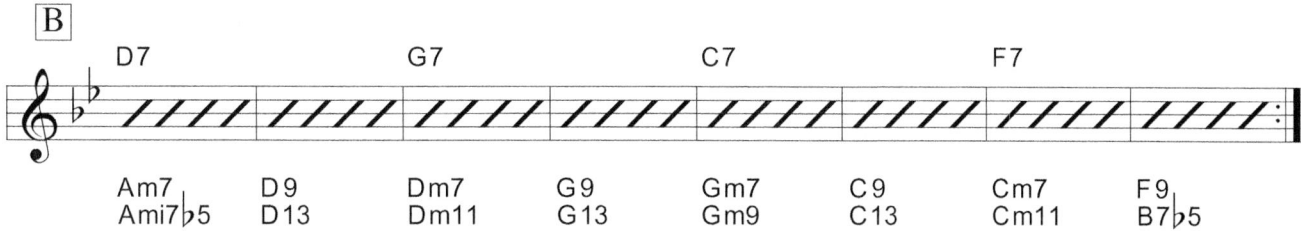

D.C. first 8 bars and take second ending.

Rhythm Changes Solo

53 Slow version

54 Fast version

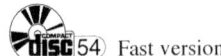

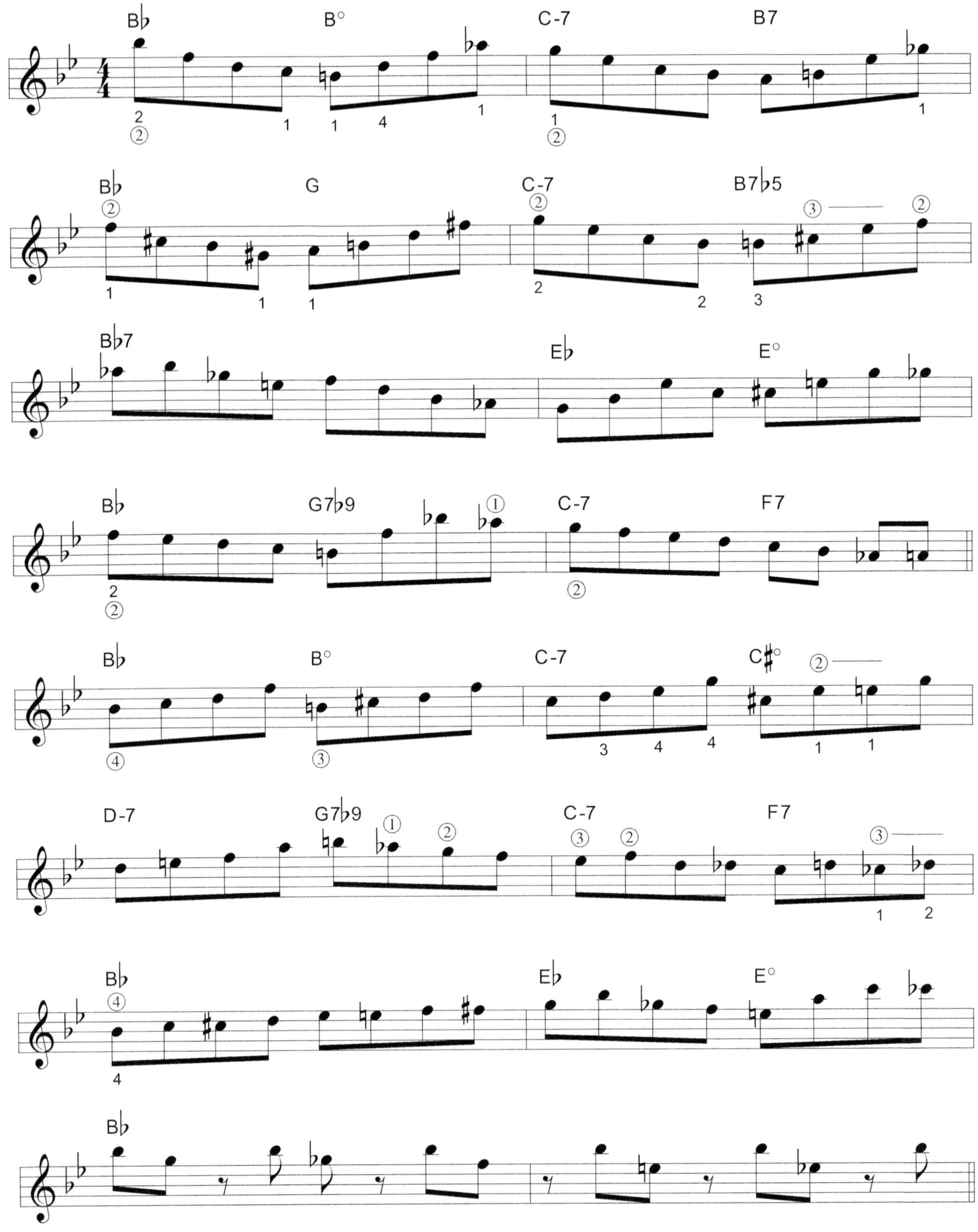

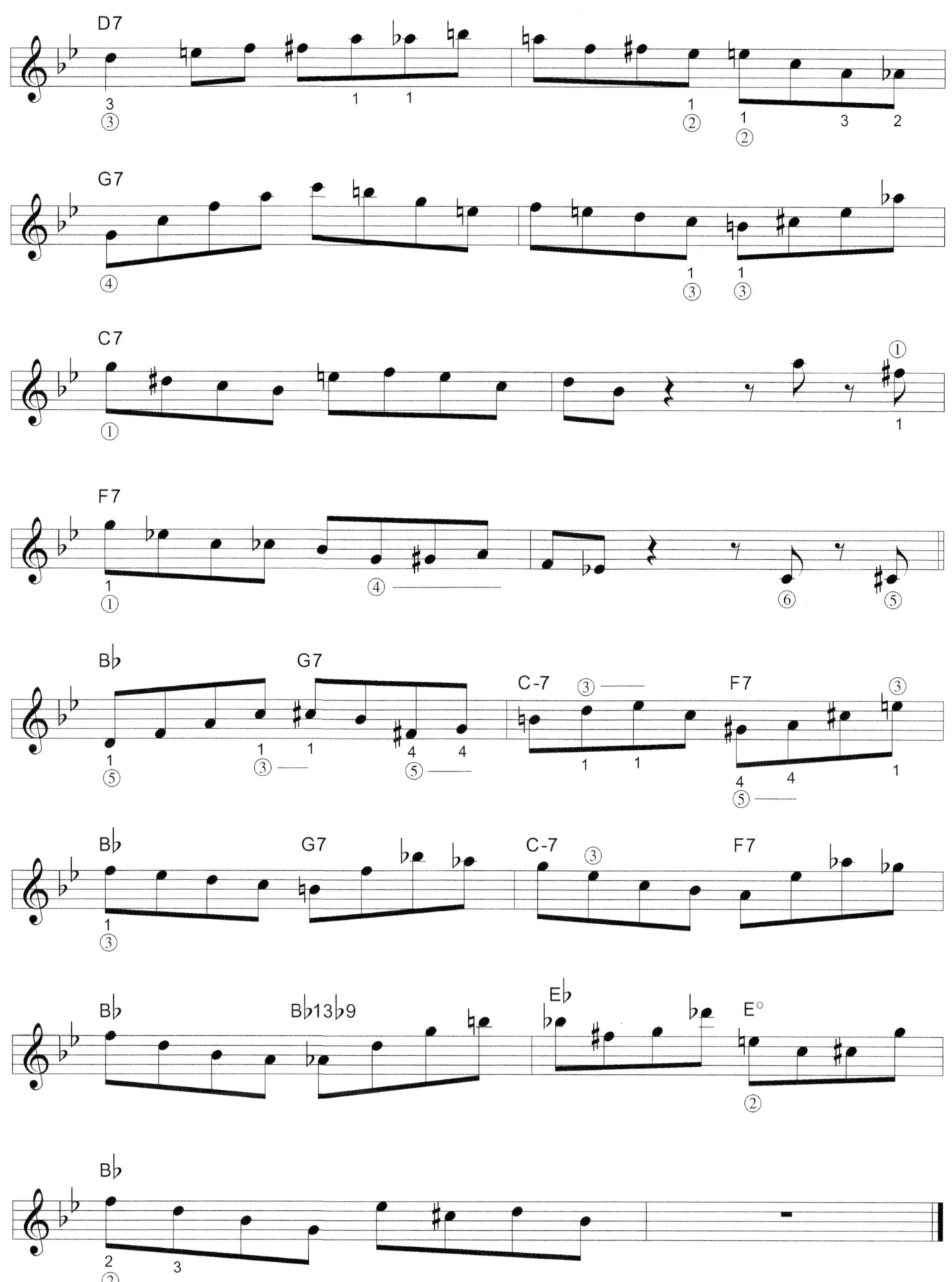

Here are some melodic ideas to be played over the 1st and 2nd measure of rhythm changes. These patterns can be applied to the 3rd and 4th measure as well.

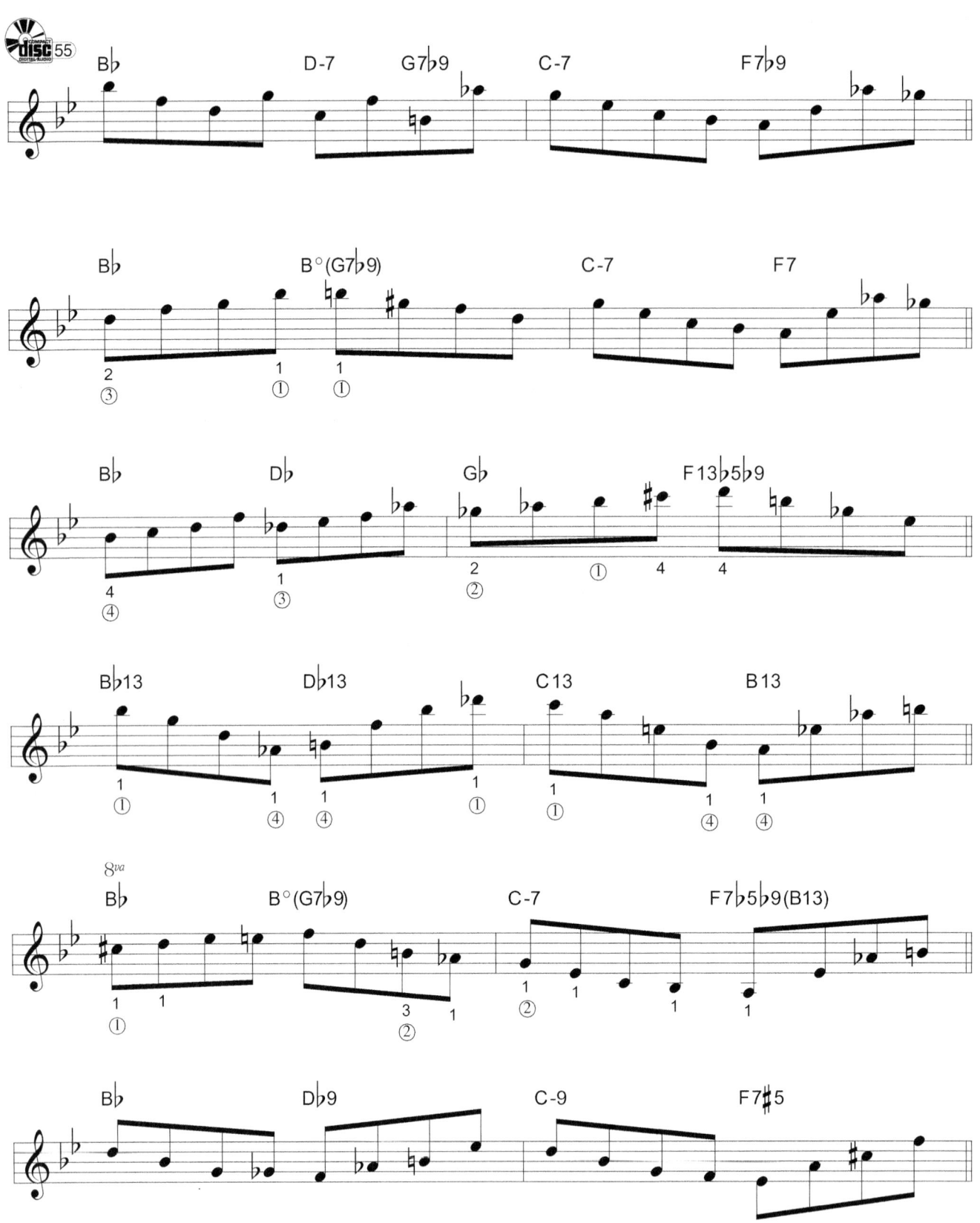

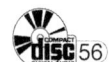

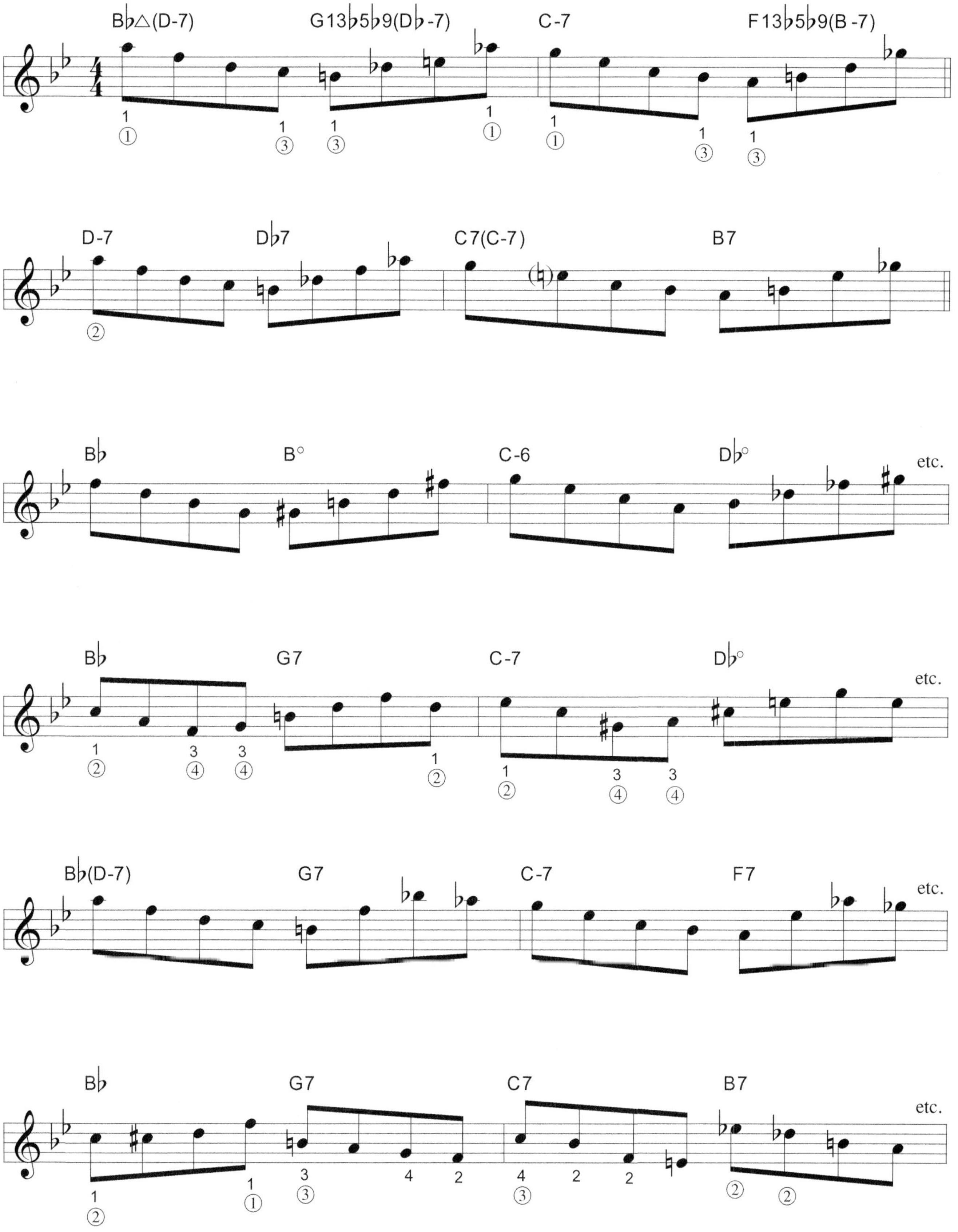
B♭△(D-7) G13♭5♭9(D♭-7) C-7 F13♭5♭9(B-7)
D-7 D♭7 C7(C-7) B7
B♭ B° C-6 D♭° etc.
B♭ G7 C-7 D♭° etc.
B♭(D-7) G7 C-7 F7 etc.
B♭ G7 C7 B7 etc.

Chord Forms

Memorizing the chord changes to the tunes I have listed is an excellent way to gain fingerboard knowledge. Here are the chord voicing variations that a guitarist would need to know to play the chord changes to most any tune. All of these chords are written in the first five frets and are moveable because there are no open strings. The letter "R" indicates which string the root is played on (example - the root of Gmi7 is the note "G"). All of the chords can be transposed to any key by finding the fret of the desired root present. In a group context the bass player supplies the root most of the time. Notice that some chords have more than one name.

When there is a chord such as E/G#, which is two letters (E and G#) separated by a diagonal line, the top left letter (E) is the name of the chord and the bottom right letter (G#) is the bass note. When there is a chord such as $\frac{F\#}{C}$, which is two letters (F# and C) separated by a horizontal line, this represents a polychord (an F# triad over a C triad). A polychord is two or more chords played at once.

Chord Symbols

Since there is a lack of standardization in chord notation, everyone should become aware of all of the chord symbols currently in use. Some of the chords on the chord pages (137 - 140) have two symbols which are currently in use. A triangle (△) usually represents a major 7th. A minus sign (-) is used for a minor chord. Sometimes a minus sign is used incorrectly to represent a flat sign (e.g. C7-9). A plus sign (+) is recommended only for augmented chords (i.e. chords with a #5). It is occasionally used as a sharp sign (e.g. C7+9). In jazz theory, there is no difference between ° and °7. A half-diminished sign (ø) represents a minor 7th b5 chord.

Major

G   D   C   A   E/G♯ (3rd in Bass)

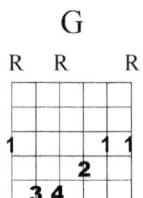 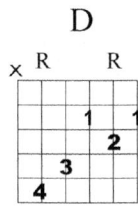 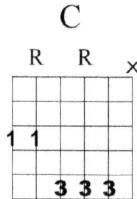 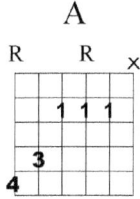 

G6   D6   G△ / Gma7   C△ / Cma7   D△ / Dma7

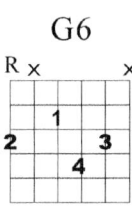 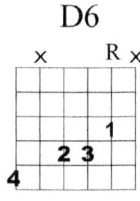 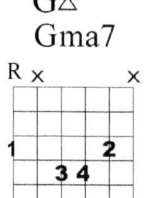 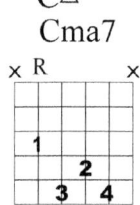 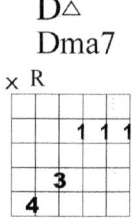

C△9 / Cma9   G△9 / Gma9   G6/9   C6/9   G△♭5 / Gma7♭5

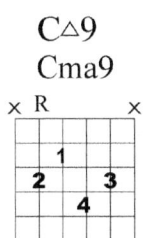 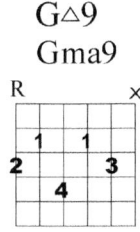 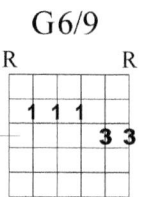 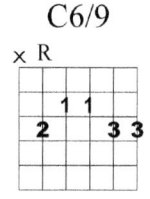 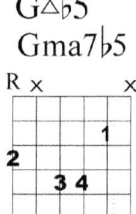

A² / A(add9)   D² / D(add9)   G² / G(add9)   C6/9♭5   Cma9♭5

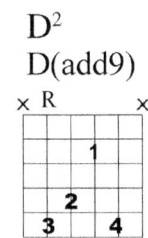 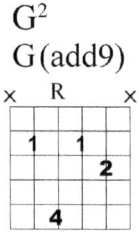 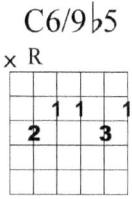 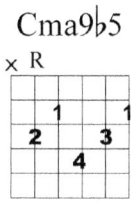

D△♯5 / Dma7♯5   B△♯5 / Bma7♯5   G△♯5 / Gma7♯5   Bma13   Dma7♭5

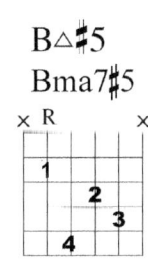 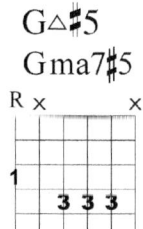 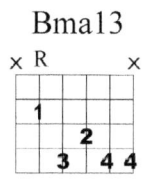 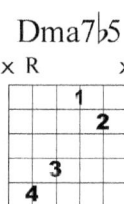

△ = ma7

Minor

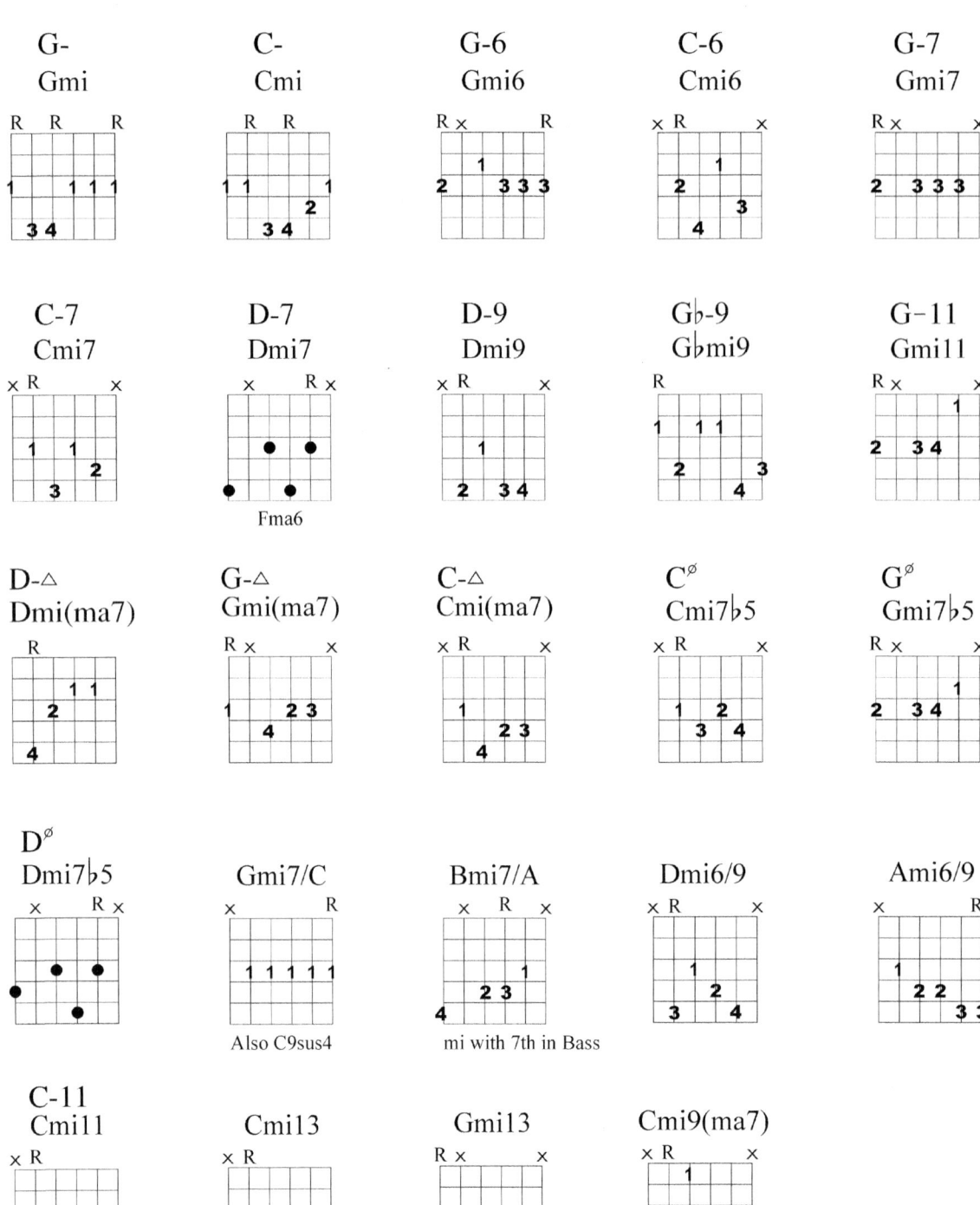

- = minor

Dominant Seventh

G7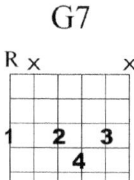
Gb7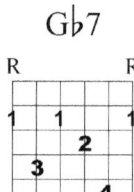
D7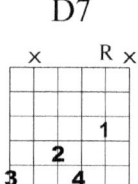
C7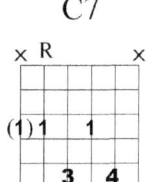
E7/G# (3rd in Bass)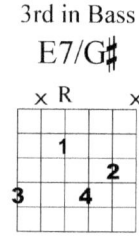

C9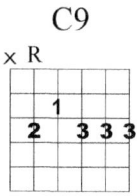
A9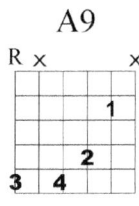
G9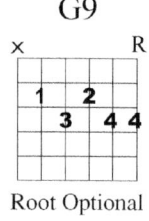
Root Optional
G7sus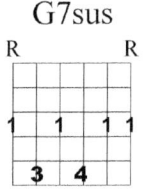
D7sus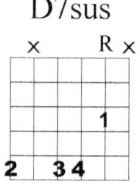

G7#5 / G+7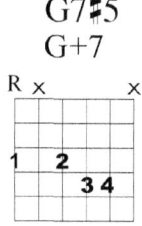
D7#5 / D+7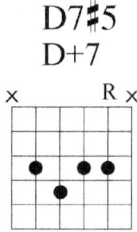
C7#9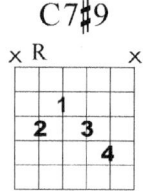
F7#9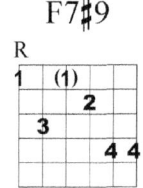
A7#9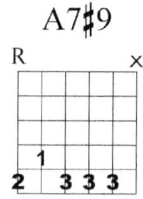

C7b9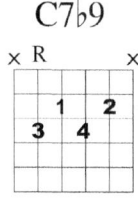
A7b9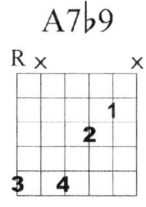
G7b9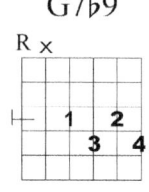
G7b5 Db7b5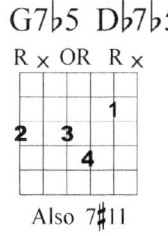
Also 7#11
C9#11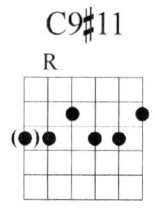

C9#5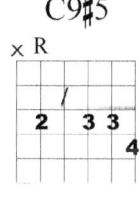
G9#5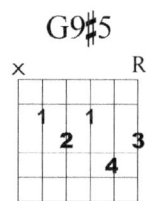
G9#5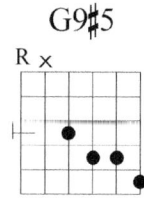
C7#5b9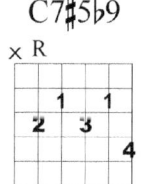
G7#5b9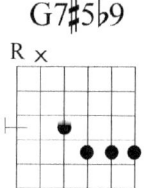

C7b5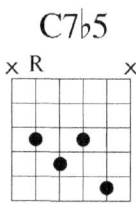
D7b5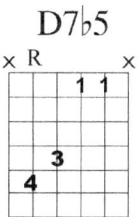

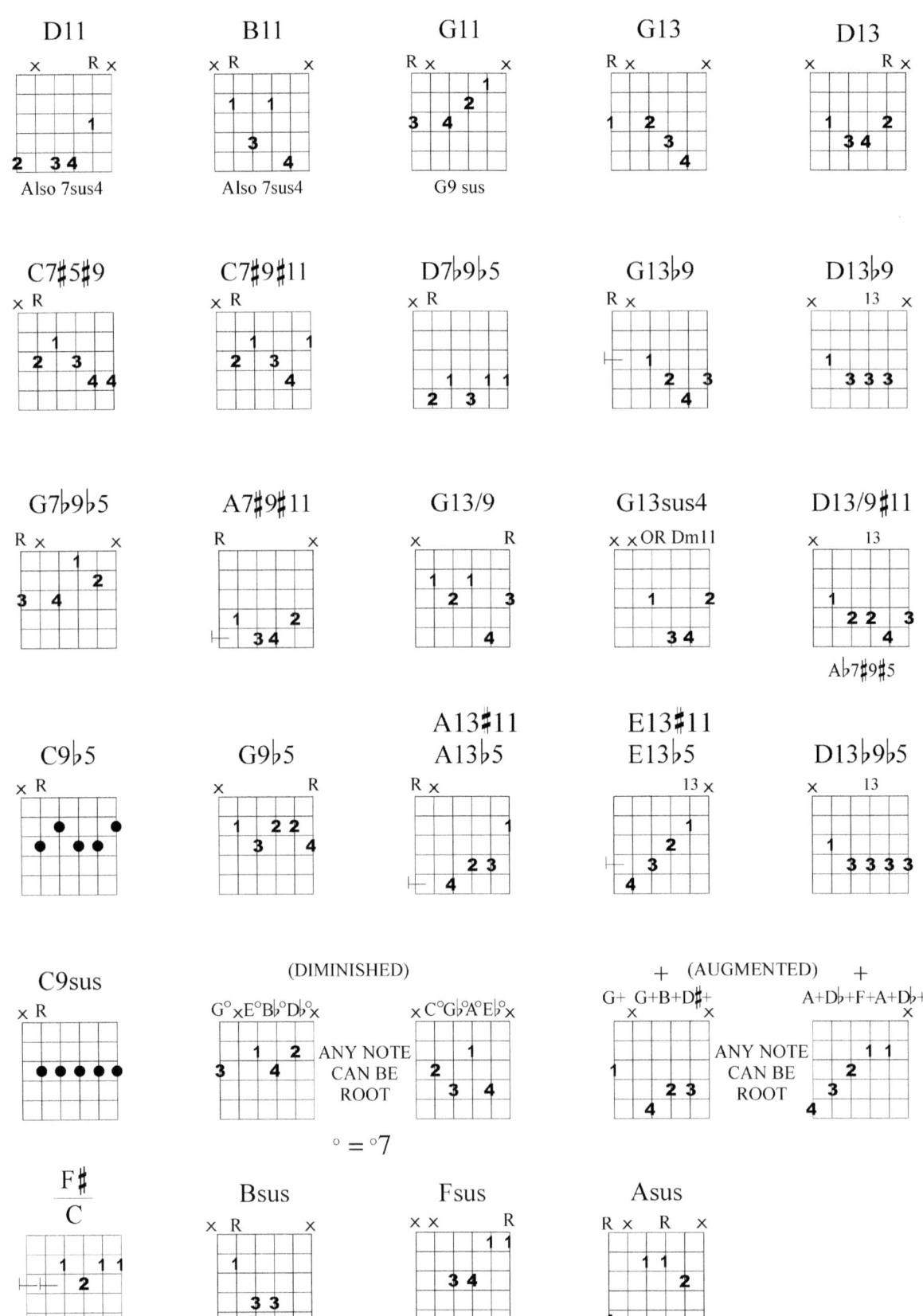

Chords with Open Strings

When comping or playing chord melodies, I like to include chords which incorporate open strings. With this technique, I'm able to voice chords which contain certain major or minor second intervals which would not be possible to finger otherwise.

In order for these chords to sound good, it is very important that your guitar is in tune with itself up and down the entire neck. You should tune your 12th fret harmonic note to your 12th fretted note by adjusting your bridge. If the fretted note is flat to the harmonic note, you should move your bridge closer to the fingerboard. If the fretted note is sharp to the harmonic note, you should move your bridge closer to the tailpiece. The use of an electronic tuner will leave no chance for error.

Old strings can cause a note to be flat. I change my strings every two weeks. Below are several examples which incorporate open string voicing.

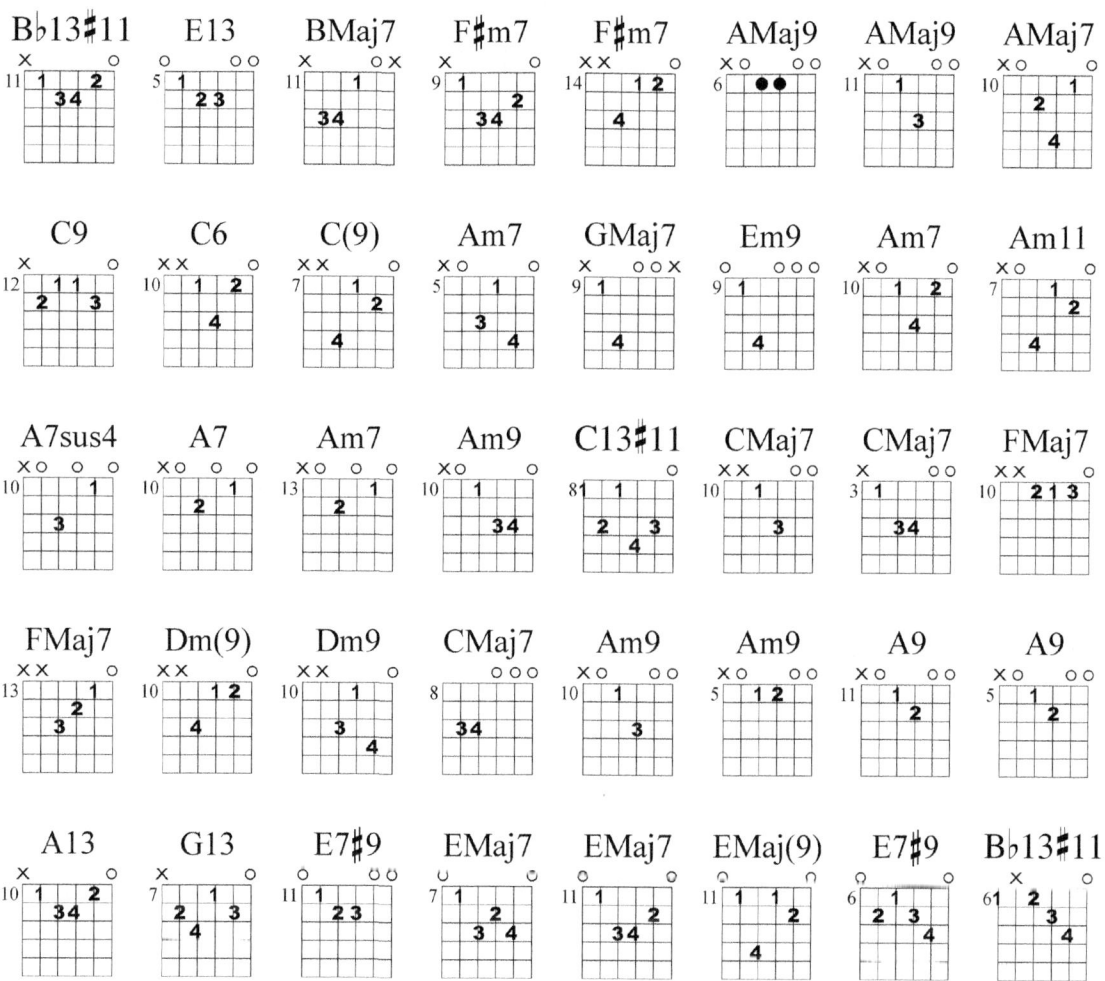

Comping

This section is related to the area of comping. The word "comping" is generally referring to the accompaniment for a soloist provided by a piano or guitar. Your approach to comping should vary according to the style of the soloist you are playing behind. Therefore, you must be intuitive and sensitive to his direction. This makes it difficult to write down any hardfast rules, but I will suggest a few guidelines which might be helpful. If the soloist is more of a horizontal (linear) player, then the accompaniment can be more vertical (progressive with extended harmonic structures). If the soloist is "busy" and more of a vertical player (implying all of the progression with substitutions), then the comping should be much more sparce. The accompanist should never get in the way or dictate the direction of the soloist. Phrasing and rhythm play an extremely important part in the art of comping. The entire rhythm section must <u>LISTEN</u> and work together. You should try to compliment but not mimic. A complete awareness of all the connecting lines within a progression should be developed. Varied experience with different styles and players provides good training. Here are a few progressions which are referred to as "turn around" changes. #5 could be used as a four bar introduction.

Comping

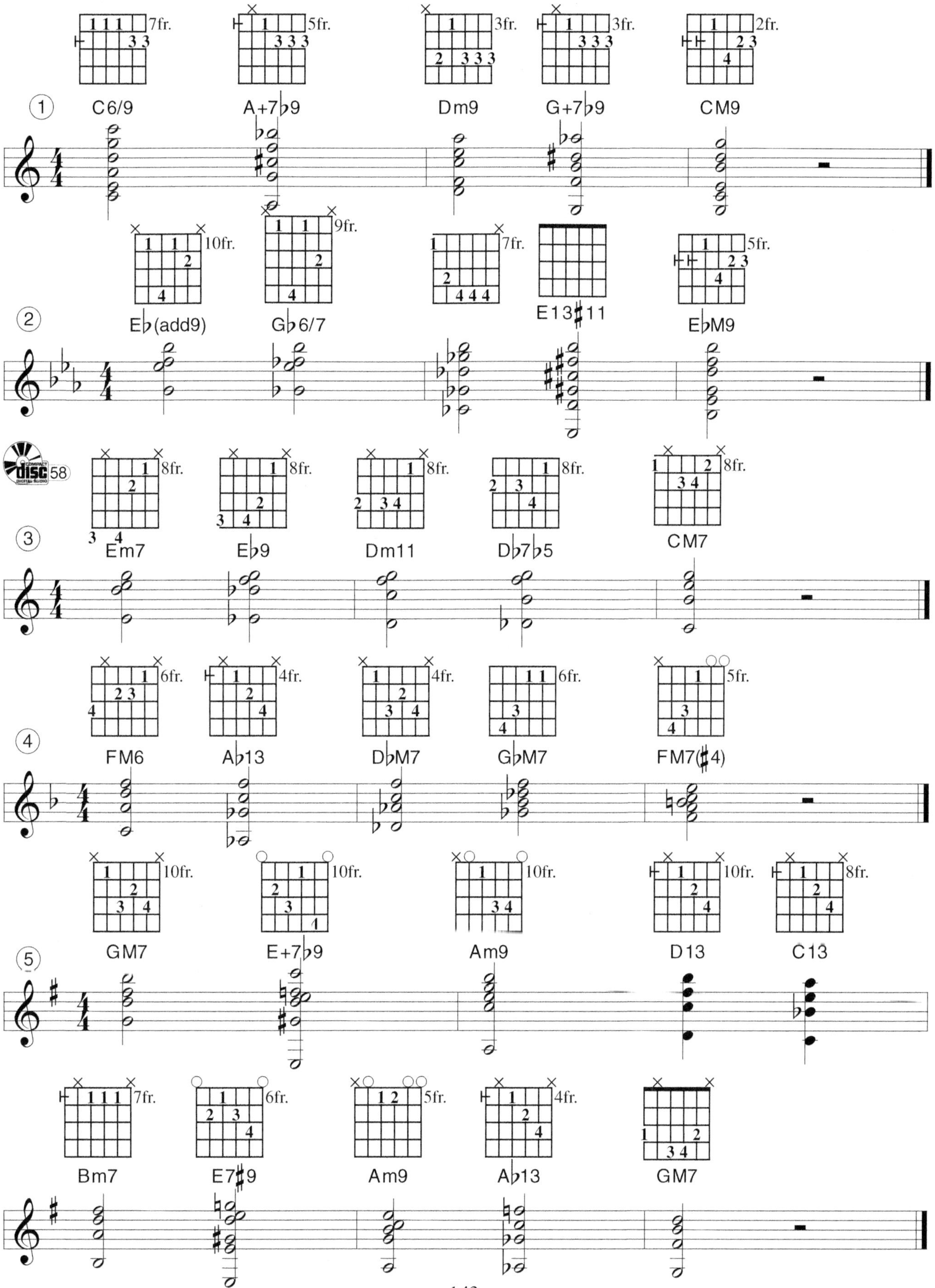

Modal Comping

Here are some triads and chords derived from C major scale which could be used when comping in modal compositions in the keys of D minor, G seventh, C major or F major. Any combination of notes in C major scale may be played when you are comping in any one of these keys. Notice that all of the three note chords are voiced with an interval of a fourth on the top in order to achieve an 'open' sound. The bottom interval of the chords in the first line is a third. The second line has the most 'open' sound because the bottom interval is a fourth, just like the top interval. The bottom interval of the third line is a second. The fourth line is an example of how to combine the chords of lines ② and ③ when comping over a modal tune. The rhythmic variations are infinite, even though I am writing only quarter notes. All of the lines on this page should be practiced descending as well as ascending.

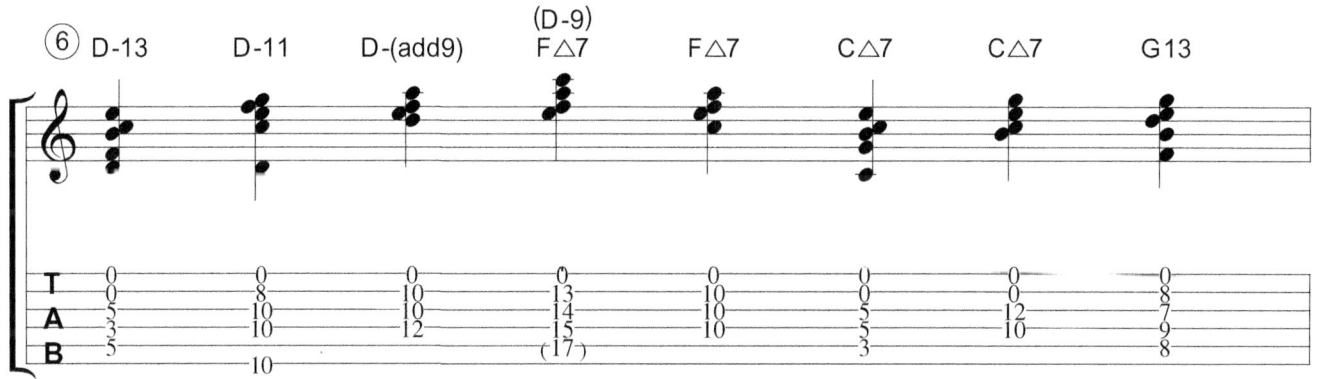

Twelve Bar Blues

Here are different examples of twelve bar blues in the key of G. You should write out your own examples of twelve bar blues by combining portions of these progressions. Notice that practically all blues progressions follow a similar basic form, which is as follows: First 4 measures - I chord; Second 4 measures - IV chord (returning to a I chord or it's substitute); Final 4 measures - V chord or (II-V substitute); Returning to a I chord. Most of the time you may use a ninth chord as a substitute for a dominant 7th.

In chord selection, your first choice should be a chord with the root on the 6th string. The second choice would be a chord with the fifth on the 6th string or the root on the 5th string. Avoid skipping up and down the neck. Try to select a chord as close as possible to the last chord and/or the next chord. The chords of the first 5 1/2 measures of example "e" should be played with the roots on the 6th string. The first and second chord of the "f" example should be played with the roots on the 5th string (index finger).

 (CD 61)
 (CD 62)
 (CD 63)

Measure	1	2	3	4	5	6
a	G7	G7	G7	G7	C7	C7
b	G7	C7	G7	G7	C7	C7
c	G7	C7	G7	Dm7 G7	C7	C#°
d	G7	C7	G7	Dm7 G7	C7	Cm7
e	Gma7	Am7 Bb°7	Bm7 Cma7	Dm7 Db7b5	C7	Cm7 F9
f	Gma7	F#m7b5 B7	Em7 A7	Dm7 G7	Cma7	Cm7 F9
g	Abm7 Db7	F#m7 B7	Em7 A7	Dm7 G7	Cma7	Cm7 F9

	7	8	9	10	11	12
a	G7	G7	D7	D7	G7	G7
b	G7	G7	D9	C9	G7	D7
c	G7	Bb° E7	Am7	D7	G7 E7	Am7 D7
d	Bm7	E7	Am7	D7	G7 E7	Am7 D7
e	Bm7 E9	Bbm7 Eb9	Am7	D7	G7 E7b9	Am7 D7
f	Bbma7	Bbm7 Eb9	Abma7	Am11 Ab7b5	Gma7 E7#9	Am7 D7b9
g	Bbma7	Bbm7 Eb9	Abma7	Am7 D7	Gma7 Bb13	A13 Ab13

Twelve Bar Progressive Blues

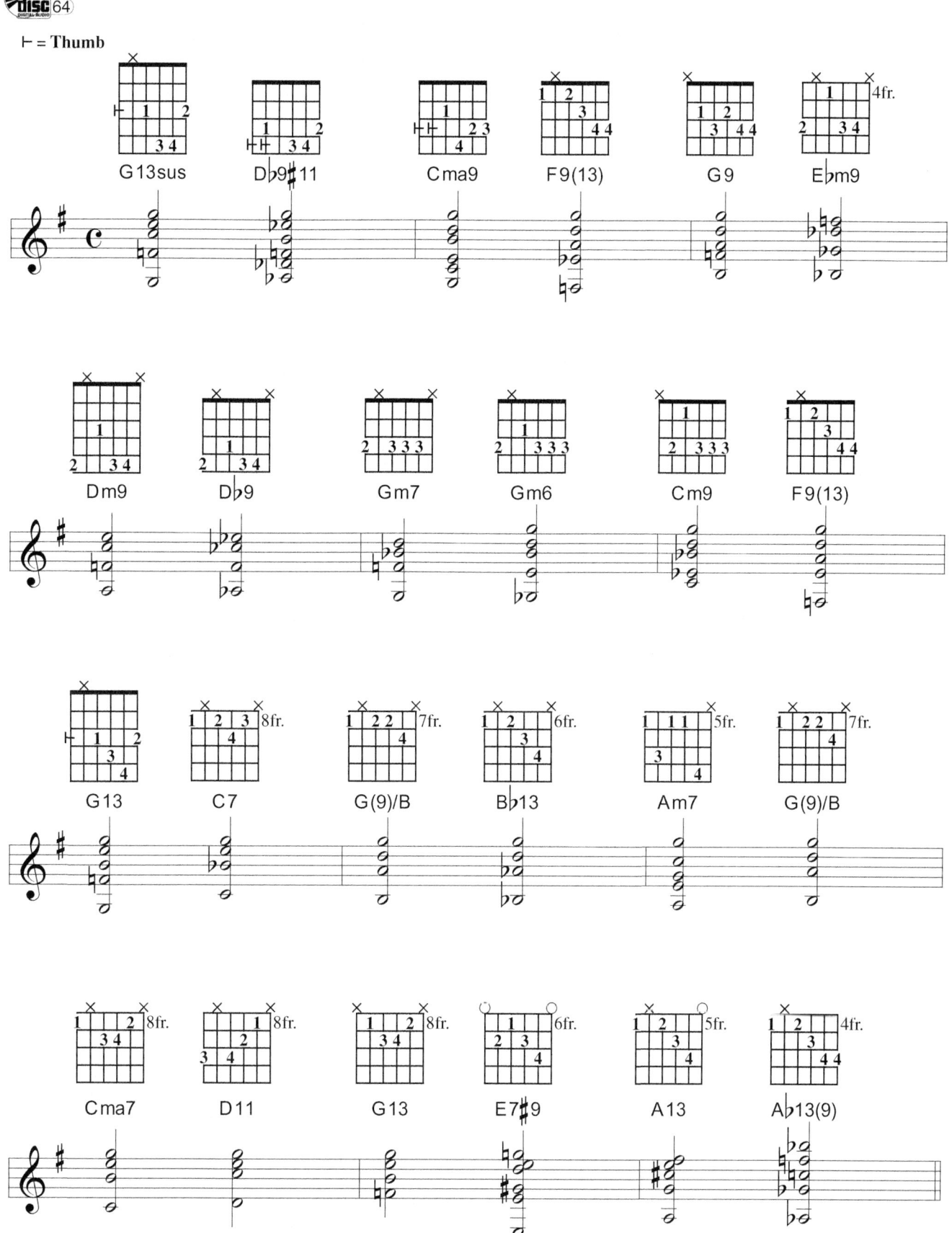

Twelve Bar Progressive Blues

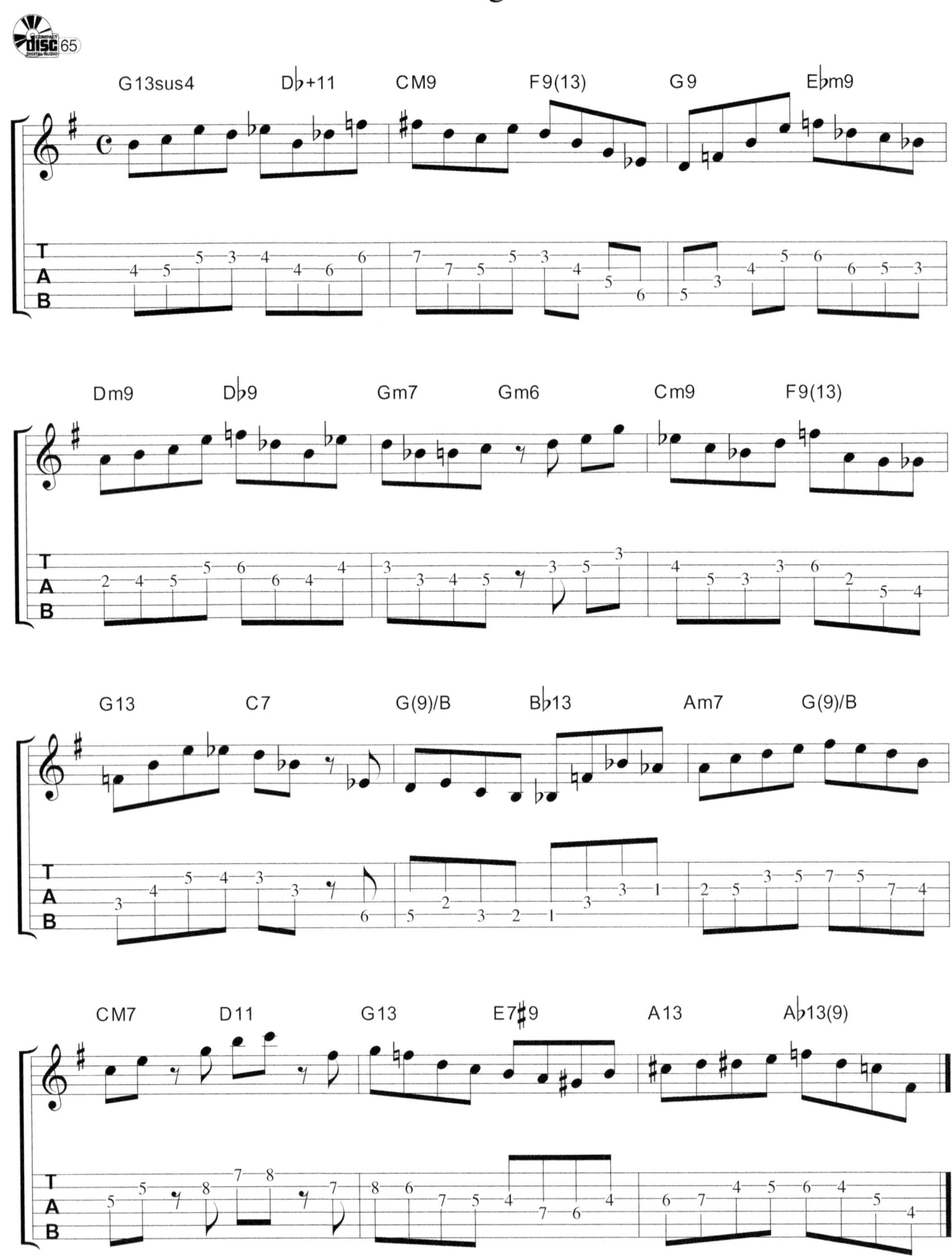

Harmonized Bass Lines

This style of rhythm playing is sometimes referred to as voice leading. This kind of jazz voice leading can be very functional when there is an absence of a bass player.

The harmonization of a bass line creates vertical patterns within a progression that facilitates a smooth transition from one tonal center to another. When we first look at a chord progression of this type, the chord relationships seem very complicated, but if we step back and view the music in terms of the basic progression, a clearer pattern emerges. Many of the chords seem to be three-part melodic elaborations between the basic chords. Some of the individual chords can be viewed as intermediate melodic steps between fundamental chords rather than as separate chords in their own right. Most of the motion in all three voices is stepwise, and the overall effect is fluid and compact.

When composing a progression in this style, much of the time the object is to move from one inversion of the basic chord to another inversion, sometimes creating diatonic or chromatic bass lines in between.

Sometimes more than one chord symbol is shown; this is because the three-note sonorities used can sometimes imply more than one chord. (For example, -A, F♯, C is by itself an F♯ diminished triad, but in context it suggests either an Am6 without the 5th or a D7 chord without the root.)

In these studies, the three-note chords contain two notes on the 3rd and 4th strings and a bass note on the 5th or 6th string. The chords, for the most part, are played on the 6th, 4th and 3rd strings. Most of the time the 6th and 3rd strings are voiced a 10th apart. This type of voicing sounds nice when you are playing rhythm guitar in a big band.

Study #1, #2 and #3 are harmonized bass lines as applied to a standard 12-bar jazz/blues progression. With the exception of the E-7 and E7 chords of the 2nd study, there are no open strings in this section. Your left hand should mute out all of the strings which are not being fretted. Play each chord with a down stroke.

Here is the basic chordal structure of the blues:

1	2	3	4	5	6	7	8	9	10	11	12
G	C	G	G7	C	C	G	G	Ami	D7	G	D7

Every one of the chords in basic blues pattern appears in the same bar as in study #1, usually on the first beat of the chord change.

Study #1 in G

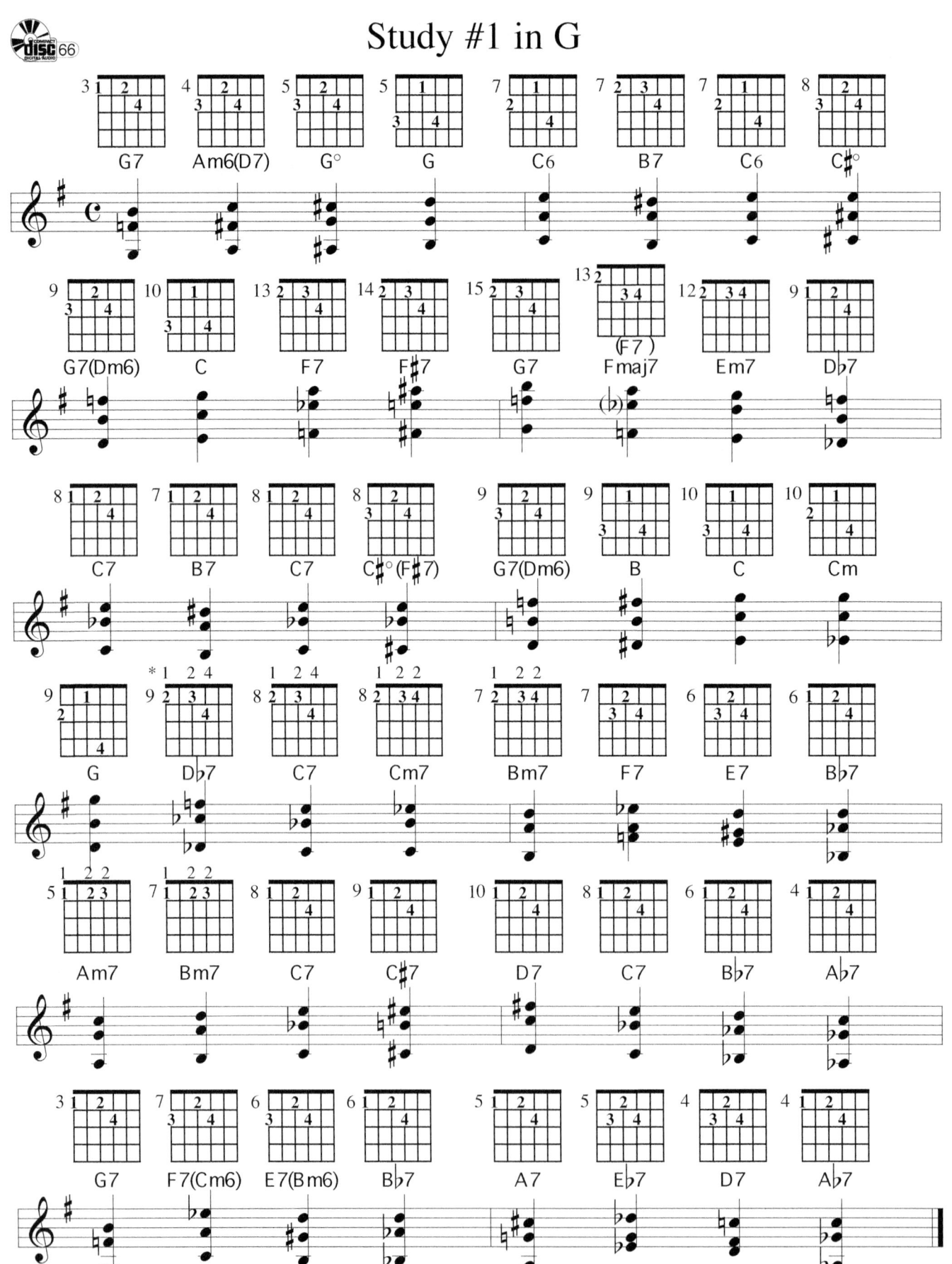

* The D♭7 and C7 chords on the fourth line can be played with 1st, 2nd and 4th fingers. The Cm7, Bm7 and Am7 chords of the fourth and fifth lines can be played with the 1st and 2nd fingers.

Study #2 in C

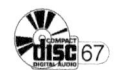

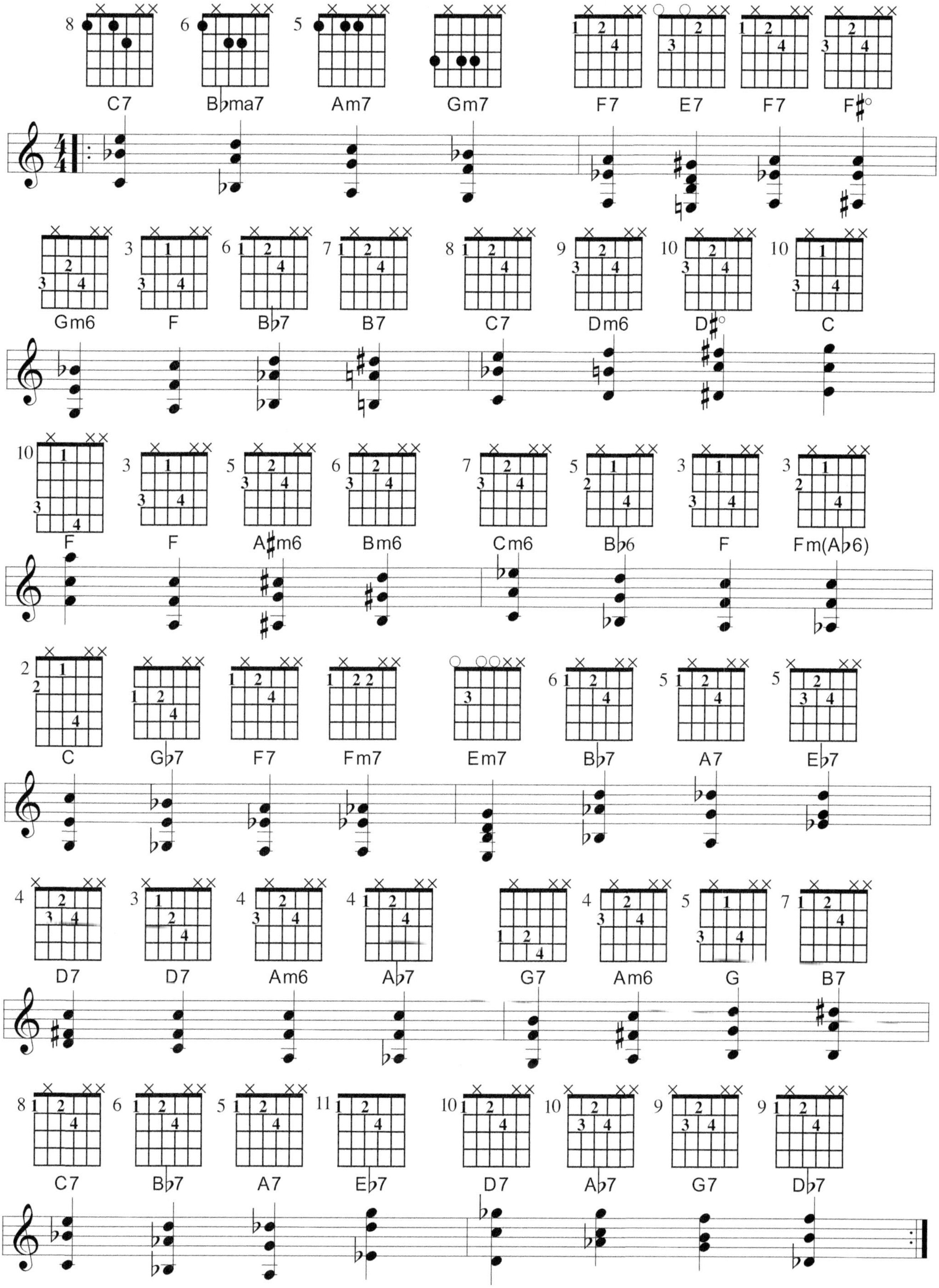
C7 B♭ma7 Am7 Gm7 F7 E7 F7 F♯°
Gm6 F B♭7 B7 C7 Dm6 D♯° C
F F A♯m6 Bm6 Cm6 B♭6 F Fm(A♭6)
C G♭7 F7 Fm7 Em7 B♭7 A7 E♭7
D7 D7 Am6 A♭7 G7 Am6 G B7
C7 B♭7 A7 E♭7 D7 A♭7 G7 D♭7

Study #3 in B♭

I have intentionally omitted the chord designations because the names are not as important as the relationship of the moving voices within the chords.

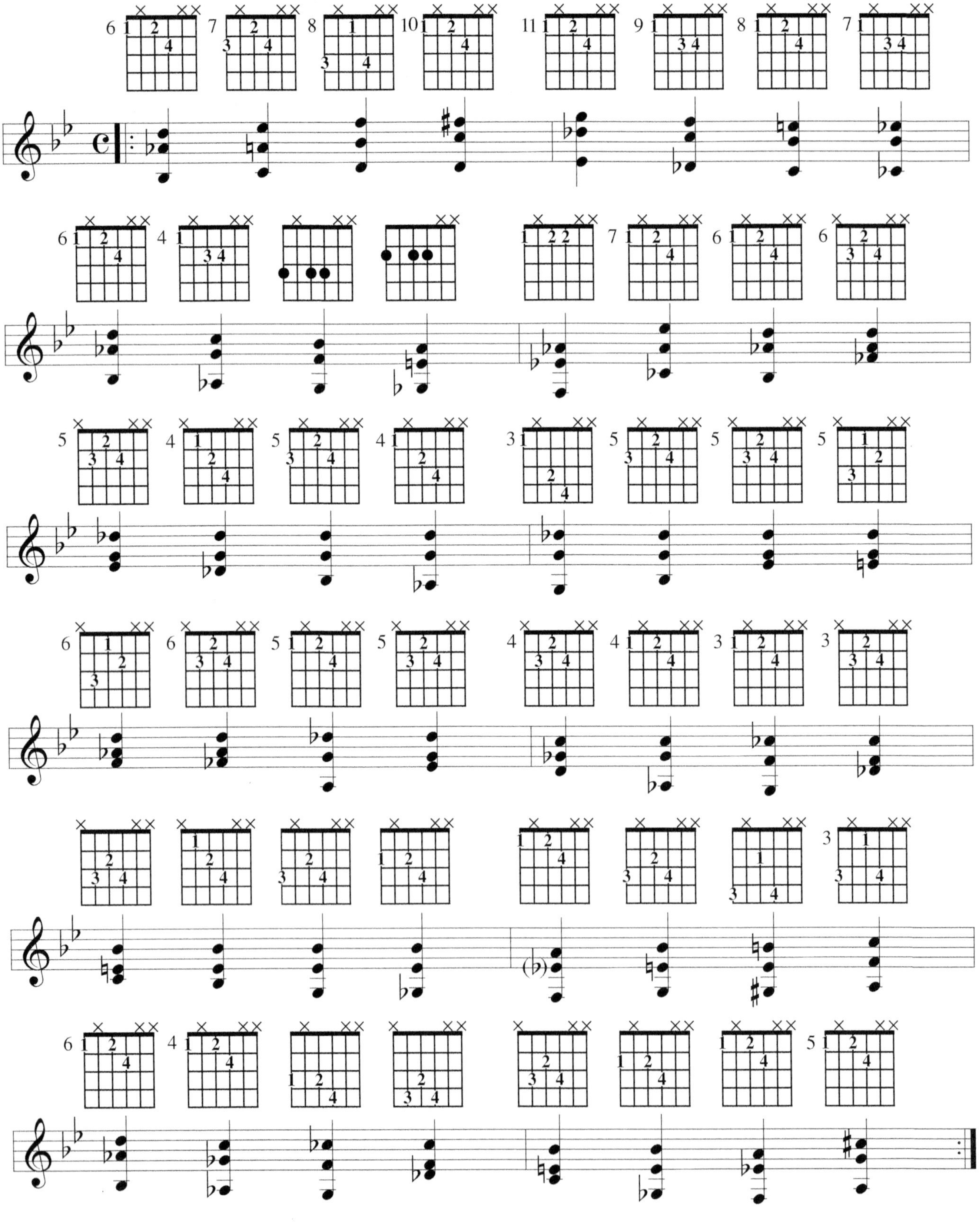

Study #4

Harmonized bass lines for changes similar to "Donna Lee" or "Indiana."

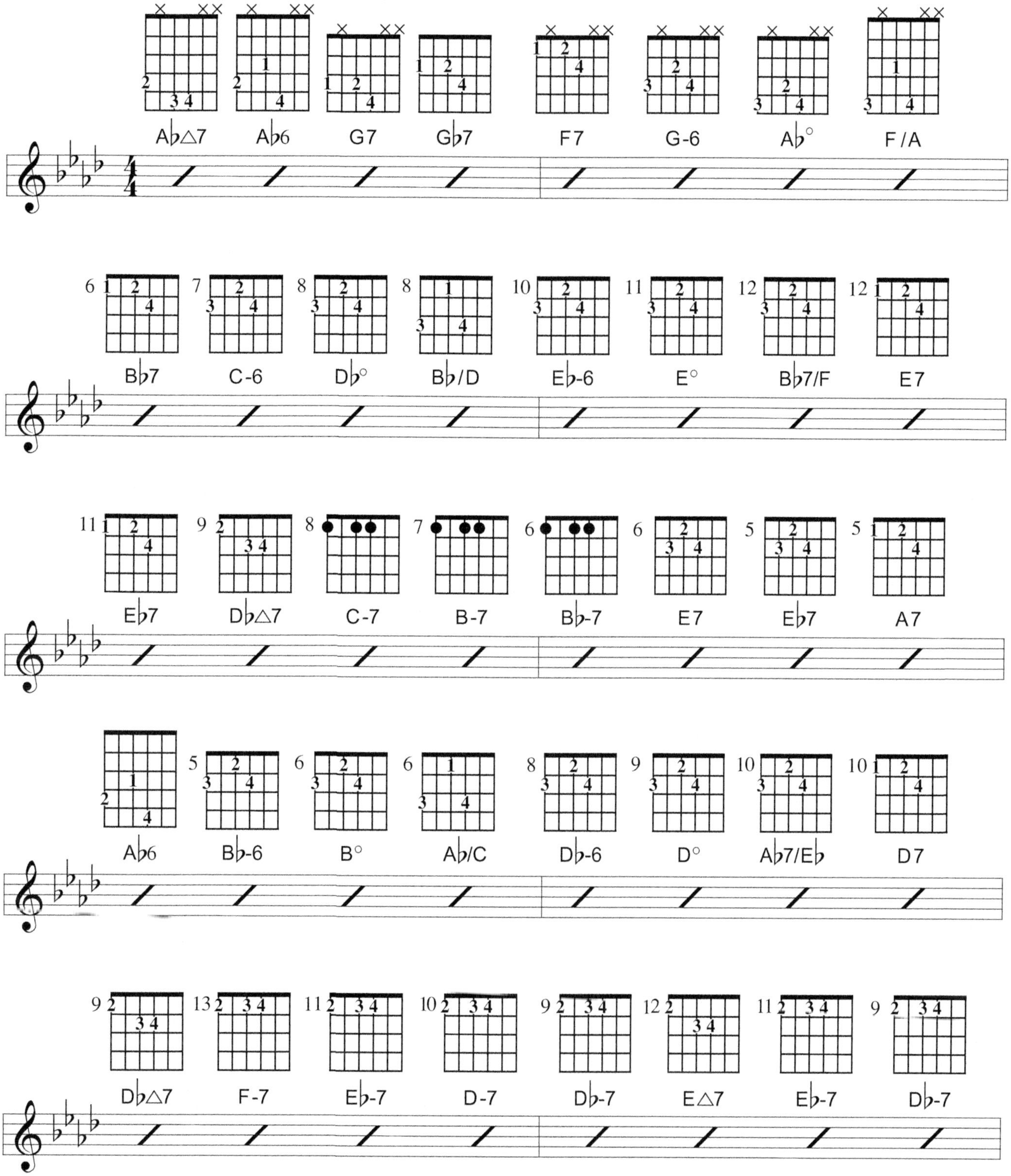

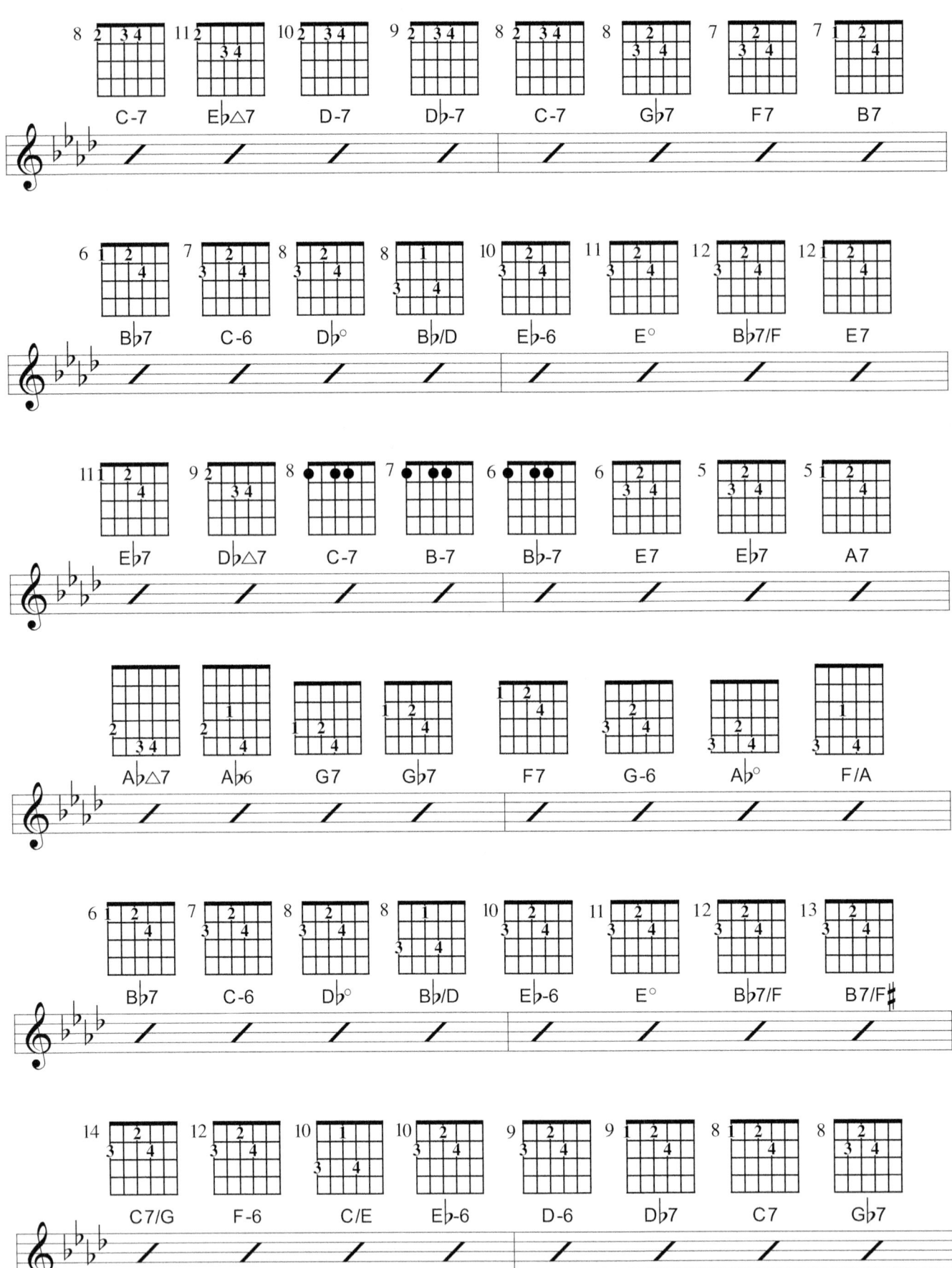

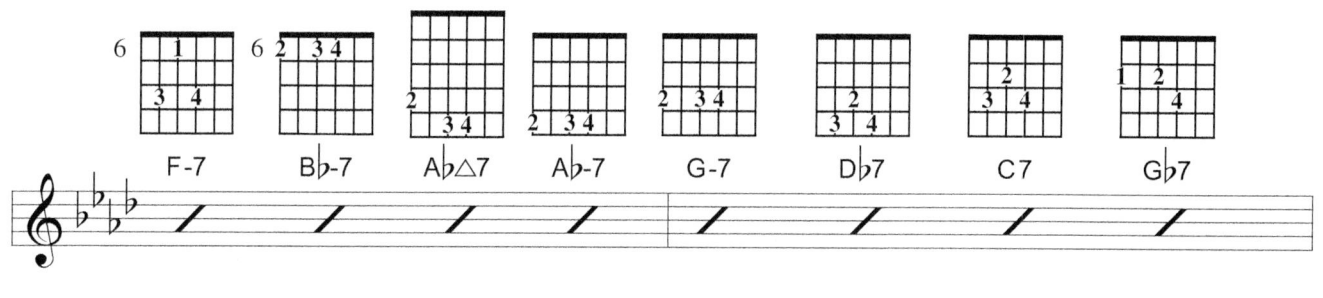

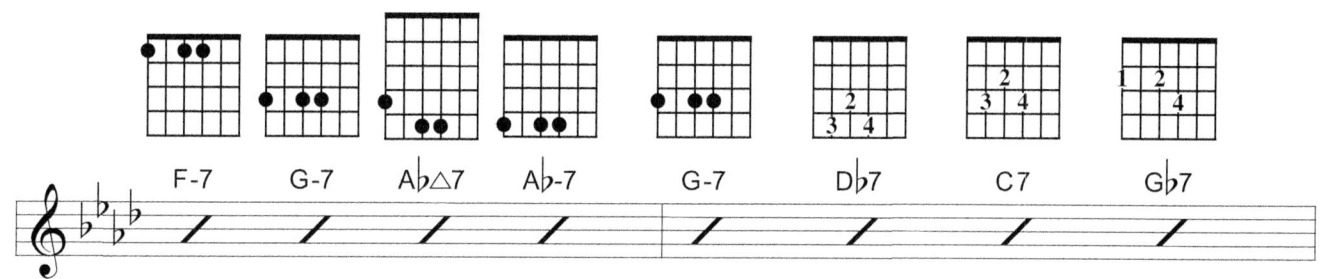

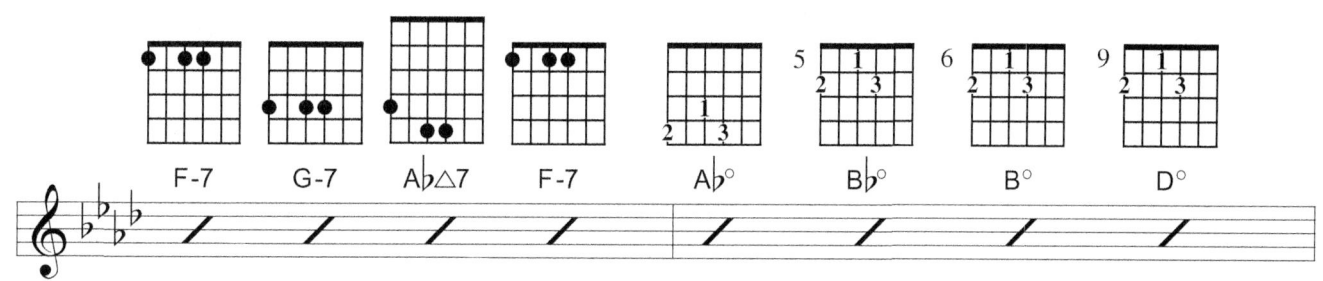

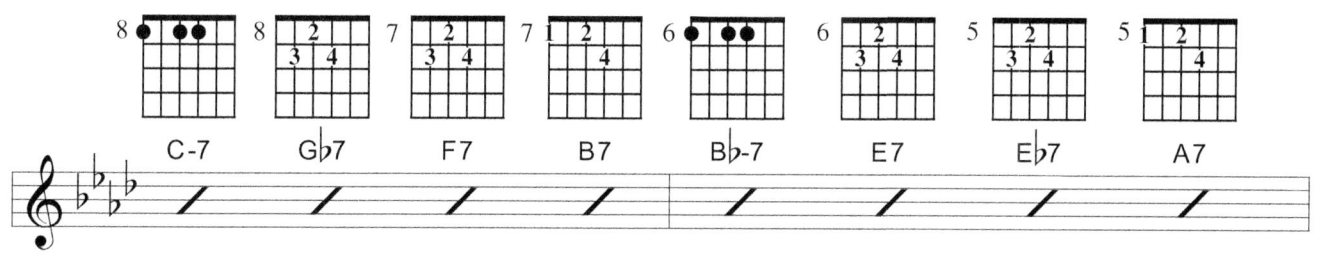

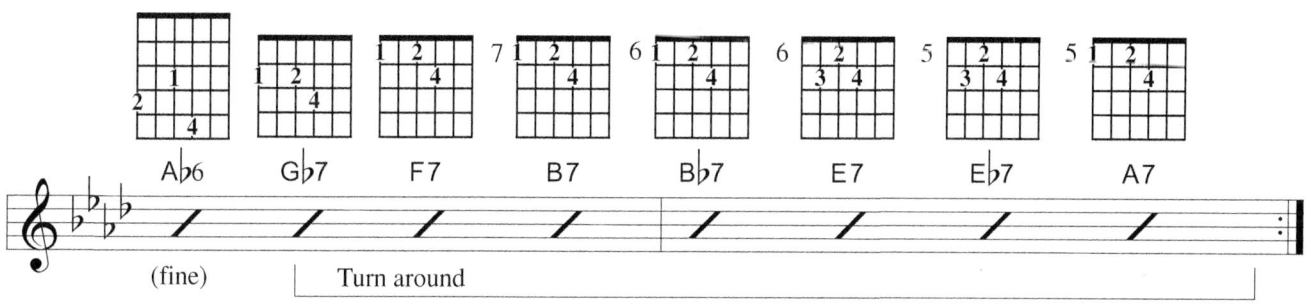

Chelsea Rose

Concert

By Jerry Hahn

Ballad

"Chelsea Rose" is written in concert for piano or two guitars. If played by two guitars, the first guitar starts in seventh position on the first string and the second guitar must read concert bass clef starting with the second finger on the sixth string. The bass player should play designated bass notes on the first and last chorus but the root changes in between.

What a Friend We Have in Jesus

Guitar Arrangement By Jerry Hahn (Written one octave above Concert)

Improvisation
LESSON I

This is the first of four lessons on jazz improvisation. Reference to lesson one will be essential when reading and studying lessons two, three and four. Write a six-measure solo in 4/4, using all of the notes of the two octave G7 scale. This solo will be used in analysis according to rule 9 and should be played and memorized in 2nd and 3rd position.

G7 scale and arpeggio (chord tones)

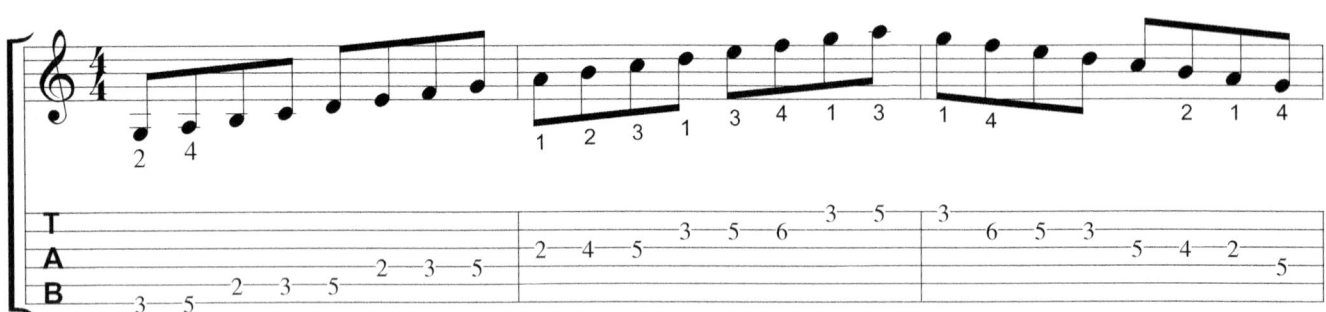

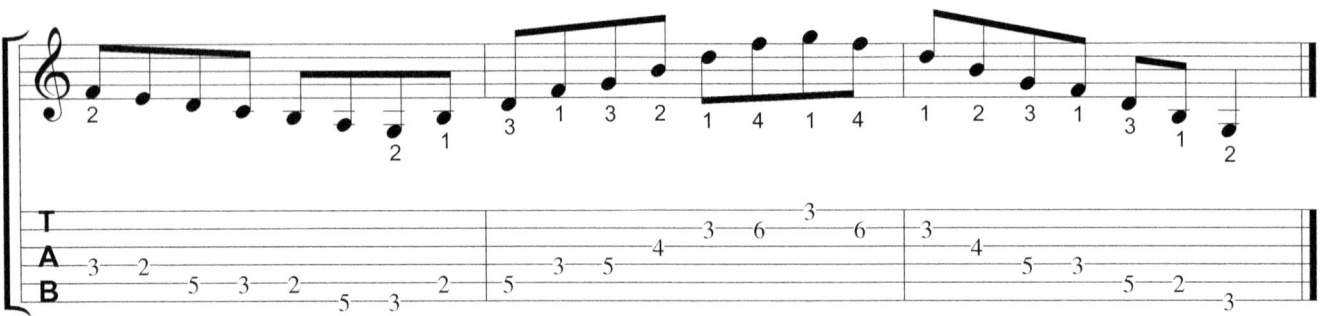

Apply the following rules for lesson one.

1. Without using an instrument, write out solos using eighth-notes which are played with jazz phrasing (♫ = ♪♪♩). All written solos should be memorized on your instrument.

2. You may insert an eighth rest anytime on the beat, but not on the "and." However, do not insert an eighth rest after a note which is the perfect 4th of the parent scale or in the middle of a series of notes related to one of the alternative rules found in lessons two and three. There should be an average of one or two eighth rests every two measures. The inclusion of a rest does not affect rule #5.

3. Do not repeat notes one right after the other.

4. The first and last note of an entire chord change must be primary chord tones. Therefore, if there are six measures of G7, the first and last note of the entire six measures must be chord tones (G, B, D or F), not necessarily the first and last notes of each measure.

5. In the solo you write out, the order of progression of notes must be either scalewise movement (moving up or down to the next note in the scale) or arpeggiated movement (moving from a chord tone to another chord tone). When on a chord tone, you have the option of skipping to another chord tone or moving scalewise. When on a non-chordal scale tone, you do not have that option. The next note must be the closest note in the scale (up or down). You can not have a skip of an interval larger than a second unless it is from a chord tone to another chord tone. You can not have a skip of an interval larger than a second from a non-chordal tone. If you have written the note "C" (a non-chordal scale tone), the next note must either be a "D" (up) or a "B" (down), but if you have written the note "B" (a chord tone), you may skip to a "G", "D" or "F" (other chord tones). Reread this rule. It is the most important yet most often misunderstood in the lesson.

6. Avoid any large skips (over a 5th) unless there is a rest between the two notes.

7. The solos should be approximately two-thirds diatonic movement (scale-wise) and one-third chord tone movement with not over three or four chord tones following consecutively.

8. Change direction in motion (up or down) at least one time per measure.

9. Label each note in the solo according to it's intervallic relationship with the root of the chord change. Here are some guidelines to help you do this correctly.

M = major (all seconds, thirds, sixths and sevenths of a major scale).
P = perfect (all unisons, fourths, fifths and octaves of a major scale).
m = minor (major intervals made chromatically a half-tone smaller).
o = diminished (perfect or minor intervals made chromatically a half-tone smaller).
+ = augmented (major or perfect intervals made chromatically a half-tone larger).

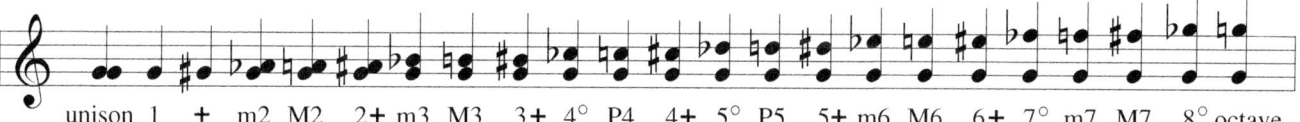

unison 1   +   m2 M2   2+ m3 M3   3+ 4° P4   4+ 5° P5   5+ m6 M6   6+ 7° m7 M7   8° octave

Do not become discouraged if you aren't really thrilled with the sound of the first solo. It will sound better if you memorize it and learn to play it fast, clean and swinging in a steady tempo without mistakes. Future solos will sound better because the rules included in lessons 2, 3 and 4 will offer more options for melodic development. After memorizing the solo in G7, learn to play the solo in A7 (move solo up two frets) and then C7 (move solo up five frets).

Here is a six-measure solo example. Complete the analysis and memorize before working on your own. Notice that all of the intervals larger than a second are from one chord tone to another. Use a metronome starting at a very slow tempo.

Improvisation
LESSON II

Facility with the G7 scale and arpeggio is important to this lesson and should be practiced everyday. Write and memorize another six-measure solo in G7 (second and third position) using rules 10 through 13 frequently in addition to the first nine rules in lesson 1. All of the rules in this lesson offer alternatives to the restrictions imposed by rule five.

10. You may consider a major 6th a chord tone; You may skip to or from a major 6th to or from another chord tone.

11. You may skip up from a chord tone to a non-chordal scale tone if you come down to the nearest chord tone.

12. You may skip a third from any scale note to another scale note if the next note is the chord tone found between the two preceding scale notes.

13. A successive series of ascending thirds, starting on a primary chord tone, are permitted if (a) the last note of the series resolves down to a chord tone (b) the last note of the series is a chord tone.

With this rule, use a Lydian mode (raised 4th) for major chords and some of the dominant 7th chords. This rule generally works better with dominant 7th chords.

EXAMPLES OF RULES

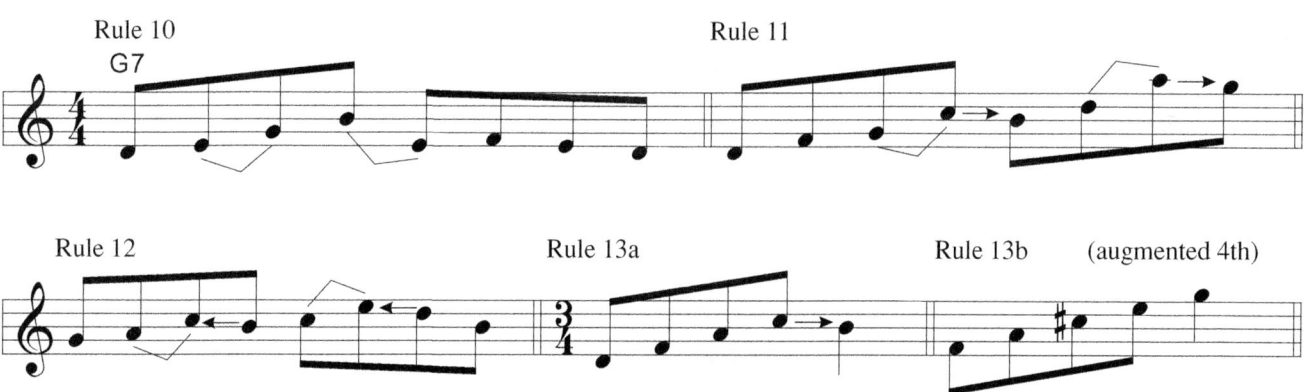

After memorizing the G7 solo you worked out, write another which covers a range from B below the staff to B above the staff. This is to be played and memorized in second and third positions and also in seventh (the first finger on the 7th fret). Here is an example of such a solo;

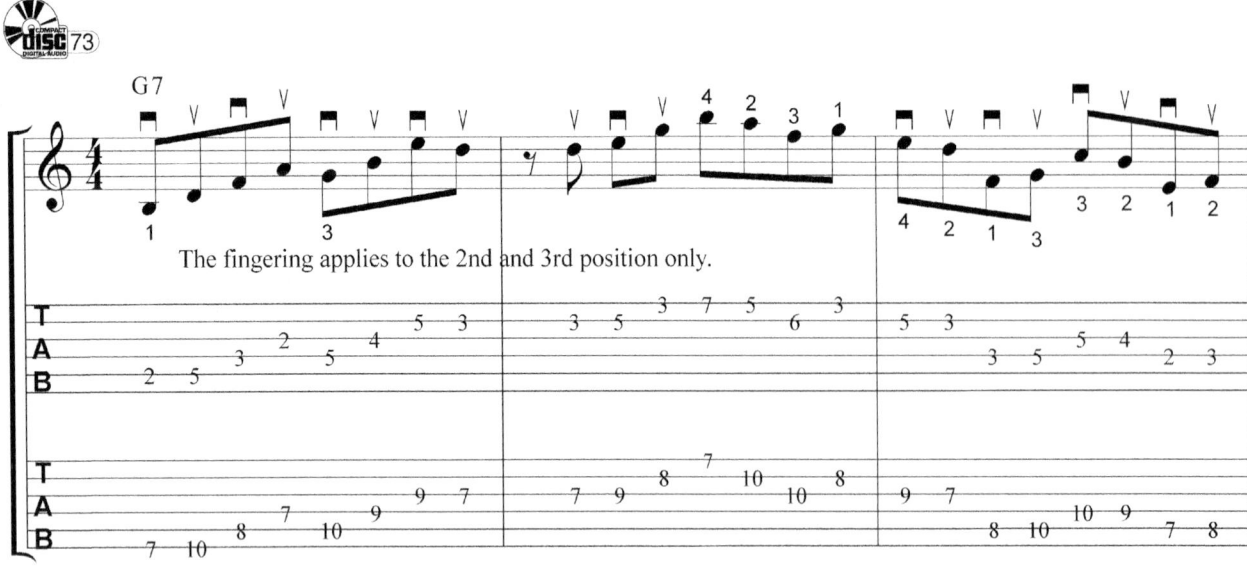

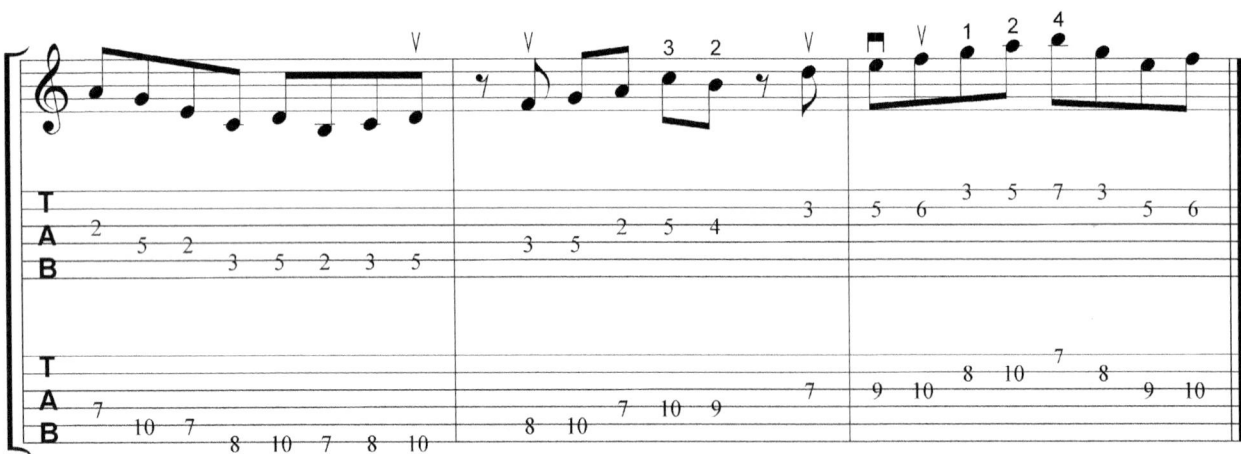

Usually, notes that occur on the beat are played with a down-stroke and notes on the upbeat are played with an up-stroke. A skip will be easier to play if you write it so that the low note falls on the beat (down-stroke), and the high note falls on the upbeat (up-stroke). In measure 3, there is a skip between the second and third notes, and sixth and seventh notes. The second and sixth notes are the high notes, which fall on the upbeat and therefore are played with an up-stroke. The third and seventh notes are the low notes which fall on the downbeat and therefore are played with a down-stroke.

After completing your G7 solo assignment, I would like to suggest that you write additional solos on different chords such as F major chord and scale, or C7 chord and scale before moving on to Lesson III.

Improvisation
LESSON III

Write and memorize an eight measure solo in G7 ranging from D below the staff to B above the staff to be played in 2nd and 3rd position, 7th position and also in 9th and 10th position. Use rules 14 through 17 as frequently as possible in addition to the first 13 rules of lessons one and two. The rules of this lesson continue to liberate us from the restrictions imposed by rule five.

14. Any note may be used to connect two diatonic scale notes to create chromatic movement.

15. Any note may be used to connect two chord tones if it is a half-step below the second chord tone.

16. You may skip to an upper register major 2nd or major 9th (not below treble clef staff) from a chord tone if the next note is a chord tone.

17. You may combine rule 11 or 12 with rule 14 even if it involves a perfect 4th (refer to measure 12 and 13 in example).

If the parent scale does not have a major 2nd (or major 9th), rule 16 is not applicable. Probably the most common chord substitution is replacing a dominant seventh chord with a ninth chord. This occurs frequently when playing the blues. When this happens, the ninth (2nd degree of the scale) becomes a chord tone. If a G7 is changed to a G9, the tone "A" becomes a chord tone along with the primary chord tones of G, B, D and F. In the fourth and ninth measures the note A (the ninth) is followed by the note F (the seventh), thus strengthening the harmonic implication in the line. I would not recommend using extension chord tones until you have become thoroughly familiar with the application of the rules to the basic dominant 7th chord/scale. This solo is to be played and memorized in all three positions. The fingering applies only to the 2nd and 3rd position. Examples of the rules are indicated above certain sections of the solo.

When creating chromaticism within a scale type passage which includes two whole steps, it is usually stronger to insert the non-scale chromatic note next to a chord tone rather than a non-chordal scale tone.

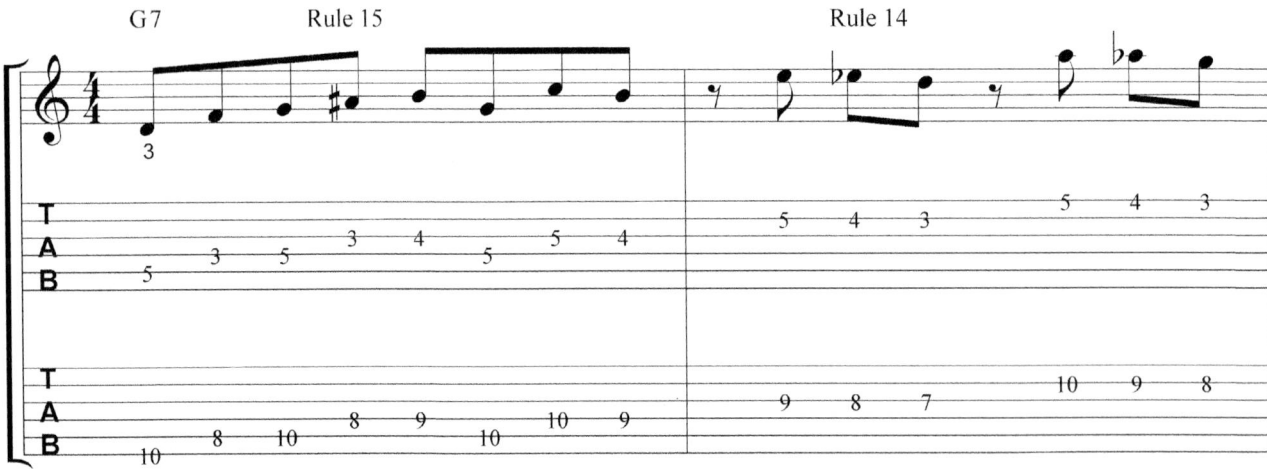
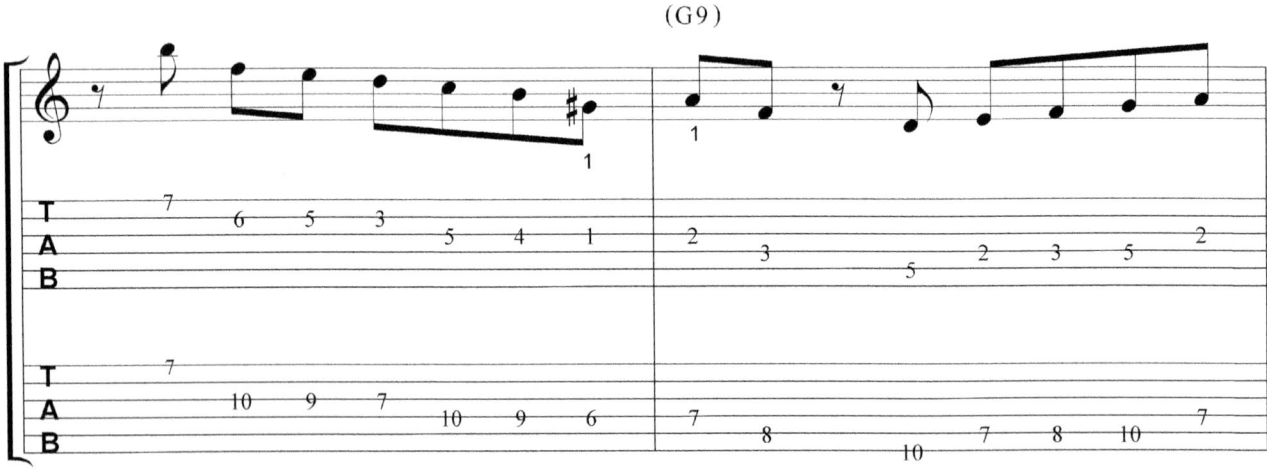
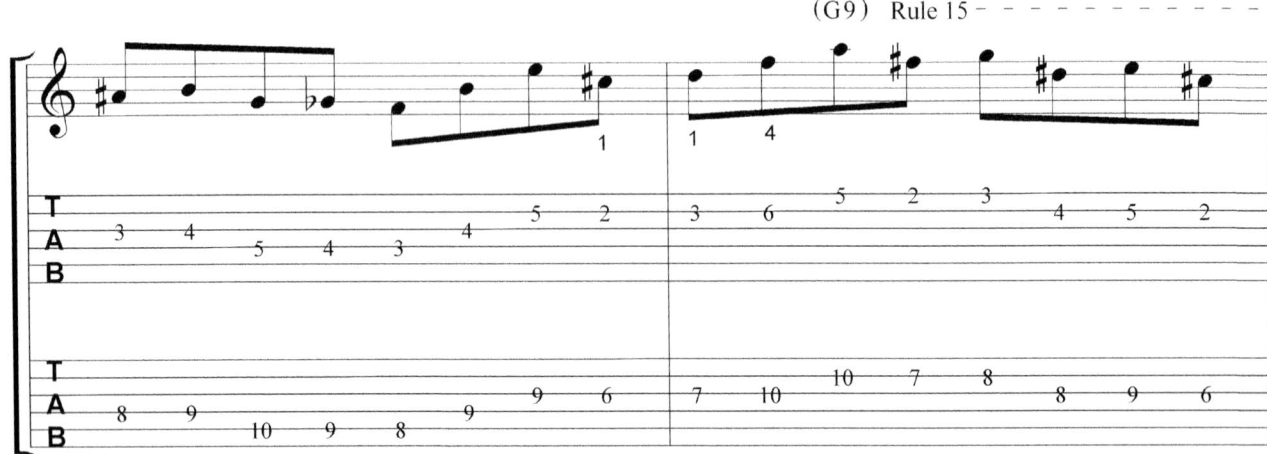

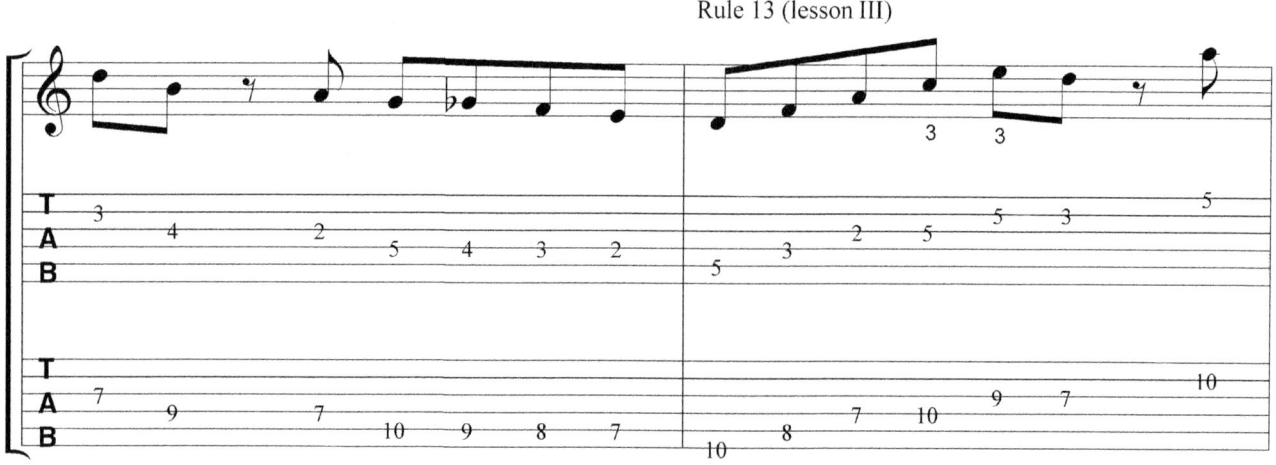
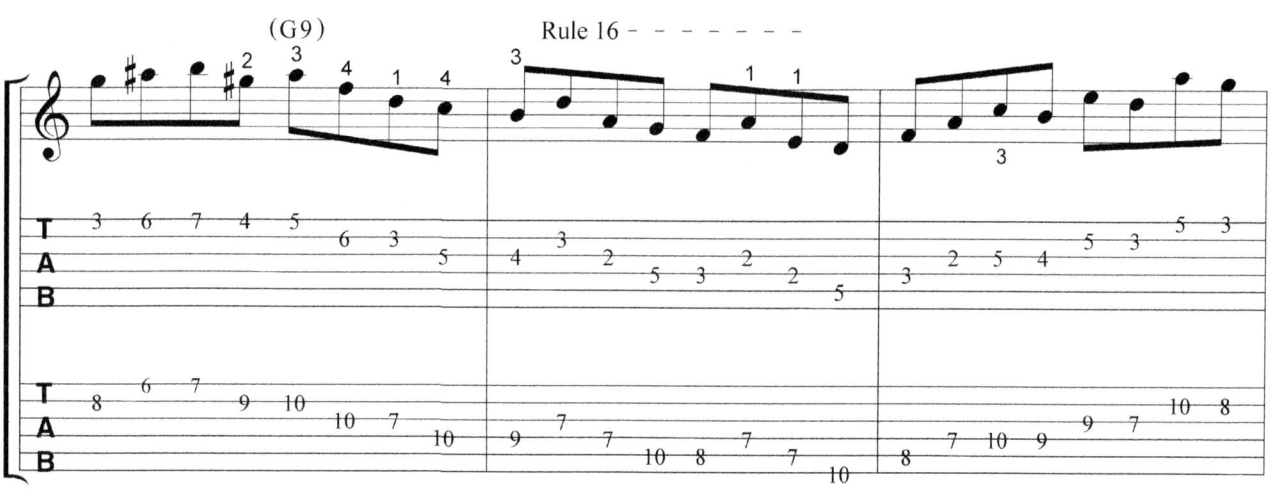
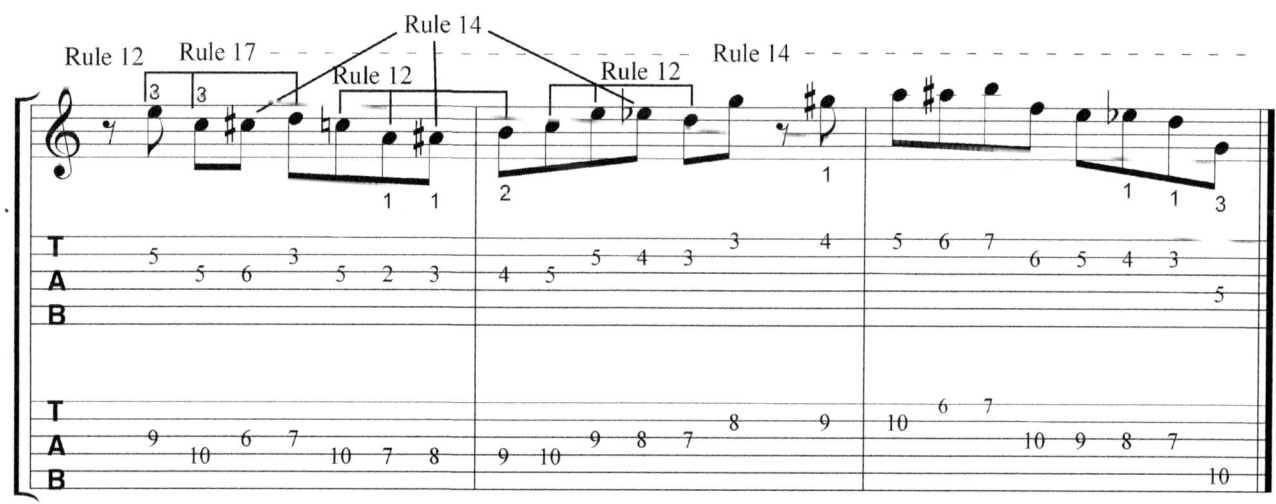

Improvisation
LESSON IV

Write and memorize a solo to the changes of "In the Breeze" using rules 1 through 21 after you study, analyze and memorize the examples I have written. From my "Parent Scales and Modes" section, transpose and write down all of the scales you will need to correspond with the changes of the tune. For example, the first chord is F major. Transpose the C major scale to F and use that scale to write out the improvisation for the first measure. The second chord is D7. Transpose the C7 (Mixolydian) scale up a whole-step to D7 and use that scale for the second measure. The C7 scale has a minor 7th (B♭). Take the D major scale and flat the major 7th (C♯) down a half-step to the minor 7th (C) and that will create the D7 scale. Apply all of the rules to the different scales and know the chord tones, scale tones and non-scale tones of each scale. You should be able to play a two octave scale and arpeggio to every chord change in the position of the solo. A guitarist should be able to play all major, minor and 7th scales and arpeggios in 5 positions in all 12 keys before he works on this lesson. Rules 18, 19 and 20 relate to chord connecting notes which are alternative choices to the restrictions imposed by rule #4. Rule 19 is related to rule 14 of lesson III and rule 20 is related to rule 15 of lesson III. The difference being we are applying these rules to two different chords (and scales).

18. You may end a chord change with a non-chordal scale note if it is a chord tone of the next chord, or if you are moving diatonically or chromatically to the first note of the next chord.

19. If the next to the last note of a chord change is a whole step away from any chord tone of the next chord, any note may be used as the last note of a chord change to connect the two notes creating chromatic movement.

20. If the next to the last note of a chord change is a chord tone, the last note of the chord change may be any note if it is a half-step below the first note of the next chord change which would be a chord tone according to rule #4.

21. You may use eighth note triplets and quarter note triplets for rhythmic variety. Triplets should always start on the beat, not on the "and."

LESSON IV

Examples for rules 18, 19 and 20

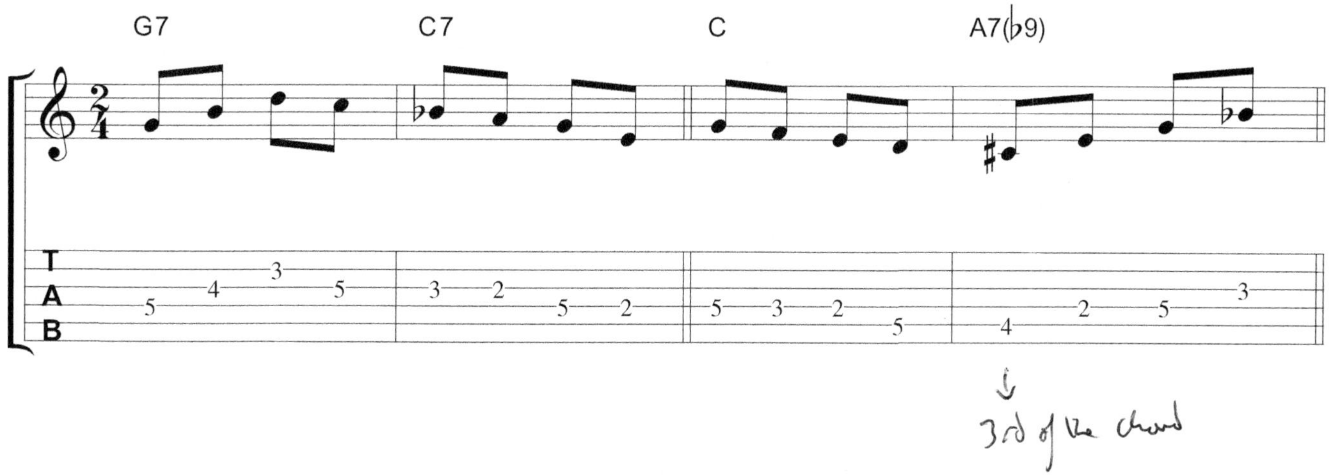

Refer to "In the Breeze" solo for rule examples.

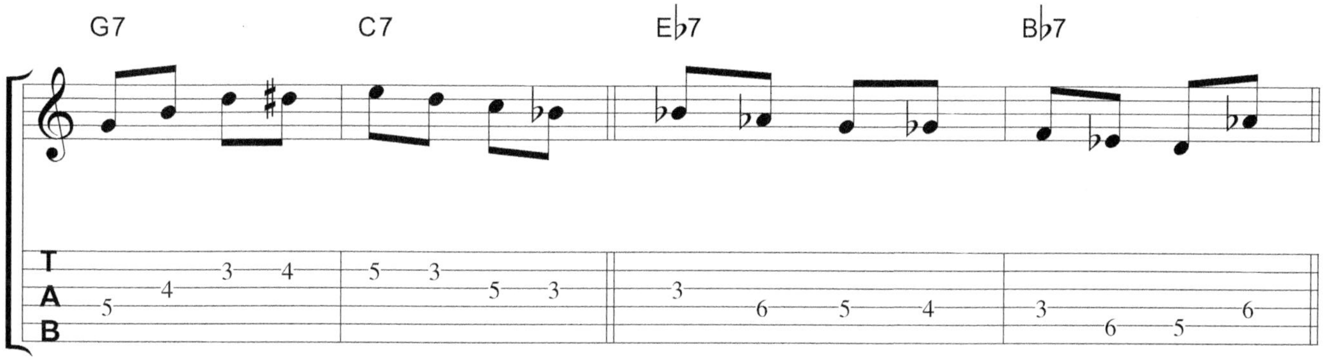

Solo To "In the Breeze"

Numbers in parentheses show the rules being used.

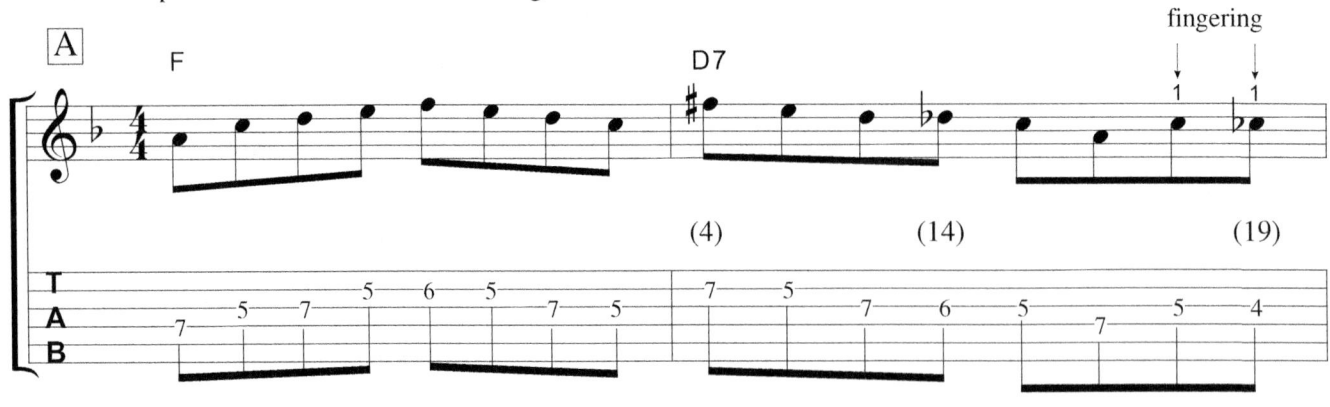
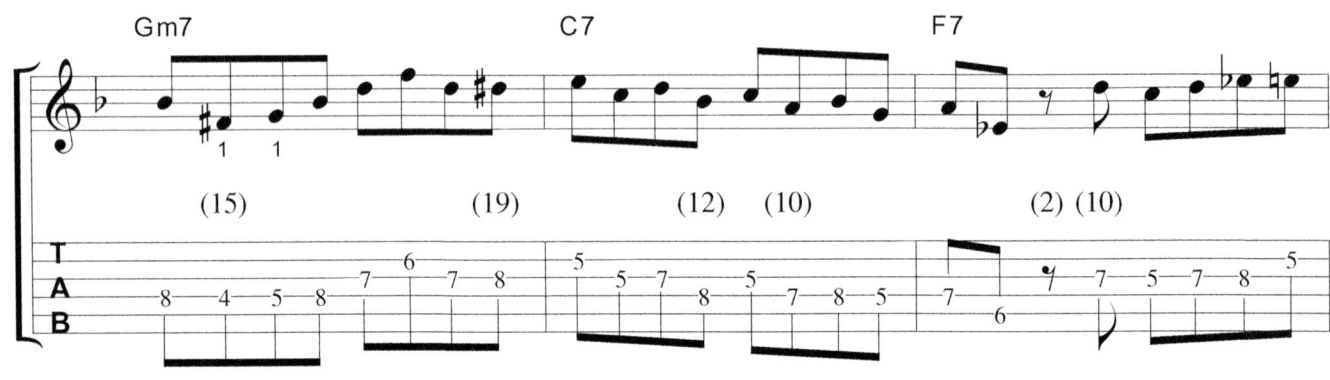
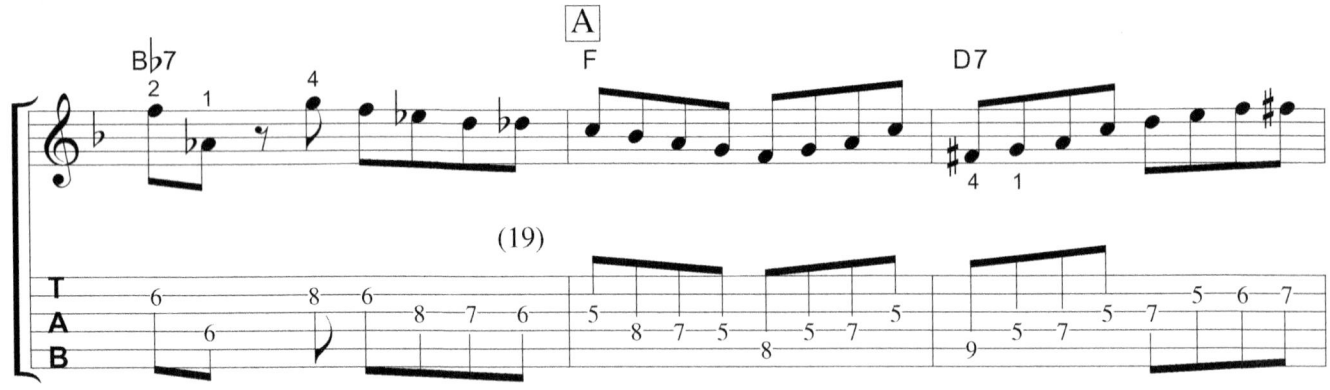
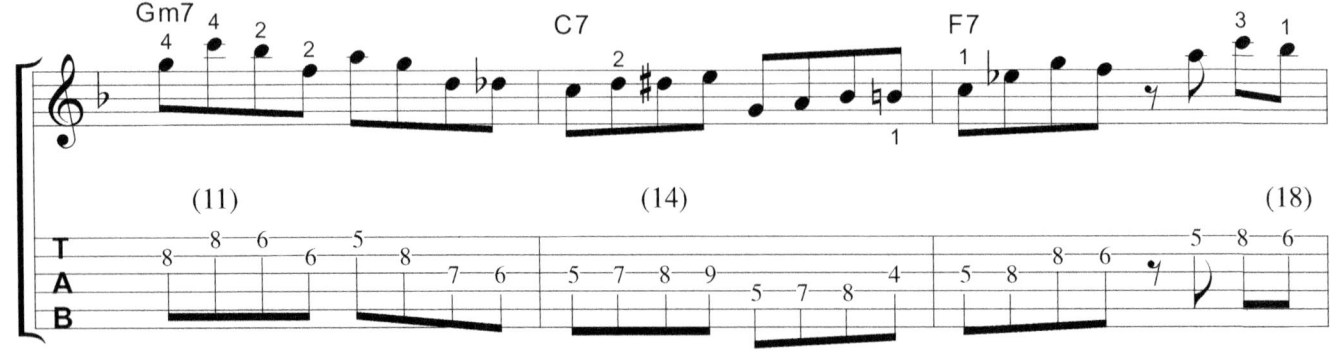

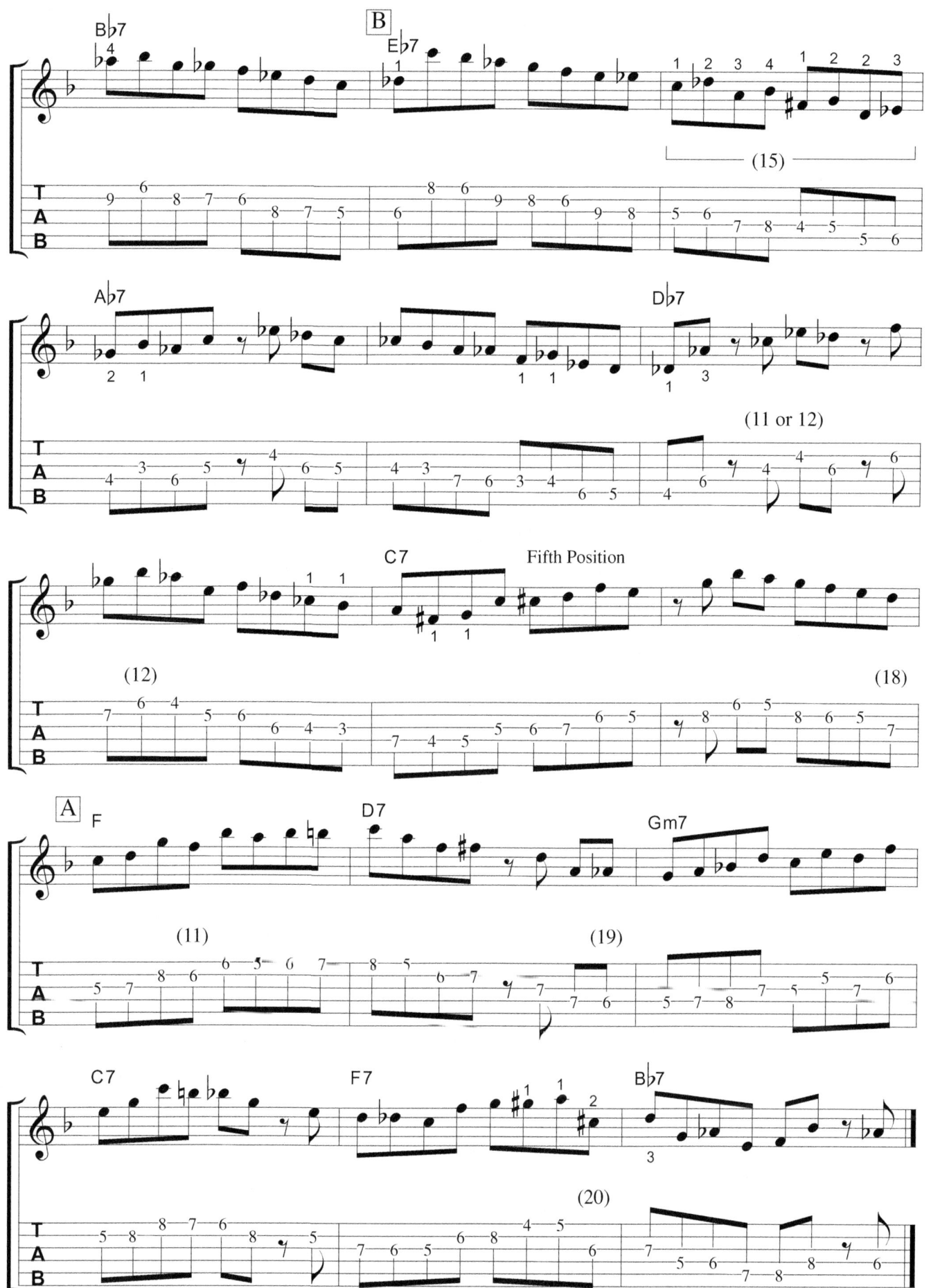

Transfiguration - 1

Fingerstyle/Classical

Transfiguration - 2

171

Transfiguration - 3

Transfiguration - 4

173

Transfiguration - 5

Listening

Listening is very important for the development of aspiring jazz guitarists.

With all the thousands of albums available today, I can see why it might be difficult for a musician who has just recently become interested in jazz to know what would be best to buy and listen to. I would like to recommend what I believe to be some of the best jazz albums ever recorded and a few of my favorite classical CD's.

I think it's good to find an excellent album and then listen to it over and over until you can sing along with solos. I did not care for many of my favorite albums the first time I heard them. Very often it seems that only after repeated listening can the best music be fully appreciated.

Notice how the Miles Davis choices are from the late 50's to late 60's. His groups were so good during this that his sidemen were "giants."

Half of the Coltrance is "early" Coltrane [early 60's]. Most of the other albums were recorded with his famous quartet, made up of Elvin Jones on drums, McCoy Tyner on piano, and Jimmy Garrison on bass.

There are not very many guitar albums on this list because I do not feel that guitarists have been among the outstanding innovators of jazz. Horn players have usually established the direction. I started listening to horn players such as Charlie Parker, Miles Davis, John Coltrane, and Ornette Coleman early in my development because they were the innovators of jazz; I felt it would be better to be influenced by horn players than guitarists, because I would be likely to develop a more original style.

My early guitar influences were Chet Atkins, Les Paul, and then Barney Kessel. The first two jazz albums I bought were Barney Kessel's *To Swing or Not to Swing, Vol. 3* (Contemporary, C3513), and *Easy Like, Vol. 1* (Contemporary, C3511). I went on to listen to Tal Farlow, Johnny Smith, Gabor Szabo, Kenny Burrell (on the recommended Jimmy Smith albums), Howard Roberts' *Good Pickins* (Verve, MGV-8305 My Favorite), and Wes Montgomery.

Most of the albums on the list have a "timeless" quality to them. I think the Miles Davis albums are the most consistent.

The Ray Charles' album, *Genius*, and Holiday's album, *Lady in Satin*, are the only two solo vocal albums listed. The depth of the soul evident on these LP's surpasses any vocal album I have ever heard. The "early" Ornette albums were chosen because of their strong influence on the direction of jazz after their appearance in the late 50's and early 60's.

Gunther Schuller's *Jazz Abstractions* features an extraordinary group of musicians including Jim Hall, Ornette Coleman, Scott LaFaro, Eric Dolphy and Bill Evans.

Village Vanguard Sessions combines the beautiful style of Bill Evans, which became a prime influence for a great many pianists of the 60's, with the interplay and rapport of the great, innovative bass playing of Scott LaFaro, who was killed in a car accident two weeks after these recordings. *Undercurrent* is really a classic piano and guitar duet album, with Bill Evans and Jim Hall.

Charles, Ray - *Genius* (Atlantic, S-1312)
Coleman, Ornette - *Tomorrow is the Question* (Contemporary, 7569)
    Shape of Jazz to Come (At., S-1317)
    This is Our Music (At., S-1353)
Coltrane, John - *John Coltrane* (Prestige, 24003)
    Giant Steps (At., S-1311)
    Black Pearls (Pres., P-24037)
    Coltrane Jazz (At., S-1354)
    "Live" at Birdland (Impulse, S-50)
    Live at Village Vanguard (4-62 Imp., S-10)
    Love Supreme (Imp., S-77)
    Expression (Imp., S-9120)
Davis, Miles - *Milestones* (Columbia, CS-9248)
    My Funny Valentine (Col., CS-9106)
    Miles Ahead (Col., CS-8633)
    Kind of Blue (Col., CS-8163)
    "Four" & More (3-66) (Col., CS-9253)
    '58 Sessions (Col., CK47835)
    Workin' & Steamin' (Pres., 24034)
    Miles Davis (Pres., 24001)
Dolphy, Eric - *Eric Dolphy* (Pres., 24008)
Evans, Bill - *Village Vanguard Sessions* w. LaFaro (2-Milestone, 47002)
Evans, Bill & Jim Hall - *Undercurrent* (United Artists, 5640)
Handy, John - *Monterey Jazz Festival* (Col., CS-9262)
Holiday, Billie - *Lady in Satin* (Col., CS-8048)
Montgomery, Wes - *Smokin' at the half note.*
The incredible Jazz Guitar of Wes Montgomery
Parker, Charlie - *Charlie Parker* (2-Pres., 24009)
    Jazz at Massey Hall (Fantasy, 86003)
    Essential (Verve, 68409)
Schuller, Gunther - *Jazz Abstractions* (At., S-1365)
Smith, Jimmy - *Organ Grinder Swing* (Verve, 68628)
    The Sermon (Blue Note, 84011)
Berg, Alban - *Concerto for Violin & Orchestra* (1935) Stern, Bernstein, NY Phil. (Col., MS-6373)
Bartok, Bela - *Quartets* (6) (complete) Juilliard Qr. (3-Col., D35-717; M-3119618)
Bream, Julian - *Art of Julian Bream* (RCA, LSC-2448)
Christian, Charlie - *The Genius of the Electric Guitar* (Columbia/Legacy)

Jerry Hahn

Selected Discography: As Leader

Solo Jazz Guitar	Bop Wire
Time Changes	ENJA-9007
Moses	Fantasy
Jerry Hahn Brotherhood	Columbia
Jerry Hahn&His Quintet	Arhoolie-9011

As Sideman
Paul Simon (first solo album) - Columbia
Ginger Baker - Falling off the Roof - Atlantic
Gary Burton - Country Roads - RCA
Gary Burton - Good Vibes - Atlantic
Gary Burton - The Throb - Atlantic
John Handy Quintet - Live at Yoshi's Nitespot
John Handy Quintet - Live at Monterey - Columbia
John Handy Quintet - The Second John Handy Album
Bennie Wallace - The Talk of the Town - ENJA
Nancy King/Glen Moore - Impending Bloom - Justice
David Friesen - The Spirit of Christmas - Burnside

Publications
Complete Jerry Hahn Method for Jazz Guitar
Book and CD
Mel Bay Publications

Jerry Hahn's Guitar Seminar - monthly column
Guitar Player Magazine - 1973 - 1978

Jazz Festivals

Montreux	Switzerland
Newport	Rhode Island
Monterey	California
Berlin	Germany
Mt. Hood	Oregon
Wichita	Kansas
Pacific	Costa Mesa, CA
Copenhagen	Denmark
Miami	Florida

Highlights
Movie Sound Track: White Men Can't Jump
Doctorate of Music - Berean Christian College
National Endowment for the Arts grant
Carnegie Recital Hall with Gary Burton
Tour of Europe and Japan with Benny Wallace
Tour of Europe and Japan with Gary Burton

Guitar Instruction
Portland State University
Director of Jazz Guitar Program - 1997 to 2004
Wichita State University
Director of Jazz Guitar Program - 1972 to 1986
Musicians's Institute of Technology
Clinician
San Francisco Conservatory
Guitar Instructor
Jamey Aebersold Jazz Camp - *Instructor*

The Penguin Guide to Jazz on CD.
"Though hardly a household name, Hahn is an extremely important figure in jazz guitar."
"-bursting with ideas-" "-oozes maturity-"
Down Beat "Impressive new recording"   *New Yorker* "Marvelous, unsung"
Guitar Player "Hahn lets off bluesy, speed-picked burst of notes-"
Jazz Times "His trademark blend of jazz, blues and country remains as fresh as ever-"
5/4 Magazine "-he's trailblazingly fast and crystal clear." "-so full of ideas that he's overflowing"

www.jerryhahn.com

Printed in Great Britain
by Amazon